D1158356

American
Sport Culture

By the Same Author

The Sporting Myth and the American Experience: Studies in Contemporary Fiction

Mythmakers of the American Dream: The Nostalgic Vision in Popular Culture

The Movies Go to College: Hollywood and the World of the College-Life Film

American Sport Culture

THE HUMANISTIC DIMENSIONS

Edited with an Introduction and Commentary by
Wiley Lee Umphlett

Lewisburg
Bucknell University Press
London and Toronto: Associated University Presses

Associated University Presses
440 Forsgate Drive
Cranbury, NJ 08512

Associated University Presses
25 Sicilian Avenue
London WC1A 2QH, England

Associated University Presses
2133 Royal Windsor Drive
Unit 1
Mississauga, Ontario
Canada L5J 1K5

Library of Congress Cataloging in Publication Data
Main entry under title:

American sport culture.

  Bibliography: p.
  1. Sports—Social aspects—United States—Addresses,
essays, lectures. I. Umphlett, Wiley Lee, 1931–
GV706.5.A44 1985   306'.483'0973   83-45967
ISBN 0-8387-5070-2

Printed in the United States of America

To my "starting five":
Reg, Don, Ed, Kipp, and Matt

Contents

Preface

Taken as a whole the pieces collected in *American Sport Culture* offer a unique approach to their subject matter. They do not concentrate on the usual ingratiating and agreeable aspects of a field that appeals to millions; nor do they dwell primarily on the defamatory and denigrating, an increasingly popular development in the literature of sport since the appearance of Jim Bouton's *Ball Four*, certainly a major force in demythologizing American sport during the 1970s. Rather, the main purpose of this collection is to focus impartially on both the positive and negative concerns of a humanistic character that have been fermenting in the American sports scene since the 1960s. These polar and often controversial issues have been brought to the attention of the American public through a continuing stream of pieces in journals and newspapers and through works of nonfiction and fiction, as well as through a steady diet of television productions, both dramatic and documentary—overall an astonishing output that ranges from the realm of pure entertainment to that of serious, even scholarly, interpretation. Judging from the current evidence around us as we encounter the harsh realities of life in the 1980s, there appears to be no letup in sight concerning the peculiar American mania for sports and their impact on our lives.

In examining the humanistic dimensions of this complex subject area through a representative sampling of significant statements about the American way of sport, this collection discloses a type of cultural conflict or ongoing debate within our society. Due to this clash of antithetical opinions and viewpoints, a number of problematic questions about the nature and function of contemporary American sport are raised here, among them some key critical queries which help underscore this book's emphasis on society's growing interest in the humanistic side of sports experience:

1. Respecting society's current attitude toward the roles of the spectator and the participant, what are the sociocultural implications of the distinction drawn between sport as entertainment and sport as a "religious" or ritualistic experience?
2. In order to enhance and foster a sense of selfhood and self-actualization in a technologically oriented and increasingly dehumanized society, how can sports participants, particularly team members, relate to sporting experience in a humanistic way?
3. Why has our creative literature, especially the form of fiction, been so obsessed with dramatizing the negative side of sporting experience in recent years?
4. How can the serious and scholarly examination of sport help us learn more about its humanistic import for society and the individual?

In response to these basic questions and their impact on the broader issues of how sport and society might meaningfully interrelate, this symposium's focus on humanistic concerns spotlights an outstanding array of "contenders" who have formulated their special cases within the framework of four general areas of experiential perception about American sport: the sociocultural approach, the individualized experience, the literary-folkloric interpretation, and the academic analysis. Presented mainly as original essays, these statements appear to center on whether or not a proponent views sports experience as either a humanistic or a dehumanizing involvement for the spectator or the participant; whether or not sports can provide humanistic involvement for the individual in search of self-realization, both in real life and in the social image of contemporary literature; and whether or not sports really deserve the degree of scholarly attention they have been accorded.

While no ready and conclusive answers about such an intricate and elusive subject as the pros and cons of our humanistic relationship to sport are arrived at here, these frequently brilliant but occasionally disconcerting opinions and insights— whether taken as constructive or critical—will undoubtedly afford the reader a heightened sensitivity to an area of experience that appears to take on more significance in the societal scheme of things with each passing year. If today's sporting events continue to come across in the guise of commercialized spectacle as a technocratic society attempts to exploit an inordinate share of our selfhood, then perhaps attending to both the agreeable and the discordant voices in *American Sport Culture* can help to enlighten us concerning the humanistic implications of this phenomenon and provide us with a clearer understanding of our roles as individuals in an increasingly complex society.

Acknowledgments

The task of putting this collection together has been largely a cooperative venture, and in addition to all those who helped make this project possible, I would like especially to thank the following:

Joseph Arbena, director of the annual Conference on Sport and Society at Clemson University; *The American Scholar* and George Core for permission to reprint "The Lower Mythology and the Higher Clichés"; *The Georgia Review* and David L. Vanderwerken for permission to reprint "The Joy of Sports Books: A Tout Sheet"; Christopher Lasch for permission to reprint "The Corruption of Sports"; Lea & Febiger Publisher for permission to reprint "Sport for All" from *Saga of American Sport* by John A. Lucas and Ronald A. Smith; Robert Lipsyte of CBS News for permission to reprint "Varsity Syndrome: The Unkindest Cut"; Christian K. Messenger for permission to reprint the introduction to *Sport and the Spirit of Play in American Fiction;* Allen L. Sack and *Notre Dame Magazine;* and Michael Novak, whose contribution to our humanistic understanding of contemporary sport speaks for itself.

Introduction:
The Humanistic Conflict in American Sport Culture

As the sources of man's identity are strangled by
technology, as his primacy and his relation to the land
are minimized, his fanaticism toward sports spectacle
increases.

—John Lahr,
"The Theater of Sports" (1969)

We will have humane, creative sports when we have
built a humane and creative society—and not until
then.

—Paul Hoch,
Rip Off the Big Game (1972)

It would appear in retrospect that my earlier analysis of the
cultural relationship of our sporting heritage with American literary tradition might have hit upon the source of a continuing
debate in our society.[1] I contended then that our literary heroes
(and antiheroes) of an athletic or sport-oriented background are
defined and conditioned in their dramatic behavior and
significance by their immediate reaction to a basic American
cultural conflict between nature and society. This antipathy is
suggested in the distinction I make between the term *sporting* (a
positive attitude toward experience derived from our frontier
heritage and its natural code of values) and *sports* (the system of
organized games invented by society primarily for its amuse-

ment and ordered by an artificial code of values).* The literary source of this conflict is James Fenimore Cooper's portrait of Natty Bumppo, the athletic hero of the Leatherstocking saga, who, in choosing to flee the social restrictions of an encroaching civilization and confront the self-fulfilling challenges of the frontier, symbolizes the basic concern of the American primordial self.

Evolving through the subsequent output of our literary tradition, the nature-society antithesis redefined itself in the 1960s and 1970s, as, for example, in Peter Gent's *North Dallas Forty* (1973), a novel about a disenchanted athlete who rejects the system of professional football in order to satisfy an innate desire to return to his natural heritage—the land. Accordingly, the fictional experience of this story's central figure is symbolic of a lively dispute which has persisted in recent years between those who espouse a decidedly humanistic interpretation of sports experience and those who contend that the overly organized and systematic approach to modern sports is essentially dehumanizing.

But since the 1960s, both sides of this cultural conflict or dialectic—whether expressed through the intensely imaginative mode of fiction or the subjectively critical and purposely sensational nonfiction accounts by figures from organized sports like baseball's Jim Bouton in *Ball Four* (1971); football's Dave Meggyesy in *Out of Their League* (1971); or basketball's Connie Hawkins in *Foul!* (1972)—have been closely related in philosophical intent. They appear, in fact, to emanate from the dramatic clash of the individual versus the demands of a system which apparently seeks to control the athlete's selfhood. Consequently, a situation has developed which ironically seems to be always asking the same question: In the face of an increasingly technocratic and impersonal approach to sports involvement, particularly that of team sports, how may the individual continue to participate in organized athletics and maintain a strong sense of personal identity and self-respect?

Reflective of numerous diverse viewpoints which have reacted sociologically and psychologically to this pervasive

---

*On the other hand, the term *sport,* as it is used in the title of this collection, suggests the cultural aspects of all sporting endeavor, particularly as they reveal the social preoccupations of contemporary American society.

question, exemplary works of fiction and nonfiction as well as journalistic pieces, television documentaries, and movies inspired by the themes of these books have been proliferating at an astonishing rate since the sixties. Some publications expressed from the participant's point of view, as, for example, Bernie Parrish's *They Call It a Game* (1972), vehemently attack or satirize the system of organized sports; while others, like Roger Kahn's *The Boys of Summer* (1972), indirectly praise or defend the role and significance of sport in contemporary life, especially from the spectator's point of view. But all this abundant output, no matter how divergent in purpose or theme, appears to be unanimous in reminding us that sport is a kind of sacrosanct refuge in a world of increasing dehumanization; that sport exists mainly to enable the individual to discover his or her essential worth and dignity as a human being, whether as participant or spectator; and that sport fails or succeeds according to how well it can afford opportunities for the individual to realize and develop these qualities. Not a few works in the literature of American sport culture have achieved a measure of power and distinction, some even a degree of notoriety, in elucidating either the positive contributions or the decided shortcomings of sport in our lives.

In 1969, the sociologist Harry Edwards published a book entitled *The Revolt of the Black Athlete,* which had grown out of his own experiences in organizing and carrying out the black athletes' boycott of the 1968 Olympic Games in Mexico City. Labeling his mission "The Olympic Project for Human Rights," Edwards presented a searing indictment of the American way of sport, observing in the process that instead of realizing racial equality through athletics, the black athlete was merely being used by them. Edwards's special concern for an ethnic group was only a prelude to what Jack Scott would come up with two years later in *The Athletic Revolution* (1971)—a bitter attack on the entire structure of American sports. Founder and director of the Institute for the Study of Sport and Society, Scott sounds as impassioned as Edwards in his stand on the dehumanizing effects of the modern sports system on the individual, particularly when he draws on Dave Meggyesy's disenchanted personal experiences as both a college and professional football player. However, Scott not only presents the reasons for his views on the evils of organized athletics, he also suggests a plan for constructive change. Underneath Scott's argument lies his basic contention that if we are to humanize athletics, then we must also humanize the American educational structure, which is really responsible for our erroneous understanding of how we think the competitive side of our sports system should function.

Ironically, in the same year that Harry Edwards's controversial book appeared, the Yale philosopher Paul Weiss produced *Sport—A Philosophic Inquiry* (1969), a book whose premise transcends polemics and politics by suggesting that the representative role of the athlete is that of a natural humanist who is imbued with the idealistic goal of attaining physical excellence in order to become, in the process, something of a public model or cultural symbol. In his or her quality of performance, the athlete, according to Weiss, rises above political and mundane concerns to express the most positive and elusive of human aspirations—self-mastery.

But the philosopher's idealistic viewpoint was also indicative of what was going on in other, more earthbound, areas of intellectual exploration at this time, especially in the social sciences, which by the early seventies had begun to espouse a counterculture ideology that centered on the need to cultivate the independent qualities of the individual in order to counteract the oppressive influence of bureaucracy and technology. On the popular front, the flood of self-help books, which openly declared their intent of making us "fuller" persons, were yet another sign of the times that one could somehow, even in the face of an increasingly automated way of life, manage to develop and retain a sense of personal identity by reading and taking seriously any one of a spate of books, which ranged from the interpersonal concerns of transactional analysis to the spiritual speculations of transcendental meditation.

The reasons behind this pervasive trend have been manifold and complex, of course, but one of the most obvious that comes to mind is that the relentlessly expanding technology which has enveloped us all during this century has created an atmosphere that demands a special choice on our part: We must either give in to what we see happening around us or come up with a more self-assertive way to circumvent or transcend the dehumanizing trends of our age. It is an end which, in its ascetic devotion to fathoming the mysteries of the self, often approaches a spiritual dimension. Along these lines, George Leonard, in *The Ultimate Athlete* (1975), has been the most articulate spokesman for the metaphysical side of sports experience and how the individual might discover, or recover, the positive powers of self through appropriate physical activity. Crying out against the system of modern team sports, whose highly competitive standards of excellence limit those who would participate, Leonard advocates direct personal identification with specially designed games and physical activities that play down the competitive element. Such involvement, he implies, allows for self-fulfillment and the realization that participation in sport can be a pleasurable end in itself.

Even though our ever-expanding technological society may be singled out as the enemy of individual expression, it has paradoxically created an age of more and more leisure time, which, in turn, has made it possible for more and more people to be curious about what it is they need to know and do to keep their bodies up to par.[2] Ironically, though, at a time when more jogging shoes and tennis racquets are being sold than ever before, many people appear to be finding their "sporting" identities through participating as spectators, either by attending live events or through watching televised activities. In fact, along with the attendant expansion of the ways in which sports enthusiasts are informed, our nation of spectators has grown to such proportions that the sports psychologist Thomas A. Tutko has been prompted to observe how a "true sports fan can now spend every hour of the waking day keeping track of the various teams and the thousands of athletes involved."[3] Indeed, with the recent establishment of an independent cable television network programming sports events around the clock, the "true sports fan" may find himself rising at the ungodly hour of 3:00 A.M. to view a taped playback of his favorite college team in action. Truly, this country's love affair with sports has extended far beyond just a need to participate in an active, physical sense.

Moreover, television, with its natural propensity for projecting the realistic details of live athletic events right into our living rooms, has conditioned viewers to expect a more down-to-earth interpretation of sports experience, addressing both its positive and negative sides; and whether today's sports journalists realize it or not, the authoritative posture of a commentator like Howard Cosell, which brazenly attempts to "tell it like it is," has had a tremendous influence and impact on reportorial styles and attitudes. If Cosell can label sport as entertainment, a kind of melodrama which contains the elements of both good and bad, then a syndicated sports columnist like Dick Young can readily adopt a similar stance in using words as weapons to keep his readers alert to what's happening within the sporting scene. Thus, while our athletes are performing their roles in the continually unfolding drama of contemporary sport, our reporters and commentators who describe the current scene seem compelled to get on stage, too, in their eagerness not only to inform but also to expose. The paradox of such an approach resides in the fact that in the attempt to lay bare the inherent problems of the sports world, the larger concerns and issues which haunt contemporary society are also revealed, whether or not readers and viewers are even aware of them and their implications.

Mirroring a growing sensitivity to this condition, popular modes of cultural communication like fiction, the movies, and the journalistic focus of the newspaper, magazine, and television have had considerable influence in conditioning the American people to what has been going on in the world of sports since the sixties. But the most significant impact, I believe, has been generated by the dozens of reputable sport-centered books which began appearing in the 1970s. These works, ranging from the specialized analysis of scholarly exposition at one pole to the predominantly entertaining realm of both light and serious fiction at the other, made the decade of the seventies the most sports-conscious era in our history and consequently the most articulate ever in keeping a sports-minded public informed. And, apparently, as publishers' lists keep insistently announcing, the end is nowhere in sight. If the inspiration for this overwhelming output derives from what I have pointed out as an ongoing debate between those who look upon sport as an experience of self-discovery and those who view its present overorganized condition as demanding and debilitating, then the sources of these antithetical postures should reveal to us a great deal about what may be wrong or right with contemporary society. To substantiate my awareness of this condition, I submit that the literature of American sport culture, which often reflects many of the partisan concerns and issues that tend to polarize today's society, has continued through the seventies and into the eighties to express itself in four general modes of experiential perception.

First, there is the sociocultural interpretation of these issues, which sees sports cutting across all the things that affect our social behavior and are therefore interwoven into the fabric of American life. Accordingly, the practitioners of this approach, while they may agree on the pervasive role that sports have played in weighing both the good and the bad sides of the American way of life, may range as far apart as the view of Michael Novak in *The Joy of Sports* (1976) that sports function as our "natural religion" and that of Christopher Lasch, whose carefully measured, but obviously pessimistic, opinions in *The Culture of Narcissism* (1978) imply that sports have been corrupted by society and that they may, in turn, have corrupted us. Other decidedly negative but influential points of view in this mode include those of Robert Lipsyte in *SportsWorld: An American Dreamland* (1975) and Paul Hoch in *Rip Off the Big Game: The Exploitation of Sports by the Power Elite* (1972), which are stated from stances as diametrically opposite as that of a former sports writer for a conservative newspaper (Lipsyte) and that of a Marxist social critic (Hoch), both of whom nevertheless agree that sports have been too much with us in their distortion and overplay by management, commercial interests, and the mass media. More recently, Richard Lipsky, in *How We Play the Game: Why Sports Dominate American Life* (1981), has attempted to demonstrate how sports function as a socializer of our political and social values while offering us an escape from the dominant realities of American life. Other outlooks, like Edwin H. Cady's analysis of intercollegiate sports and their impact on today's society in *The Big Game: College Sports and American Life* (1978) and Allen Guttmann's brilliant exposition of the American preference for team rather than individual sports in *From Ritual to Record: The Nature of Modern Sports* (1978), assume the more controlled and objective posture of the scholar. In spite of their academic stances, though, both Cady's and Guttmann's approaches to their subject matter reveal an inherent sensitivity to the emotional aura surrounding American sport, a characteristic that points out the underlying complexity of a subject which appears ultimately to defy in-depth analysis.

The output of the second mode, which centers on the dramatic revelations and implications of individualized experience, attempts, in the main, to expand upon either the detrimental or the beneficial side of personal involvement in organized sports. It is exemplified, on the one hand, by such a book as former college player Gary Shaw's vitriolic exposé of the vicious tactics of football coaches who are out to win at all costs—*Meat on the Hoof: The Hidden World of Texas Football* (1973)—and, on the other, in autobiographical accounts like John Brodie's *Open*

Field (1974), in which the former professional quarterback concentrates on the rewards of athletic participation from both a materialistic and an idealistic standpoint. Some works in this vein have been more speculative, however. George Leonard's *The Ultimate Athlete,* mentioned earlier, compellingly assesses the personal satisfaction derived from exploring the spiritual side of athletic experience, while Roger Angell's delightful essay collection, *The Summer Game* (1972), lyricizes about the simple, but almost transcendental, pleasures experienced by the spectator who is knowledgeable of the subtle and mystical profundities of baseball. The intensity of feeling in both these books approaches the poetic. But the most popular works in the mode of personalized sports experience have been the autobiographical accounts of well-known athletes and their rise to success. These books may range from the generally positive tone and manner of Bill Russell's *Go Up for Glory* (1966) or Bill Bradley's *Life on the Run* (1977) to the defiantly militant stance of one of sport's most dynamic and narcissistic individualists, Muhammad Ali, in a variety of books about this controversial figure.

However, the sociopolitical issues suggested by the aggressive pose of an Ali have served mainly to echo the human rights concerns of ethnic and minority athletes, which have come to the fore in recent years, particularly as these concerns have been expressed through the unique experiences of black and women athletes. But while the Jim Crow problems that a baseball player like Jackie Robinson faced in the 1940s have largely disappeared with the black man's acceptance into the mainstream of amateur and professional athletics, the cause of the woman athlete in America has grown more pronounced. Promulgated by a multitude of publications and media productions, the movement to create a positive athletic identity for women presents us with even more evidence of the current crusade to humanize sports experience, suggesting, too, that the system has been gradually giving in to the demands that equal opportunity be afforded all those who would participate in the arena of athletic competition. Beneath any critical outlook in sport culture literature expressed from the personal point of view, though, there exists the emotional sensitivity of a lover's quarrel, an intimate relationship which, perhaps, James Michener has caught better than anyone else in the epilogue to *Sports in America* (1976), his testimonial to what he feels has been both good and bad about our involvement with sports. After taking the American sports establishment to task for its multitude of sins and misdirected goals, Michener states his belief that because of our sports' special role in the "enlarging of the human adventure," they need to be protected, augmented, and made readily available to our citizens.[4] Such an outlook helps crystallize the premise of this anthology, which seeks to point out that, at bottom, the humanistic debate carried on by the literature of American sport culture is dialectical in nature and inherently concerned with improving athletic opportunity for the individual in order to enhance self-fulfillment.

In our day, the fictional and folkloric approach to interpreting sport—the third mode of experiential perception cited here—has become an increasingly meaningful vehicle for dramatizing the vicissitudes of human relationships. The contemporary fiction writer, in contrast to his predecessors, is more sensitive to the folkloric sources, as well as the rituals of sporting activity with which today's sports-indoctrinated reader can culturally identify. Deriving from the nature-society conflict of our literature's prototypal athlete—the Natty Bumppo character created by Cooper—and evolving, for example, into the alienated experience of *North Dallas Forty*'s football hero searching for his natural heritage, a significant number of works in the American literary tradition have revealed how our serious writers have taken care to integrate the cultural import of athletic activity into their personal visions of what may be right or wrong with American life. Along the way, an indigenous folklore about American sporting experience has sprung up, particularly around the team sports of baseball and football, providing the writer with an infinite variety of inspirational subject matter. Nevertheless, in portraying the popular character types created by this folklore tradition, fiction initially restricted its revelation of conventional sports experience to the standardized formula stories demanded by naïve juvenile and pulp magazine audiences. The Hollywood movie followed suit from the twenties through the fifties with its idealized but highly fantasized version of collegiate and professional athletics. Then suddenly, during the sixties and seventies, both serious fiction and film discovered the expansive possibilities of capturing the precise metaphor for the American experience through athletic activity—and from a negative as well as a positive point of view. In fact, in writing a work of fiction inspired by a sports background, the contemporary novelist—as much as he may relish or personally identify with the act of athletic involvement itself—rarely visualizes sport as having any redemptive value or positive meaning for the individual. In marked contrast to Ernest Hemingway's earlier vision of sports experience as a test of manhood and individual integrity, especially in the more solitary activities like hunting and fishing, fiction writers of recent years have produced works which draw on sports experience, particularly organized sports, as a metaphor for the negative and pejorative aspects of modern life. This viewpoint is strikingly apparent in contemporary novels as disparate in underlying intent as John Updike's *Rabbit, Run* (1962), Don DeLillo's *End Zone* (1972), Dan Jenkins's *Semi-Tough* (1972), and, of course, Peter Gent's *North Dallas Forty* (1973), as well as in a number of more recent novels, which also come across as variations on the nature-society antithesis.[5]

Consequently, the output of American literature with pervasive or tangential sport themes and backgrounds has recently inspired a number of critical interpretations which substantiate my contention that sports experience has become a rich and boundless source for a writer to draw on for comment on the human condition. Since my own study of the mythical significance of the athlete in American fiction, three important studies have appeared: Robert J. Higgs's *Laurel and Thorn: The Athlete in American Literature* (1981), Christian K. Messenger's *Sport and the Spirit of Play in American Fiction* (1981), and Michael Oriard's *Dreaming of Heroes: American Sports Fiction 1868–1980* (1981). Each of these scholarly works contains perceptive and stimulating analyses of the influence of athletic experience on American literary achievement, demonstrating that our writers have found in sports activity a highly useful metaphor for the struggles and concerns of American life, as well as for that most archetypal of all our literary themes—the individual against the system.[6]

The achievement of literary scholarship has been complemented by the wide range of research embracing historical, philosophical, sociological, and psychological meaning in the American sports experience, and, in the process, additional insights into the humanistic conflict pervading our sport culture have been revealed by this last area of experiential perception. Naturally, many of the selections included in this collection belong to the scholarly category, but it would be helpful here to categorize, in the main, those books and anthologies which adopt an obviously specialized approach to the American sports scene. Because this mode includes, in addition to the specialized studies, the innumerable texts and thematic readers which have appeared as the popularity of sport-oriented courses at schools around the country has grown, perhaps singling out here some of the outstanding works in the Addison-Wesley Series in the Social Significance of Sports (John W. Loy, general editor) will exemplify the high standards of recent sport scholarship.

From a generally historical perspective, John Betts's *America's Sporting Heritage* (1974) is a highly readable account of the rise of American sport during the period 1850–1950, providing us with considerable sociocultural insight into the growing interrelationship between sport, culture, and society during the hundred years the book covers. Since Paul Weiss's speculative book in 1969, philosophical thought about sports experience has been given a more down-to-earth treatment by Harold J. Vanderzwaag in *Toward A Philosophy of Sport* (1972), while the cause of the woman athlete has been advanced in a collection of essays edited by Ellen Gerber et al. entitled *The American Woman in Sport* (1974). The Addison-Wesley Series has even produced a geographical study of American sport culture in John F. Rooney's well-documented *A Geography of American Sport* (1974). Of the astronomical number of books and readers with sociological and psychological themes turned out by other publishers, the provocative collection edited by Jeffrey H. Goldstein serves as a good example of the interdisciplinary scholarship inspired by contemporary sport culture. *Sports, Games, and Play: Social and Psychological Viewpoints* (1979) not only presents a variety of perspectives on the experiences of both participant and spectator, it also focuses on the competitive factors which have contributed to the humanistic conflict in modern sports. Undoubtedly, as our present cultural climate attests, brave new studies and thematic essay collections will continue to appear, raising possibilities for stimulating and developing even further areas of productive research.

In spite of the solid body of sport scholarship that has been turned out in recent years, there are those who naturally persist in questioning the validity and quality of what has been done and even whether or not sports as a legitimate subject area should fall within the purview of the scholar or simply be left to the diurnal whims of the journalist. In refuting the contention that the concerns and issues of sports are too superficial and ephemeral to attract the attention of the serious scholar, David L.

Vanderwerken has forcefully stated the case for continued exploration by recognizing the remarkable achievements of the recent past and declaring that the seventies will probably come to be known as the "golden age of sports studies."[7] Actually, the question of whether or not sports are worthy of academic scrutiny makes for a lively debate, too, and the repercussions of this argument could provide us with continued insights into the humanistic conflict at the heart of this country's flourishing sport culture. Evaluating the extensive and varied output of the literature inspired by American sport since the sixties will undoubtedly help us to realize that sport has been important enough in our lives to merit even closer attention and that we are now into a decade which will probably outshine the seventies in determining how sport, through the complementary experiences of participating and observing, can add new meaning to our lives.

—W. L. U.

Notes

1. See Wiley Lee Umphlett, *The Sporting Myth and the American Experience* (Lewisburg, Pa.: Bucknell University Press, 1975).

2. Note that this area of interest has in itself opened up a highly successful publishing field in which books on dietary methods, physical fitness, jogging techniques, and special improvement methods in individualized sports like golf and tennis have attained tremendous popularity.

3. Thomas A. Tutko, "Personality Change in the American Sport Scene," in *Sports, Games, and Play: Social and Psychological Viewpoints,* ed. Jeffrey H. Goldstein (Hillsdale, N.J.: Lawrence Erlbaum Associates, 1979), 102.

4. James A. Michener, *Sports in America* (New York: Random House, 1976), 451.

5. That organized sports continue to be a favorite source for fiction writers to mirror the humanistic concerns of contemporary life is revealed in the subject matter of a number of recently published novels (1982), among them, for example, David Small's *Almost Famous,* Michael Schiffer's *Ballpark,* and Frank Deford's *Everybody's All-American.*

6. I might mention here the sections which deal with sport and literature in Neil Isaacs's *Jock Culture, USA* (1978) and Allen Guttmann's *From Ritual to Record* (1978), both highly insightful discussions from entirely different perspectives. Mention should also be made of the appearance of a number of anthologies of sport-oriented literature, of which the best, I think, is *The Sporting Spirit: Athletes in Literature and Life* (Harcourt Brace Jovanovich, 1977), edited by Higgs and Isaacs.

7. David L. Vanderwerken, "The Joy of Sports Books: A Tout Sheet," *Georgia Review* 33 (Fall 1979): 707. Reprinted in the present volume as chapter 21.

American
Sport Culture

PART I
The Sociocultural Approach

Sports owe more to the ritual grammar of religion
than to the laws and forms of entertainment. Millions
become involved in the rituals of sport to a depth of
seriousness never elicited by entertainment.

—Michael Novak,
The Joy of Sports (1976)

What began as an attempt to invest sport with religious significance, indeed to make it into a surrogate
religion in its own right, ends with the demystification
of sport, the assimilation of sport to show business.

—Christopher Lasch,
The Culture of Narcissism (1979)

Issues and Contentions

Do sports—especially our major public spectacles like baseball, football, and basketball—perform a necessary function in keeping society conscious of its national purpose and moral sense, as Michael Novak suggests in the leadoff piece of this symposium ("American Sports, American Virtues")? Or do sports, at least in their present form, tend to corrupt society because, as Christopher Lasch implies in "The Corruption of Sports," their true role has been distorted and misinterpreted by the socially narcissistic demands of an industrialized society? Regardless of whose view we may find more acceptable, both Novak and Lasch present highly perceptive and deeply concerned expositions of what may be right or wrong with sports in contemporary life and to what extent they mirror cultural characteristics and societal preoccupations.

In a special sense, Richard Lipsky's attempt to formulate a sociopolitical theory of American sport ("The Political and Social Dimensions of Sports") appears to bridge both Novak's and Lasch's antithetical outlooks. In elaborating on Robert Lipsyte's "SportsWorld" metaphor, Lipsky informs us that to analyze the sociocultural ramifications of this concept is to understand "something of the structural malaise of American politics and society." Ironically, at the same time, observing and participating in sports can provide "a 'utopia of escape' that refreshes," thus allowing sports enthusiasts "to return with renewed vigor to their places in the political and social system."

Lipsyte's contention in *SportsWorld: An American Dreamland* that a number of ills, particularly that of commercialism, has created a "grotesque distortion of sports" finds further substantiation in Richard C. Crepeau's essay, which cites some possible reasons for society's changing attitudes toward the American sports hero in our time. According to Crepeau, the overwhelming commercialization of sports has resulted in a celebrity culture in which anti-heroes abound; thus it appears that the new type of sports hero could well be a tycoon like Ted Turner, a personality whose entrepreneurial success with sports has assured him of high-level celebrity status. In fact, Crepeau goes so far as to suggest that our "envy of celebrity" may be all that remains for a society that apparently has lost sight of the sense of shared values which contributed to the perpetuation of sports heroes in the past.

Since the 1960s, television has played a dominant role in conditioning the spectator's reaction to major sporting events, and its pervasive influence has induced many of us to conclude that this medium has prostituted the traditional values of American spectator sports to the monetary reward of lucrative network contracts. However, Joan Chandler, in "American Televised Sport: Business as Usual," refutes this charge by declaring that "TV has not changed sport; rather, the societal values which sport epitomized have changed in the last thirty years, and TV has reflected those changes." In demonstrating that our mass spectator sports, particularly professional baseball, has always been "in search of dollars rather than accolades," Chandler convincingly argues her case for how "television unwittingly ripped the mask off the sports industry, and in so doing, unmasked spectators as well." From a humanistic point of view, then, Chandler's contention that we need to learn how to control the power of television is well taken, for, as she asserts, the fault does not lie so much within television as it does within ourselves.

Another ill pervading contemporary American sports that Neil D. Isaacs describes as being "interrelated and interlocked" with television and its "prevailing atmosphere of commercialized exploitation" is gambling. Considering the proliferation of fixes and scandals which the sports fan has been exposed to over the years, gambling abuses may well be another significant reason for the public's negative assessment of the sports hero's image today. In "Rotten Apples of Gold: Gambling in American Sports," Isaacs, a longtime observer of our sporting scene, compiles his tongue-in-cheek list of the "Ten Greatest Sports Figures in American History," a fascinating lineup of individuals who have in one way or another affected sports gambling in this country. The rationale behind his ironic choices is based on a perception of the professional gambler as having exerted a powerful influence on our "jockocracy's focus on sports, where the money is, the real money, the big money." However, Isaacs goes on to argue that if the widespread gambling in sports cannot be stopped, then its pervasive corruption should be, perhaps through the legalization of gambling practices, if no other way. Like the other contributors to this section, Isaacs contends that sports and games "reflect and teach the value systems of the whole culture"; therefore, we had better heed the obvious signs of decadence and make reparation before it is too late.

1

American Sports, American Virtues

MICHAEL NOVAK

When the Chinese premier flew over the territories called "the United State of America" in early 1979, it is apocryphally reported that he asked his expert on American culture the meaning of those oval buildings and mammoth domes that are, from above, a distinctive mark of every major American city and every university. As through some great keyhole—the observer from faraway China might muse from his aerial window—whoever could learn the secret of *those* structures might be able to unlock the riddles of the American character. The more he would learn about the involvement Americans have in those buildings, the more impressed he would become.

For what happens in the three major American sports played in those buildings—baseball, football, and basketball—is far more intense than entertainment, and involves millions of citizens in rigorous disciplines and a taste for high excellence. If a visitor could campare the atmosphere in a motel bar when Monday night football is seen (or attend one of those little altars in the family shrine of every American home, through which visions of sacred events are communicated), and contrast that atmosphere with the flatter, duller attitudes of the other days of the week, he would recognize instantly the difference between sports and entertainment. Sports involve spectators far more; many of the more fervent become active participants. They refuse to permit their attention to be diverted, especially during the high holy moments. They are elated or dejected—their mood altered sometimes for days—by the outcome. Mood? It is more than mood. Something having to do with their own self-image, their own identity.

To be sure, a visitor from abroad would discover that our culture is also composed of many nonbelievers, who seldom if ever darken the doorway of such magnificent buildings. To them, the movements on the field are "paleological gibberish," primitive rites in which they see no dignity and have no interest. There is nothing for a believer to do (especially if married to an unbeliever) except to fast and to pray that, one day, they might come to understand.

The anthropologically trained visitor would soon comprehend that, in America (as, indeed, all through human history), certain sports are (1) more than entertainment and (2) far more than hygiene and exercise. Baseball, football, and basketball are highly organized, institutionalized rituals; they are public liturgies; they are symbolic statements, dramas, narratives. The ancient root word *fanum,* temple, shows up in the word *fan.* Even the category "play" is inadequate for expressing what is involved in such sports. Play may be unorganized, spontaneous, private. Sports of this type are public, highly ritualized, thoroughly thought through. Indeed, the actors on the field are more like workers than like players. They are paid. More significantly, they are subject to elaborate disciplines and routinized exertions simply to maintain their skills and their endurance at the high levels demanded by their exhibitions. The relation of the athlete to the sports event is rather like that of the clergy to the Solemn High Mass—except that their perfection at the fulfillment of their tasks is far more rigorously subjected to instant public disapproval. The lay participant at Mass may attend for purposes of inner renewal; the minister is performing his essential work and, while trying likewise to enjoy the liturgy in a prayerful and playful way, must also attend to its duties and requirements quite independently of his own feelings. The minister works.

Our major sports, then, are more like liturgies—symbolic public dramas—than like entertainment or exercise. What do they symbolize? One notes first that while many nations play basketball with enthusiasm, only a few have learned to love baseball, and, to this point, none have learned to love American football (save Canada). Only in America does this precise set of symbolic public dramas respond to some profound need in the national consciousness. No other major sports (hockey, tennis, golf, soccer, auto racing) have cut across regional, class, and other cultural lines so as to become truly national sports in quite the same sense.

A mistake is made by many analysts of the impact of our sports upon our character and our morals. Character is usually understood in too moralistic a sense; too much attention is paid to the content of intellectual principles and acts of will. Confronted with the word *ethics,* most Americans seem to think of the voluntarism of Sunday school lectures and college courses in Hume, Kant, and Camus. Not nearly enough attention is paid to the subconscious soil of the psyche: the terrain of myth, symbol, story, and imagination. Sports as liturgies appeal to the same stratum of the person as do novels and plays, the stratum of an imagined world view, the stage on which agents in conflict decide, act, and meet their destiny. For this reason, the most illuminating route to an understanding of sports lies through the fields and valleys of our historical imagination.

1

Put yourself for a moment in the shoes of those first Europeans, fleeing from other cultures or attracted to an open, new, unexplored future, the first to tread upon American soil. The continent they faced was vast. Not a few were the first to look upon a given valley, to push a canoe into a smooth river never seen before by one of their own kind, part the leaves and look upon a range of hills. On their errand into the wilderness, many must have questioned whether their God could travel with them from Europe. Alone, unseen, able to do whatever they wished, without censure or even observation, they must have wondered what would happen to them in this lawless virgin land. They felt unbound. They could start fresh. In Eden, what ought they to do? Call upon new gods? Invent new laws? Imagination lay open as the land before them.

It is striking how their imagination was drawn to the "athletes of the wilderness," to the new type of human being they discerned in the American Indian, "the noble savage," reports of whom traveled back to Europe. Early American literature is full of moral excitement at the beauty of newly discovered athletic skills: skills in tracking the forest, in marksmanship, in craft, and in wiles; skills, too, in feats of bodily agility and endurance. Daniel Boone, Leatherstocking, Chingachgook, Davy Crockett, the outdoorsman and the pioneer, even Captain Ahab, are among the first representations of the new type of athlete in the American imagination.

There developed, I think, a form of American Zen, the necessary precondition to the attraction of later generations of Americans for Eastern religions. This American Zen is distinctive, and, as a first stab at analyzing it, I discern in it four characteristic marks.

1. *Transcendence in perfect acts.* In many primitive cultures, there was a profound sense that human beings, in moments of excellence, are possessed momentarily by the gods and lifted up to live in a higher form of existence. The ideal form of human action is, to this sensibility, a form of godliness. Indeed, a distinction is drawn between profane time, the time of prosaic, humdrum daily acts, and sacred time, the time proper to the life of the gods, surrounding, encompassing, and occasionally penetrating ordinary time, and the time of the heroes, the moments of high and perfect or near-perfect achievement under stress. Not everybody got to share in this last time, and no one lived in it constantly. It required intense preparation and instant readiness. Thus, to shoot an arrow through a designated leaf, to fell a buffalo with a single arrow, to strip the bark of a tree with perfect grace, to detect an almost invisible clue on the forest floor—such acts of highly perfected human skills were understood as special graces. One transcends the ordinary human limits by individual perfect acts. Thus, too, a football player called upon in the last seconds of a whole string of games to perform a difficult act perfectly is lucky to be chosen for this role, and lifted up out of the ordinary by perfect achievement. Skill alone does not explain such perfection under pressure. For even the most skillful human fails a rather substantial proportion of the time. To make the act count when it is needed is to achieve a sort of immortality, not so much because others will remember the great deed, as because it is a deed not always given to mortals. The fast draw, the deadly shot—such instances of the perfect act formed a kind of aesthetic code in American life. It is still effective.

2. *Union with nature.* Perfect acts, learned in part from observation of the athletes of the forest, were early seen to follow from a particular kind of union with nature. Nature and humankind are part of one whole; man does not so much walk *on* the

earth (a stranger) as walk *in* it (a part of it, nature streaming through him and in him). One must, therefore, learn how to "listen" to nature, adapt oneself to its rhythms and possibilities, glimpse its energies, dynamisms, and impulses, learn to respect its limits and laws.

The image of a wholly natural man began to appear, a man who by superior sensitivity and craft lived up to the potentialities of nature. The idea, in a sense, is that nature, even our own nature, is greater than our present level of instinct, comprehension, and agency. We must become what we are not yet, in order to fulfill what, in potentiality but not in act, we are. To encourage one another by the imperative, "Let us be men," is not redundant, for we are not yet what we can become. And the secret of such becoming lies in deeper and more exact fidelity to the nature within us. There is a kind of self-knowledge involved here, an exploring of our own personal capacities and limits. General rules are helpful—craft can be passed from teacher to student—but in the end each person must learn to listen for guidance to his own personal nature. Emerson, here, is not far in the distance; or Walt Whitman. But before the writers put the attitude in words, Americans learning the skills of the wilderness were beginning to live it out. Far more than observers of our civilization have noted, stressing as they tend to do our voluntarism, activism, industry, and dominion over nature, our civilization also inculcates a profound sense of the individual's union with nature, a great need to absorb the silences of nature on mountaintops and in the wilderness, on the plains and in the desert, at night in the swamps and on the sparkling seas *(Moby Dick, Two Years before the Mast)*.

3. *Competition with nature.* Yet nature in the American imagination is not solely beneficent. "Dan'l Boone kilt a b'ar," but the b'ar might, as well, have killed Daniel Boone. Dust storms lifted the top soil off entire sections of large states. Nature's waters were often poisonous or brackish. Blizzards killed. Deserts and mountains exposed the bleached bones of many settlers who did not survive the westward trek. Hordes of locusts wiped out an entire summer's arduous manual work. So nature is, in part, at war with humankind. There is no guarantee that humans can or will survive this deadly competition. Hence, humankind's union with nature is also a struggle with death. Nature is "red in tooth and claw." Humans alone do not pollute the earth; nature herself

pollutes with ash, wind, erosion, flood, earthquake, and blizzard. Yet in the struggle between humankind and nature, life continues to win reprieve; after winter, spring; after death, new life. The ritual that would perfectly capture the spirit of this struggle would have to be a ritual in which the taste of death is left in the mouths of some, while others experience the rush of life, the possibilities or resurrection, death and resurrection in (as it seems) endless and cyclical repetition: seasons following seasons, new individual contests tomorrow following contests closed today. The human being—in American Zen—is constantly being tested; loves the contest; dislikes the humdrum in between.

4. *Victory over nature.* Nature, of course, inevitably wins. The young brave slows a step, loses power in the arm, feels muscles tighten with age, withers, dies. Over the individual human being, nature is the inexorable victor. The sting is taken from this victory, however, by the inducting of new generations into the lore and craft of survival—and not survival, merely, but real progress. The land is cleared. Crops are raised. Children are sent to school. The arts begin to flourish. Civilization becomes possible. And, with it, a new round of victories and defeats. A new struggle. Indeed, the structure of the struggle shifts. Each "victory" over nature becomes, in due time, a new sort of threat. Halt the deaths of infants and soon millions of human individuals survive who, in preceding generations, would not have survived. They require new resources, new sorts of institutions to support their lives. They acquire new sorts of ailments (cancer, heart diseases, and the like begin to kill many who in previous ages had died earlier of other maladies). The instinct for survival is very strong. The belief in its possibility is rooted in life itself: the will to live. And thus the impulse of American Zen is tremendously overbalanced on the side of life. The preposition *up (up-*beat, looking *up,* picking *up,* trend is *up)* is singularly important in our daily speech. There is, overall, at least upon the surface, a tremendous innocence about America, a belief in the possible. Fatalism does not set our typical national self-image at ease. Total cynicism of the Mediterranean sort does not seem becoming to us. Outrage is our typical response to things unfair. We do not accept what seems to be unfair as natural. With Robert Kennedy, we like to face the future with "Why not?"

There is, of course, an undertow of fatalism. A great whale

somewhere lurks beneath the ship of state, as yet incompletely
known and never neutralized, a threat of which we are at least
remotely and unconsciously aware. Our experiment might fail.
We might betray ourselves. We may not be worthy of carrying
through what we have begun. We may have become a danger to
ourselves and to the world. We may be losing our nerve. We may
be coming to the end of what seemed, at times, to be a lovely
game. We may need new gods. We may need new sports. Prefer-
ably, less competitive sports; less disciplined sports; more spontaneous sports.

That is to say, American Zen is in crisis. Our sense of ourselves is reflected in our sports. Or so it seems.

Perhaps, though, it is only an invented crisis. For the first time
in history a civilization is being bombarded by new and totalistic
instruments of propaganda. We are awash in oceans of symbols,
images, and distorting mirrors. Moreover, these instruments of
instantaneous mass communications are in the hands of a very
small class of opinion-setters, whose world views, tastes, and
uncritical, undisciplined passions are inflicted relentlessly upon
the rest of us. The "Style" sections, cover stories, and talk
shows have generated a new public reality which no civilization
ever had to cope with before. These are not the nation's most
saintly, noble, wise, or morally self-disciplined spokespersons
who fill our imaginations, minds, and hearts with their instant
feelings and opinions. Nobody elected them to anything. By the
accidents of celebrity they have been imposed upon us, through
no one's plan. The life of the spirit is daily corrupted by their
meanderings. Striking moral poses—trying to do what is right—
they try at once to enlighten and to entertain us. No civilization
before us ever drowned in its own entertainment.

Against this sluice, American Zen may not survive—nor any
other moral virtue needed by a democratic society, a republican
form of government, an economy based upon individual and
corporate private virtue. Against this sluice, not even the elements of character celebrated in our national games may be able
to survive. Still, before they perish, it may be worth a moment's
reflection to examine the *mythos* embodied in America's three
national games, to discuss the ideal type of human action we
once desired to emulate. Human beings are free to choose their
models. These were—and may yet once again become—our
models, presented before our eyes in ritual narrative.

2

The Mythos of Baseball, Football, and Basketball. It would be far too simple to hold that each nation's national sport mirrors the national character. Still, not all sports catch on equally everywhere. In 1836, Alexis de Tocqueville noted with interest that Americans didn't play much, that there were no sports here. In those early days, the skills and crafts of the frontier nourished America's longing for the aesthetic and the discipline of sports. But even as de Tocqueville was writing, baseball was being invented. The first of our national games, baseball, was some forty years old when football was invented here, and some sixty years old when, in 1891, Dr. James Naismith, practically overnight, invented basketball. All three of these sports have captured the imaginations of millions of Americans, in every region and of every social class, as other games have not. One might include other sports as national sports; I am not trying to exclude. But it is of some interest to note that only in the United States have these three sports, together, seized the national imagination. Many other nations play basketball (although nations of lower normal height are a little less enthusiastic about it); a few nations with a very high sense of the lonely individual, honor, and personal dignity (Japan, several Latin American nations) play baseball; and almost no one else, American football. Each of these three sports has a unique mythic substance and a unique narrative form.

Some persons, of course, find all three of these sports either boring or without much significance. The imaginations of others are excited by one of these games, but not by the other two. If one were to look at these games as one would look at dance, or opera, or the theater, one would notice at once that they involve quite different formal genres and obey quite different formal rules.* Each, for example, has a different relationship to time. Baseball is clockless and, in principle, endless so far as a timepiece goes. Its ending is internal to its own rules; barring an act of God (against which there is protection in the raincheck), a baseball game lasts as long as it takes to go through nine innings of six outs each, according to the rules, and otherwise belongs to the realm of the infinite. By contrast, a clock, frequently inter-

*[Ed. note] Compare Joan Chandler's observation, p. 97 (note 36).

rupted by a stopwatch, contains football within sixty sacred minutes. Yet each actual play on the field lasts an average of about four seconds, and there are on the average about 140 plays in a complete game. Compressed all as one, the actual action requires considerably less than ten minutes. The game is, nonetheless, so intense that everybody at the end is exhausted, even though a majority of the playing time was spent in huddling up and breaking from the huddle. As for basketball, the college game is limited to forty minutes, but the game flows at an extremely high speed.

The relationship of each of these games to the individual is also different. In baseball, the individual is always at the center of attention. Singled out by the tiny white ball, each individual, one by one, is the focus of action. The central dramatic action consists of a duel between the pitcher and the batter, a duel of direct intimidation. (The most painful undercutting accusation in baseball is "choke.") Whereas the batter goes to the plate in baseball in total solitude, the runner or passer in football is part of a committee, even a corporation. Baseball dramatizes the myth of the lonely individual; football the myth of the collective. A hitter hits alone, but a passer is no better than his blockers and receivers. Football grew up with the unions; it is a game of class struggle, collective action, and liberation ("running for daylight"). It is not an acquisitive game. It is not the team that acquires the most yardage that wins—one no sooner acquires yardage than one must give it back—but the team that breaks free for most points. Basketball is as corporate as football, but it gives more latitude to the individual impresario. The individual can show off in football, but then he is grandstanding, whereas in basketball the individual signature gives the game more than half its pleasure. Basketball is like jazz: several instrumentalists each going his own way along a common line.

Each of these games also has a different relationship to the law. Baseball invokes tremendous dependence upon the force of law, as represented by the umpire, on virtually every single play. It is a game of exquisite checks and balances. It is a game almost perfectly contrived to exemplify the workings of republican government (one may even change managers, like a president, in midterm without severe dislocation to the game's participants). Football is a far more violent game, and given the number of players taking part and the rapidity of collective action, it is a game impossible completely to police; a certain lawlessness is essential to it. Violence is tempered by rules, regulations, traditions, expectations, and specified items of equipment. Thus, its lawlessness is reduced, at least, to recognizable forms. But there is no doubt whatever that it is a celebration of physical and psychological aggression.

Its form is socialist; it is the least liberal, nice, and gentle of games. Reasoning is terribly important to it; almost every physical move can be charted on a graph, its angles, speed, and force vectored in and reduced to a computer printout. For all that, it is a disorderly game, and in actual practice it seldom looks like the abstract diagrams of x's and o's by which it is mentally graphed.

By contrast again, basketball flows by so fast that human memory finds it difficult to record any one single play, or to abstract out one single play from the swift ebb and flow of constant individual movement. It is a game of much fakery and deception. Although it was designed to be a noncontact sport, in fact it is an exceedingly physical game. On virtually every play there is a violation of the game's clearly stated laws, and these violations are, moreover, essential to the game's perfection. It teaches, in a sense, a constant violation of the law in order to achieve a kind of perfection of the law. Legally, one ought never to touch anyone, but to play the game properly one must be in frequent, powerful, and well-executed physical contact. The referees control the game in roughly the same way that police along the highway control traffic: they by no means try to halt every single speeder, but they do make symbolic arrests in order to preserve the general rule of law within the abiding scope left to individual discretion.

Gunnar Myrdal remarked at some length in *An American Dilemma* on the American ambivalence toward law. Among peoples of the world, he judged, Americans are at once among the most law-abiding, and yet also the most law-resisting. We are forever thinking of new laws by which to constrain the behavior of others, complaining about irksome laws that limit our own freedoms. These characteristic American ambivalences toward the law are mirrored in our national games, in several unique ways.

There are many more things that can be said about the different narrative lines of each of our major games. I have written about them at greater length in *The Joy of Sports* (Basic Books, 1976) and do not wish too much to repeat myself. But it is important to insist upon two points concerning the relationship of sports to moral character. First, the relationship does not have to do with personal morality directly, but rather with the more remote formation of the moral imagination. In every human action, a human being necessarily imagines the self as an actor within a concrete world, on a specific stage, in an established narrative line. It is the work of the imagination to create the concrete world in which our actions make sense, are part of a story, are connected to a concrete world. The world of imagination suggested in our three national sports is a world that grows out of the American experience. There are in it rural elements, elements from the experience of industrialization, the fast pace of a jazz that is at once Dixieland and also from our urban centers. (Basketball is not merely a city game; it is also a rural, solitary game.) Secondly, the kind of virtues celebrated in our sports are not so much moralistic virtues as, so to speak, ontological virtues. That is, they have more to do with helping us to understand the elemental human situation than with offering us practical guides to moral behavior.

By this I mean that our major sports form our character at a level in some ways deeper than the merely ethical dimension. They show us, rather, what it is to be an individual confronted with one's own terrors, and what it is to show persistence and courage. They establish one of the most fundamental of all meanings of that difficult word "Community," not the community of person-to-person encounter, full of sensitivity and communication, but the sort of community that occurs in teamwork under great stress and great provocation. This is the sort of community characterized not so much by tender feelings toward one another, although these may indeed often be both present and quite powerful, but rather by the ability to accomplish together a common task, picking up one another at the point of weakness of each, gaining strength from one another, adapting almost unconsciously to one another's needs and requirements, and coming to learn to recognize and to achieve effortlessly the "click" of disparate individuals finally acting together as one. This is a rare and precious experience. There are many other meanings for the word "community," but this is a critically important, foundational meaning, in some ways more basic than any other. It is above all a meaning crucial in pluralistic societies. It is not entirely an accident that in later life many who have experienced it look back on this experience of community as one of the most profound of their lives, in whose light they judge all other meanings.

It is not by accident, either, that the world of sports has supplied so many metaphors to many of our poets, novelists, and dramatists. For the world of imagination upon which our sports draw is also the same concrete world upon which our literature draws. The expanse of green grass that delights the eye in a game of baseball carries the imagination back to the days when America was a largely agricultural nation, sleepy and rural in culture, almost fanatically individualistic and idiosyncratic, Protestant and ordered, and delighted with the sound, magic, and computation of numbers: three strikes, four balls, three outs, four bases, 360 feet (like 360 degrees around the world) to "home," seventh-inning stretch, nine innings, etc.

At the kickoff in a football game, the imagination reels backward in time to the era in which men became hunters and, once the hunted one was designated (in this case by receiving the ball), sped swiftly toward the kill. One relives, too, the dream of opportunity and liberation which met the first immigrants: a dream which simultaneously, in reality, placed between the immigrant and his goal at the very least eleven obstacles determined to halt his progress. It suggests the long intellectual labor of bringing a sort of collective consciousness to moderate the individualism of American life. As more and more Americans have entered into a corporate way of life (today, fewer than 15 percent work solely for themselves), football has added to the ritual mirror held up to our own existence a dimension we can hardly discern in baseball. As the tempo of our lives has speeded up, so also has the ritual of our games: and, thus, our delight in the almost urban frenzy of basketball, that discotheque of games.

Interestingly enough, each of our national games is, in a powerful way, a game decided by fate. The way the ball bounces decides many a baseball game. The football was deliberately designed so as not to be round, so as to be unpredictable in its bounces. Many astute football coaches have well understood that close games are decided by the breaks; they train their teams, accordingly, to wait patiently for the breaks and then suddenly to exploit them. As for basketball, on any given night, almost any team, getting hot, can defeat almost any other, and even in the closest and most evenly matched contests, the contingencies and high fortune of the last few seconds usually decide the outcome. The player who makes 80 percent of his free throws over a season either does or does not make the one critical free throw *drop*. Often the last shot of the game, surely as much by luck as by skill, decides the outcome.

We are supposed to be a puritan, pragmatic, calculating people. Yet it is astonishing how inwardly satisfied we are by liturgical images of luck and fortune. Indeed, luck may be the most fundamental assumption in the American view of the world. We believe in equal opportunity; yet experience teaches us there is no equality of results. We believe in hard work; yet we can see quite vividly that rewards are not equivalent to hard work, but decisively affected by a little luck here or there. By freedom and by equality, we seem to have in mind a kind of lottery in which luck might strike anyone at any time, regardless of social class or position. Not mere, random luck, of course, but a luck for which one has trained and prepared oneself—but luck, nevertheless. Our greatest athletes have a knack for "coming through" at the most critical moments. That is, they are graced. Fortune blows with them. They have prepared themselves, they have trained, they have worked hard, but at the last moment it is the flight of the dove that bears them aloft, not the patient climbing of the mountain. This, at least, is what our games seem to celebrate. It happens to fit, as well, what our scholars have to tell us about the actual practice of equality in the United States. Nothing seems to correlate with results as much as luck or chance, according to Christopher Jencks and his associates, in *Equality*.

We see, then, that those oval stadiums and circular domes within which our three national liturgies are consummated are indeed feminine in their symbolism, built in honor of a goddess, whose name is Fortune. Fortune does not smile simply at command; she chooses whom she will. Blessed are they on whom, often through no special merit of their own, she smiles. Rejected do they feel indeed who, even after superhuman effort to execute the best laid plans, through no fault of their own fall short. The better team, better on paper, often does not win. America, like Fortune, loves the underdog.

3

Many of the human experiences essential to an understanding of the literature of Western civilization are embodied in the rituals of our sports. In teaching the humanities, a professor does well to imagine that many of the experiences upon which American youngsters might draw in order to understand the words they read have been accessible to them in their experiences of our major sports.

Consider only a few of many examples. Over a lifetime, no athlete wins all the time. Teaching oneself how to lose, how to learn from errors, how not to make excuses, and how to rise to struggle again on another day is learned in every battle with oneself to master every element of a given sport. Most athletes, like most teams, lose more than half the time. Each athlete discovers in himself certain limitations and finds himself inferior to others in certain skills. Moreover, our major sports take place under the eyes of connoisseurs, and ridicule for failures is quite open and unabashed. One of the most important experiences in sports, therefore, is the experience of public failure. Failure to which is added, sometimes in good humor and sometimes meanly, an element of humiliation. Since every exercise of freedom involves the risk of failure, there is in sports an excellent preparation for learning how to try things publicly, even at the risk of public failure, and of learning how to accept both failure and defeat with a certain grace.

To learn all such things is not quite the same as acquiring moral virtue. It is, rather, to learn how to be reconciled to one's own human nature. Here, too, the virtues are rather ontological than moral. They suggest more about the human situation, the uses of craft, and the limits of will, about "character" in this sense, rather than about "character" as it is spoken of by Sunday school teachers or by moralists. Athletes, like artists, may acquire a certain excellence and create works of considerable beauty, while not excelling in the moral virtues, even while in their personal lives being moral failures. Often, indeed, like the rest of us, they are moral mediocrities. Excellence in the arts and excellence in sports are far from being the same as excellence in moral behavior.* Virtues taught by sports, like the virtues involved in artistic excellence, are in this sense of a nonmoral nature. To learn how to think clearly under the pressures of impending defeat and humiliation is not easy for human beings. The conditions of an athletic contest are appropriate condi-

---

*I am alluding here, of course, to Jacques Maritain, *Art and Scholasticism.*

tions under which to learn such skills, which appertain to the
survival, even to the possible improvement, of the human race.
These are not inconsiderable skills.

It is, to repeat, a common analytic error to leap too easily from
athletics to moral virtue. Coaches are quite right to speak of the
importance of "character" in sports, to speak of discipline, and
temperance, and courage, and endurance, and the rest. They are
right to speak of teamwork and even of love. But it must always
be understood that they are speaking of these things liturgically,
in a certain symbolic context, which is quite different from the
complete context of a full human life. Learning how to be moral
is *like* learning how to be a good athlete. But being a good human
being calls for a far larger and more detailed set of attributes than
simply learning how to be a good athlete. No doubt, there is
some transference from one field of endeavor to another, but the
scope of this transference should not be exaggerated. Rather, the
one realm provides a kind of metaphor for the other. It provides
basic experiences of considerable human interest. These experiences may be drawn upon as a field of examples and parables, to
be applied differently in other and different moral terrain. They
are far from exhausting the whole moral terrain. As the poet or
the humanist in his actual living practice can fall far below the
level of the moral insight expressed in his poetry or humanistic
wisdom, so also the athlete can excel in the athletic virtues while
falling far short on the terrain of human living. Indeed, this cir-
cumstance is quite common. It is difficult enough to be a poet; it
is far more difficult to be a saint. It is difficult to become as good
an athlete as one can; it is even more difficult to become as good
a human being as one can. The acquittal of the one task does not
suffice to acquit one's obligations in the other.

It is quite striking, nonetheless, that American universities
have been preeminent in the world in their emphasis upon the
importance of athletics. It is equally striking that so many professors and students seem, in their actual thinking and academic
research, to avert their eyes from the powerful realities of the
world of sport around them. It is not at all necessary to be so
blind. The world of American sport is rich in materials for the
humanistic imagination; rich, too, in the actual experience of
human realities basic to the humanistic tradition. It is a shame to
overlook this field of fundamental human experience from which
most Americans have tacitly learned so much of harsh humanistic virtue. Overlooking it, indeed, is a little like squandering a

precious natural resource. Our philosophers and theologians, our literary scholars and our historians, our psychologists and anthropologists, our sociologists and even our theoreticians about democratic capitalism, if they would but pay attention to the sports which thrive around them, would discover a world rich in symbol, narrative, and mythic material, which sheds much light on the meaning of this quite lovely but fragile civilization which goes by the name of the United States of America. Without the games we have, we would be far poorer than we are. Their loveliness, though limited, deserves to be sung. Many of us are extremely grateful to them for the beauty they have brought us, the longing for excellence they taught us, the willingness to endure pain and humiliation they demanded of us. These are part of the patrimony of being American.

2

The Corruption of Sports

CHRISTOPHER LASCH

Among the activities through which men seek release from everyday life, games offer in many ways the purest form of escape. Like sex, drugs, and drink, they obliterate awareness of everyday reality, not by dimming that awareness but by raising it to a new intensity of concentration. Moreover, games have no side effects, produce no hangovers or emotional complications. Games satisfy the need for free fantasy and the search for gratuitous difficulty simultaneously; they combine childlike exuberance with deliberately created complications.

By establishing conditions of equality among the players, Roger Caillois says, games attempt to substitute ideal conditions for "the normal confusion of everyday life."[1] They re-create the freedom, the remembered perfection of childhood and mark it off from ordinary life with artificial boundaries, within which the only constraints are the rules to which the players freely submit. Games enlist skill and intelligence, the utmost concentration of purpose, on behalf of utterly useless activities, which make no contribution to the struggle of man against nature, to the wealth or comfort of the community, or to its physical survival.

In communist and fascist countries sports have been organized and promoted by the state. In capitalist countries the uselessness of games makes them offensive to social reformers, improvers of public morals, or functionalist critics of society like Veblen, who saw in the futility of upper-class sports anachronistic survivals of militarism and tests of prowess. Yet the "futility" of play, and nothing else, explains its appeal—its artificiality, the

First printed in *The New York Review of Books* © 1977. Reprinted by permission of the author.

arbitrary obstacles it sets up for no other purpose than to challenge the players to surmount them, the absence of any utilitarian or uplifting object. Games quickly lose part of their charm when pressed into the service of education, character development, or social improvement.

Modern industry having reduced most jobs to a routine, games in our society take on added meaning. Men seek in play the difficulties and demands—both intellectual and physical—which they no longer find in work. The history of culture, as Huizinga showed in his classic study of play, *Homo Ludens,* appears from one perspective to consist of the gradual eradication of the elements of play from all cultural forms—from religion, from the law, from warfare, above all from productive labor. The rationalization of these activities leaves little room for the spirit of arbitrary invention or the disposition to leave things to chance. Risk, daring, and uncertainty, important components of play, have little place in industry or in activities infiltrated by industrial methods, which are intended precisely to predict and control the future and to eliminate risk. Games accordingly have assumed an importance unprecedented even in ancient Greece, where so much of social life revolved around contests. Sports, which satisfy also the starved need for physical exertion—for a renewal of the sense of the physical basis of life—have become an obsession not just of the masses but of those who set themselves up as a cultural elite.

The rise of spectator sports to their present importance coincides historically with the rise of mass production, which intensifies the needs sport satisfies while at the same time creating the technical capacity to promote and market athletic contests to a vast audience. But according to a common criticism of modern sport, these same developments have destroyed the value of athletics. Commercialized play has turned into work, subordinated the athlete's pleasure to the spectator's, and reduced the spectator himself to a state of passivity—the very antithesis of the health and vigor sport ideally promotes. The mania for winning has encouraged an exaggerated emphasis on the competitive side of sport, to the exclusion of the more modest but more satisfying experiences of cooperation and competence. The cult of victory, loudly proclaimed by such football coaches as Vince Lombardi and George Allen, has made savages of the players and rabid chauvinists of their followers. The violence and partisanship of modern sports lead some critics to

insist that athletics impart militaristic values to the young, irra-
tionally inculcate local and national pride in the spectator, and
serve as one of the strongest bastions of male chauvinism.

Huizinga himself, who anticipated some of these arguments
and stated them far more persuasively, argued that modern
games and sports had been ruined by a "fatal shift toward over-
seriousness." At the same time, he maintained that play had lost
its element of ritual, had become "profane," and consequently
had ceased to have any "organic connection whatever with the
structure of society." The masses now crave "trivial recreation
and crude sensationalism" and throw themselves into these pursuits with an intensity far beyond their intrinsic merit. Instead of
playing with the freedom and intensity of children, they play
with the "blend of adolescence and barbarity" that Huizinga
calls puerilism, investing games with patriotic and martial fervor
while treating serious pursuits as if they were games. "A far-
reaching contamination of play and serious activity has taken
place," according to Huizinga:

> The two spheres are getting mixed. In the activities of an
> outwardly serious nature hides an element of play. Recognized
> play, on the other hand, is no longer able to maintain its true
> play-character as a result of being taken too seriously and
> being technically over-organized. The indispensable qualities
> of detachment, artlessness, and gladness are thus lost.

An analysis of the criticism of modern sport, in its vulgar form
as well as in Huizinga's more refined version, brings to light a
number of common misconceptions about modern society. A
large amount of writing on sports has accumulated in recent
years, and the sociology of sport has even entrenched itself as a
minor branch of social science. Much of this commentary has no
higher purpose than to promote athletics or to exploit the journalistic market they have created, but some of it aspires to social
criticism. Those who have formulated the now familiar indictment of organized sport include the sociologist Harry Edwards;
the psychologist and former tennis player Dorcas Susan Butt,
who thinks sport should promote "competence" instead of competition; disillusioned professional athletes like Dave Meggyesy
and Chip Oliver; and radical critics of culture and society, notably Paul Hoch and Jack Scott.[2]

Critics of sport, in their eagerness to uncover evidence of

corruption and decline, attack intrinsic elements of athletics, elements essential to their appeal in all periods and places, on the erroneous assumption that spectatorship, violence, and competition reflect conditions peculiar to modern times. On the other hand, they overlook the distinctive contribution of contemporary society to the degradation of sport and therefore misconceive the nature of that degradation. They concentrate on issues, such as "overseriousness," that are fundamental to an understanding of sports, indeed to the very definition of play, but that are peripheral or irrelevant to the ways they have changed in recent history.

Take the common complaint that modern sports are "spectator-oriented rather than participant-oriented." Spectators, in this view, are irrelevant to the success of the game. What a naïve theory of human motivation this implies! The attainment of certain skills unavoidably gives rise to an urge to show them off. At a higher level of mastery, the performer no longer wishes merely to display his virtuosity—for the true connoisseur can easily distinguish between the performer who plays to the crowd and the superior artist who matches himself against the full rigor of his art itself—but to ratify a supremely difficult accomplishment; to give pleasure; to forge a bond between himself and his audience, a shared appreciation of a ritual executed not only flawlessly but with much feeling and with a sense of style and proportion.

In all games, particularly in athletic contests, the central importance of display and representation serves as a reminder of the ancient connections between play, ritual, and drama. The players not only compete, they enact a familiar ceremony that reaffirms common values. Ceremony requires witnesses: enthusiastic spectators conversant with the rules of the performance and its underlying meaning. Far from destroying the value of sports, the attendance of spectators is often necessary to them. Indeed one of the virtues of contemporary sports lies in their resistance to the erosion of standards and their capacity to appeal to a knowledgeable audience. Norman Podhoretz has argued that the sports public remains more discriminating than the public for the arts and that in sports "excellence is relatively uncontroversial as a judgment of performance." The public for sports still consists largely of men who took part in sports during boyhood and thus acquired a sense of the game and a capacity to make discriminating judgments.

The same can hardly be said for the audience of an artistic performance, even though amateur musicians, dancers, actors, and painters may still comprise a small nucleus of the audience. Constant experimentation in the arts, in any case, has created so much confusion about standards that the only surviving measure of excellence, for many, is novelty and shock-value, which in a jaded time often resides in a work's sheer ugliness or banality. In sport, on the other hand, novelty and rapid shifts of fashion play only a small part in its appeal to a discriminating audience.

Yet even here, the contamination of standards has already begun. Faced with rising costs, owners seek to increase attendance at sporting events by installing exploding scoreboards, broadcasting recorded cavalry charges, giving away helmets and bats, and surrounding the spectator with cheerleaders, usherettes, and ball girls. Television has enlarged the audience for sports while lowering the quality of that audience's understanding; at least this is the assumption of sports commentators, who direct at the audience an interminable stream of tutelage in the basics of the game, and of the promoters, who reshape one game after another to conform to the tastes of an audience supposedly incapable of grasping their finer points.

The American League's adoption of the designated hitter rule, which relieves pitchers of the need to bat and diminishes the importance of managerial strategy, provides an especially blatant example of the dilution of sports by the requirements of mass promotion. Another example is the "Devil-Take-the-Hindmost Mile," a track event invented by the San Francisco *Examiner,* in which the last runner in the early stages of the race has to drop out—a rule that encourages an early scramble to avoid disqualification but lowers the general quality of the event. When the television networks discovered surfing, they insisted that events be held according to a prearranged schedule, without regard to weather conditions. A surfer complained, "Television is destroying our sport. The TV producers are turning a sport and an art form into a circus." The same practices produce the same effects on other sports, forcing baseball players, for example, to play World Series games on freezing October evenings. Substituting artificial surfaces for grass in tennis, which has slowed the pace of the game, placed a premium on reliability and patience, and reduced the element of tactical brilliance and overpowering speed, commends itself to television producers because it makes tennis an all-weather game and even permits it to be played indoors, in sanctuaries of sport like Caesar's Palace in Las Vegas.

As spectators become less knowledgeable about the games they watch, they become more sensation-minded and blood-thirsty. The rise of violence in ice hockey, far beyond the point where it plays any functional part in the game, coincided with the expansion of professional hockey into cities without any traditional attachment to the sport—cities in which weather conditions, indeed, had always precluded any such tradition of local play. But the significance of such changes is not, as such critics as Jack Scott and Paul Hoch imagine, that sports ought to be organized solely for the edification of the players and that corruption sets in when sports begin to be played to spectators for a profit. It is often true that sport at this point ceases to be enjoyable and becomes a business. Recent critics go astray, however, in supposing that organized athletics ever serve the interests of the players alone or that "professionalization" inevitably corrupts all who take part in it.

In glorifying amateurism, equating spectatorship with passivity, and deploring competition, recent criticism of sport echoes the fake radicalism of the counterculture, from which so much of it derives. It shows its contempt for excellence by proposing to break down the "elitist" distinction between players and spectators. It proposes to replace competitive professional sports, which notwithstanding their shortcomings uphold standards of competence and bravery that might otherwise become extinct, with a bland regimen of cooperative diversions in which everyone can join in regardless of age or ability—"new sports for the noncompetitive," having "no object, really," according to a typical effusion, except to bring "people together to enjoy each other."[3] In its eagerness to strip from sport the elements that have always explained its imaginative appeal, the staged rivalry of superior ability, this "radicalism" proposes merely to complete the degradation already begun by the very society the cultural radicals profess to criticize and subvert.

What corrupts an athletic performance, as it does any other performance, is not professionalism or competition but the presence of an unappreciative, ignorant audience and the need to divert it with sensations extrinsic to the performance. It is at this point that ritual, drama, and sports all degenerate into spectacle. Huizinga's analysis of the secularization of sport helps to clarify this issue. In the degree to which athletic events lose the elements of ritual and public festivity, according to Huizinga, they deteriorate into "trivial recreation and crude sensationalism." But even Huizinga misunderstands the cause of this development. It hardly lies in the "fatal shift toward over-seriousness." Huizinga himself, when he is writing about the theory of play rather than the collapse of "genuine play" in our own time, understands very well that play at its best is always serious; indeed that the essence of play lies in taking seriously activities that have no purpose, serve no utilitarian ends. He reminds us that "the majority of Greek contests were fought out in deadly earnest" and discusses, under the category of play, duels in which contestants fight to the death, water sports in which the goal is to drown your opponent, and tournaments for which the training and preparation consume the athletes' entire existence.

The degradation of sport, then, consists not in its being taken too seriously but in its subjection to some ulterior purpose, such as profit-making, patriotism, moral training, or the pursuit of health. Sport may give rise to these things in abundance, but ideally it produces them only as by-products having no essential connection with the game. When the game itself, on the other hand, comes to be regarded as incidental to the benefits it supposedly confers on participants, spectators, or promoters, it loses its peculiar capacity to transport both participant and spectator beyond everyday experience—to provide a glimpse of perfect order uncontaminated by commonplace calculations of advantage or even by ordinary considerations of survival.

The recent history of sports is the history of their steady submission to the demands of everyday reality. The nineteenth-century bourgeoisie suppressed popular sports and festivals as part of its campaign to establish the reign of sobriety. Fairs and football, bullbaiting and cockfighting and boxing offended middle-class reformers because of their cruelty and because they blocked public thoroughfares, disrupted the daily routine of business, distracted the people from their work, encouraged habits of idleness, extravagance, and insubordination, and gave rise to licentiousness and debauchery.

In the name of "rational enjoyment" and the spirit of "improvement," these reformers exhorted the laboring man to forsake his riotous public sports and "wakes" and to stay at his hearth, in the respectable comfort of the domestic circle. When exhortation failed, they resorted to political action. In early nineteenth-century England, they were opposed by a conservative coalition that crossed class lines, the commoners having been joined in the defense of their "immemorial" enjoyments by the traditionalists among the gentry, especially the rural gentry not yet infected with evangelical piety, sentimental humanitarianism, and the dogma of enterprise. "What would be the Consequence," they asked, "if all such Diversions were entirely banished? The common People seeing themselves cut off from all Hope of this Enjoyment, would become dull and spiritless. . . : And not only so, but thro' the absolute Necessity of diverting themselves at Times, they would addict themselves rather to less warrantable Pleasures."[4]

In the United States, the mid-nineteenth-century campaign against popular amusements, closely associated with the crusade against liquor and the movement for more strict observance of the Sabbath, took on the character of an ethnic as well as a class conflict. The working class, largely immigrant and Catholic in composition, struggled, often in uneasy alliance with the "sporting element" and with "fashionable society," to defend its drink and its gambling against the assault of middle-class respectability. The passage of blue laws, which rendered many popular amusements illegal and drove them underground, testifies to the political failure of this alliance. Middle-class reformers, usually associated first with the Whig party and then with the Republicans, enjoyed the advantage not merely of superior access to political power but of a burning sense of moral purpose. The spirit of early bourgeois society was deeply antithetical to play.

Not only did games contribute nothing to capital accumulation, not only did they encourage gambling and reckless expenditure, but they contained an important element of pretense, illusion, mimicry, and make-believe. The bourgeois distrust of games reflected a deeper distrust of fancy, of histrionics, of elaborate dress and costume. Veblen, whose satire against bourgeois society incorporated many of its own values, including its hatred of useless and unproductive play, condemned such upper-class sports as hunting, fishing, and football on the grounds of their "futility"; nor did he miss the connection between sport and histrionic display.

It is noticeable, for instance, that even very mild-mannered and matter-of-fact men who go out shooting are apt to carry an

excess of arms and accoutrements in order to impress upon
their own imagination the seriousness of their undertaking.
These huntsmen are also prone to a histrionic, prancing gait
and to an elaborate exaggeration of the motions, whether of
stealth or of onslaught, involved in their deeds of exploit.

Veblen's satire against the "leisure class" miscarried; in
America, where leisure found its only justification in the capacity to renew mind and body for work, the upper class for the
most part refused to become a leisure class at all. Fearful of
being displaced by the rising "robber barons," it mastered the art
of mass politics, asserted its control over the emerging industrial
corporations, and embraced the ideal of the "strenuous life."
Sports played an important part in this moral rehabilitation of
the ruling class. Having suppressed or driven to the margins of
society many of the recreations of the people, the *haute
bourgeoisie* proceeded to adapt the games of its class enemies to
its own purposes. In the private schools which prepared its sons
for the responsibilities of business and empire, sports were enlisted in the service of "character" building. The new ideology of
imperialism, both in England and in the United States, glorified
the playing field as the source of qualities essential to national
greatness and martial success. Far from cultivating sports as a
form of display and splendid futility, the new national
bourgeoisie—which at the end of the nineteenth century replaced the local elites of an earlier day—celebrated precisely
their capacity to instill the "will to win."
    At a time when popular preachers of success were redefining
the work ethic to stress the element of competition, athletic
competition took on new importance as a preparation for the
battle of life. In a never-ending stream of books turned out to
satisfy the rising demand for sports fiction, popular authors upheld Frank Merriwell and other athletes as models for American
youth. The young man on the make, formerly advised to go into
a business at an early age and master it from bottom to top, now
learned the secret of success on the playing field, in fierce but
friendly competition with his peers. Proponents of the new
strenuousness insisted that athletics developed the courage and
manliness that would promote not only individual success but
upper-class ascendancy. "In most countries," according to
Theodore Roosevelt,

the "Bourgeoisie"—the moral, respectable, commercial, middle class—is looked upon with a certain contempt which is justified by their timidity and unwarlikeness. But the minute a middle class produces men like Hawkins and Frobisher on the seas, or men such as the average Union soldier in the civil war, it acquires the hearty respect of others which it merits.

Roosevelt believed that sports would help to produce such leaders, at the same time warning his sons not to regard football, boxing, riding, shooting, walking, and rowing as "the end to which *all* your energies must be devoted, or even the major portion of your energies."

Athletic competition also laid the foundations of national greatness, according to ideologues of the new imperialism. Walter Camp, whose tactical innovations at Yale brought into being the modern game of football, argued during World War I that the "grand do-or-die spirit that holds the attack on the one-yard line was what made Chateau-Thierry." General Douglas MacArthur echoed these platitudes in World War II: "Upon the fields of friendly strife are sown the seeds which, on other days, on other fields, will bear the fruits of victory."

By this time, however, the cult of the strenuous life was as obsolete as the explicit racism that once informed imperialist ideology. MacArthur himself was an anachronism in his flamboyance and his faith in clean living and high thinking. As American imperialism allied itself with more liberal values, the cult of "manly arts" survived as an important theme only in the ideology of the far right. In the 1960s, reactionary ideologues extolled athletics as "a fortress that has held the wall against radical elements," in the words of the head football coach at Washington State University; or as Spiro Agnew put it, "one of the few bits of glue that hold society together." Max Rafferty, California Superintendent of Schools, defended the view that "a coach's job was to make men out of wet-behind-the-ears boys" and tried to reassure himself that "the love of clean, competitive sports is too deeply imbedded in the American matrix, too much a part of the warp and woof of our free people, ever to surrender to the burning-eyed, bearded draft-card burners who hate and envy the athlete because he is something they can never be—a *man*."

Left-wing critics of sport have made such statements the center of their attack—another example of the way in which cultural radicalism, posing as a revolutionary threat to the status quo, in reality confines its criticism to values already obsolescent and to patterns of American capitalism that have long ago been superseded. Left-wing criticism of sport provides one of the most vivid examples of the essentially conformist character of the "cultural revolution" with which it identifies itself. According to Paul Hoch, Jack Scott, Dave Meggyesy, and other cultural radicals, sport is a "mirror reflection" of society, which indoctrinates the young with the dominant values. In America, organized athletics inculcate militarism, authoritarianism, racism, and sexism, thereby perpetuating the "false consciousness" of the masses. Sports serve as an "opiate" of the people, diverting the masses from their real problems with a "dream world" of glamor and excitement. They promote sexual rivalry among males—with "vestal virgins" leading the cheers from the sidelines—and thus prevent the proletariat from achieving revolutionary solidarity in the face of its oppressors.

Competitive athletics, so the indictment goes, force the "pleasure-oriented id" to submit to "the hegemony of the repressed ego" in order to shore up the nuclear family—the basic form of authoritarianism—and to divert sexual energy into the service of the work ethic. For all these reasons, organized competition should give way to "intramural sports aimed at making everyone a player." If everyone "had fulfilling, creative jobs," moreover, "they wouldn't need to look for the pseudo satisfactions of being fans."

This attack, offensive in the first place in its assumption that cultural radicals understand the needs and interests of the masses better than the masses themselves do, also offends every principle of social analysis. It confuses adapting to a society's patterns—"socialization"—with indoctrination, and takes the most reactionary pronouncements at face value, as if athletes automatically imbibed the right-wing opinions of some of their mentors and spokesmen. Sport does play a part in socialization, but the lessons it teaches are not necessarily the ones that coaches and teachers of physical education seek to impart. The mirror theory of sport, like all reductionist interpretations of culture, makes no allowance for the autonomy of cultural traditions. In sport, these traditions come down from one generation of players to another, and although athletics do reflect social values, they can never be completely assimilated to those values. Indeed they resist assimilation more effectively than many other activities, since games learned in youth exert their own demands and inspire loyalty to the game itself, rather than to the programs ideologues seek to impose on them.

In any case, the "reactionary values" allegedly perpetuated by sport no longer reflect the dominant needs of American capitalism at all. The champions of "cultural radicalism" do not begin to understand the society they profess to criticize. If a society of consumers has no need of the Protestant work ethic, neither does it need the support of an ideology of manliness and martial valor. The professionalization of sport and the extension of professional athletics into the universities, which now serve as a farm system for the major leagues, have undercut the old "school spirit" and given rise among athletes to a thoroughly businesslike approach to their craft. Athletes now regard the inspirational appeals of old-fashioned coaches with amused cynicism, nor do they readily submit to authoritarian discipline. The proliferation of franchises and the frequency with which they move from one locality to another undermine local loyalties, both among participants and spectators, and discourage attempts to model "team spirit" on patriotism.

In a bureaucratic society, all forms of corporate loyalty lose their force, and although athletes still make a point of subordinating their own achievements to those of the team, they do so in order to promote easy relations with their colleagues, not because the team as a corporate entity transcends individual interests. On the contrary, the athlete as a professional entertainer seeks above all to further his own interests and willingly sells his services to the highest bidder. The better athletes become television celebrities and supplement their salaries with endorsements that often exceed the salaries themselves.

All these developments make it difficult to think of the athlete as a local or national hero, as the representative of his class or race, or in any way as the embodiment of some larger corporate unit. The recognition that sports have come to serve as a form of "entertainment" alone justifies the salaries paid to star athletes and their prominence in the media. As Howard Cosell has candidly acknowledged, sports can no longer be sold to the public as "just sports or as religion." "Sports aren't life and death. They're entertainment." Even as the television audience demands the presentation of sports as a form of spectacle, however, the widespread resentment of star athletes among followers of sport—a resentment directed against the inflated salaries negotiated by their agents and against their willingness to become hucksters, promoters, and celebrities—indicates the persistence of a need to believe that sports represent something more than entertainment, that though neither life nor death in themselves, they retain some lingering capacity to dramatize and clarify those experiences.

The secularization of sport, which began as soon as athletics were pressed into the service of patriotism and character building, was complete only when sport became an object of mass consumption. The first stage in this process was the establishment of big-time athletics in the universities and their spread from the Ivy League to the large public and private colleges, thence downward into the high schools. The unprecedented emphasis, in late nineteenth-century commercial life, on competition and the will to win, stimulated the growth of sports in another way. It made the acquisition of educational credentials essential to business or professional careers and thus created in large numbers a new kind of student, utterly indifferent to higher learning but forced to undergo it for economic reasons. Large-scale athletic programs helped colleges to attract such students, in competitive bidding for enrollments, and to entertain them once they enrolled.

In the closing years of the nineteenth century, according to Donald Meyer, the development of an "alumni culture" centering on clubs, fraternities, alumni offices, money drives, homecoming ceremonies, and football, grew out of the colleges' need not only to raise money in large amounts but to attract "a clientele for whom the classroom had no real meaning but who were by no means ready to send their sons out into the world at age eighteen."[5] At Notre Dame, as Frederick Rudolph has pointed out, "intercollegiate athletics . . . were consciously developed in the 1890's as an agency of student recruitment." As early as 1878, President McCosh of Princeton wrote to an alumnus in Kentucky: "You will confer a great favor on us if you will get . . . the college noticed in the Louisville papers. . . . We must persevere in our efforts to get students from your region. . . . Mr. Brand Ballard has won us great reputation as captain of the football team which has beaten both Harvard and Yale."

In order to accommodate the growing hordes of spectators, the colleges and universities, sometimes aided by local business interests, built lavish athletic facilities—enormous field houses, football stadia in the pretentious imperial style of the early twentieth century. The growing investment in sports led in turn to a growing need to maintain a winning record: a new concern with system, efficiency, and the elimination of risk. Walter Camp's innovations at Yale emphasized drill, discipline, teamwork. As in industry, the attempt to coordinate the movements of many men created a demand for "scientific management" and for the expansion of managerial personnel. In many sports, trainers, coaches, doctors, and public relations experts soon outnumbered the players. The accumulation of elaborate statistical records arose from management's attempt to reduce winning to a routine, to measure efficient performance. The athletic contest itself, surrounded by a vast apparatus of information and promotion, now appeared almost incidental to the expensive preparation required to stage it.

The rise of a new kind of journalism—the yellow journalism pioneered by Hearst and Pulitzer, which sold sensations instead of reporting news—helped to professionalize amateur athletics, to assimilate sport to promotion, and to make professional athletics into a major industry. Until the twenties, professional sports, where they existed at all, attracted little of the public attention lavished on college football. Even baseball, the oldest and most highly organized of professional sports, suffered from the faintly unsavory associations that seemed to surround it—its appeal to the working class and the sporting crowd, its rural origins. When a Yale alumnus complained to Walter Camp about the overemphasis on football, he could think of no better way of dramatizing the danger than to cite the example of baseball: "The language and scenes which are too often witnessed [in football games] are such as to degrade the college student and bring him down to a par with or even lower than the average professional baseball player."

The World Series scandal of 1919 confirmed baseball's bad reputation, but it also set in motion the reforms of Kenesaw Mountain Landis, the new commissioner brought in by the owners to clean up the game and give it a better public image. Landis's regime, the success of the eminently respectable and efficient New York Yankees, and the idolization of Babe Ruth soon made professional baseball "America's number-one pastime." Ruth became the first modern athlete to be sold to the public as much for his "color, personality, crowd appeal" (Grantland Rice) as for his remarkable abilities. His press agent,

Christy Walsh, developer of a syndicate of ghostwriters who sold books and articles under the names of sports heroes, arranged on behalf of the "Sultan of Swat" barnstorming tours, endorsements, and movie roles, thus contributing to "the bally-hoo," in the words of Warren Susman, "that promoted a professional athlete into a celebrity of ever exaggerated proportions."[6]

In the quarter-century following World War II, entrepreneurs extended the techniques of mass promotion first perfected in the marketing of college football and professional baseball to other professional sports, notably hockey, basketball, and football. Television did for these games what mass journalism and radio had done for baseball, elevating them to new heights of popularity while at the same time reducing them to entertainment. In his recent study of sport, Michael Novak notes that television has lowered the quality of sports reporting, freeing announcers from the need to describe the course of play and encouraging them instead to adopt the style of professional entertainers.[7]

The invasion of sport by the "entertainment ethic," according to Novak, breaks down the boundaries between the ritual world of play and the sordid reality from which it is designed to provide escape. Broadcasters like Howard Cosell, who embody the "virulent passion for debunking in the land," mistakenly import critical standards more appropriate to political reporting into the coverage of sports. Newspapers report the "business side" of sports on the sports page, instead of confining it to the business section where it belongs. "It is important," Novak argues, ". . . to keep sports as insulated as we can from business, entertainment, politics, and even gossip. . . . The preservation of parts of life not drawn up into politics and work is essential for the human spirit." Especially when politics has become "a brutal, ugly business" and work (not sport) the opiate of the people, athletics alone in Novak's view, offer a glimpse of the "real thing." Games take place in a "world outside of time," which must be sealed off from the surrounding corruption.

The anguished outcry of the true fan, who brings to sports a proper sense of awe, only to find them corrupted from within by the spread of the "entertainment ethic," sheds more light on the degradation of sports than the strictures of left-wing critics, who wish to abolish competition, emphasize the value of sports as health-giving exercise, and promote a more "cooperative" conception of athletics—in other words, to make sports an instrument of personal and social therapy. Novak's analysis, however, minimizes the extent of the problem and misconstrues its cause.

In a society dominated by the production and consumption of images, no part of life can long remain immune from the invasion of spectacle.

Nor can this invasion be blamed on the "spirit of debunking." It arises, in a paradoxical fashion, precisely out of the attempt to set up a separate sphere of leisure uncontaminated by the world of work and politics. While play has always, by its very nature, set itself off from workaday life, at the same time it retains an organic connection with the life of the community, by virtue of its capacity to dramatize reality and to offer a convincing representation of the community's values. The ancient connections between games, ritual, and public festivity suggest that although games take place within arbitrary boundaries, they are nevertheless rooted in shared traditions, to which they give objective expression. Games and athletic contests offer a dramatic commentary on reality rather than an escape from it—a heightened reenactment of communal traditions, not a repudiation of them. It is only when games and sports come to be valued purely as a form of escape that they lose the capacity to provide this escape.

The appearance in history of an escapist conception of "leisure" coincides with the organization of leisure as an extension of commodity production. The same forces that have organized production as an assembly line have now organized leisure as well, reducing it to an appendage of industry. As Martha Wolfenstein observed in her essay on "fun morality," work now tends "to be permeated with behavior formerly confined to after work hours"—the manipulation of personal relations in the interest of political or economic advantage—while play is "measured by standards of achievement previously applicable only to work."[8]

Modern sport is dominated not so much by the undue emphasis on winning as by the desperate urge to avoid defeat. Coaches, not quarterbacks, often call the plays, and the managerial apparatus makes every effort to eliminate the risk and the uncertainty that contribute so centrally to the ritual and dramatic success of any contest. When sports can no longer be played with appropriate abandon, they lose the capacity to raise the spirits of players and spectators, to transport them into a higher realm. Prudence and calculation, so prominent in everyday life but so inimical to the spirit of games, come to shape sports as they shape everything else.

While he deplores the subordination of sport to entertainment, Novak takes for granted the separation of work and leisure that gives rise in the first place to this invasion of play by the standards of the workaday world. He does not see that the degradation of play originates in the degradation of work, which creates both the need and the opportunity for commercialized "recreation." As Huizinga has shown, it is precisely when the element of play disappears from law, statecraft, and other cultural forms that men turn to play not to witness a dramatic reenactment of their common life but to find diversion and sensation.

At that point, games and sports, far from taking themselves too seriously, as Huizinga mistakenly concluded, become, on the contrary, a "thing of no consequence." As Edgar Wind suggested in his analysis of modern art—which raised some of the same issues that are posed by the recent history of sport—the trivialization of art was already implicit in the modernist exaltation of art, which assumed that "the experience of art will be more intense if it pulls the spectator away from his ordinary habits and preoccupations."[9] The ideology of modernism tends to guarantee the socially marginal status of art at the same time that it opens art to the invasion of commercialized aesthetic fashion—a process that culminates, by a curious but inexorable logic, in the postmodernist demand for the abolition of art and its assimilation to "reality."

The development of sport follows a similar pattern. The attempt to create a separate realm of pure play, totally isolated from work, gives rise to its opposite—the insistence, in Cosell's words, that "sports are not separate and apart from life, a special 'Wonderland' where everything is pure and sacred and above criticism," but a business, subject to the same standards and open to the same scrutiny as any other. The positions represented by Novak and Cosell are symbiotically related and arise out of the same historical development: the emergence of the spectacle as the dominant form of cultural expression. What began as an attempt not only to invest sport with religious significance but to make it into a surrogate religion in its own right ends with the demystification of sport, the assimilation of sport to show business.

Notes

1. Roger Caillois, "The Structure and Classification of Games," in John W. Loy, Jr., and Gerald S. Kenyon, eds., *Sport, Culture, and Society* (New York: Macmillan, 1969), 49.

2. See Harry Edwards, *The Sociology of Sport* (Homewood, Ill.: Dorsey Press, 1973) and *The Revolt of the Black Athlete* (New York: Free Press, 1969); Dorcas Susan Butt, *Psychology of Sport* (New York: Van Nostrand-Reinhold, 1976); Dave Meggyesy, *Out of Their League* (Berkeley, Calif.: Ramparts, 1970); Chip Oliver, *High for the Game* (New York: Morrow, 1971); Paul Hoch, *Rip Off the Big Game: The Exploitation of Sports by the Power Elite* (New York: Anchor Books, 1972); Jack Scott, *The Athletic Revolution* (New York: Free Press, 1971).

3. "Games Big People Play," *Mother Jones,* September–October 1976, 43.

4. Robert W. Malcolmson, *Popular Recreations in English Society, 1750–1850* (Cambridge: Cambridge University Press, 1973), 70.

5. Donald Meyer, "Early Football" (unpublished paper). I am indebted to this brilliant essay not only for the observations on alumni culture but for the material on Walter Camp in the following paragraphs.

6. Warren Susman, "Piety, Profits, and Play: the 1920's," in Howard H. Quint and Milton Cantor, eds., *Men, Women, and Issues in American History* (Homewood, Ill.: Dorsey Press, 1975, vol. 2), 210–14.

7. Michael Novak, *The Joy of Sports* (New York: Basic Books, 1976), chap. 14.

8. Martha Wolfenstein, "Fun Morality," in Warren Susman, ed., *Culture and Commitment: 1929–1945* (New York: Braziller, 1973), 91.

9. Edgar Wind, *Art and Anarchy* (New York: Vintage Books, 1969), 18.

3
The Political and Social Dimensions of Sports

RICHARD LIPSKY

I have been involved with sports all my life as a player, reporter, and fan. In my youth literally thousands of hours were invested in the perfection of a jump shot, the honing of batting skills, and in the fantasy imitation of athletic gods.

Despite, or rather because of my involvement and expertise, developing a political and social theory about American sports has not been a simple task. Sports have always been my refuge from what has often been a harsh and difficult reality. The escape into sports provided me with a place to let go, a place of clear understanding and undeniable feelings. Naturally, putting this sacrosanct and personal area under a lens has caused me considerable discomfort.

The more I thought about studying sports, however, the more I realized how my own personal attachments were, in one sense, just the tip of an iceberg of intensity. Involvement with sports through playing and watching, reading, and talking dominates many people's everyday lives. Michael Novak's "Holy Trinity" of baseball, basketball, and football is nurtured on the fields of rural America, the streets of urban ghettos, and the manicured play areas of suburbia. From its local and personal beginnings, the world of sports has become a major form of national and social communication to the extent that interest in and knowledge of sports make Americans of every region and class "available" to one another. Sport is the "magic elixir" that feeds personal identity while it nourishes the bonds of communal solidarity. Its myths transform children into their adult heroes while allowing adults to once again become children. All this rich excitement is part of a dramatic and symbolic world with important political as well as social ramifications.

SportsWorld is actually an infrastructure that penetrates the core of individual identity.[1] It is intensely personal, yet shared through community rituals and the heat of sports conversations. Despite this obvious depth and breadth of involvement, the attempt to study sports has met with much resistance. This resistance is, in some ways, analogous to my own initial hesitation to study sports, but other factors are important as well.

The attempt to develop a political theory of American sports faces many obstacles. Sports and politics in America have traditionally been regarded as separate institutions. The gatekeepers of SportsWorld itself have encouraged the belief that sports are "fun and games" and have vigorously fought any attempt at "outside" regulations. The separation of sports from the rest of society received judicial sanction in 1922 when the Supreme Court ruled that baseball was not a business engaged in interstate commerce and therefore was not subject to national judicial sanctions.

The separation of sports and politics has had ethical overtones as well. Sport, in contrast to politics, has been seen as a moral realm where character is built and virtue is pursued. As a result, the traditional lionizing of the sports hero clashes with the negative public perception of politicians. This difference is the source of the fierce vigilance SportsWorld's gatekeepers exhibit over the slightest appearance of corruption. An inability to police their own realm would lead, it is feared, to political interference that would destroy the moral and jurisdictional autonomy of sports. Robert Lipsyte has captured sports fans' perception of the sports-politics separation:

> All their lives they have been told that politics was dirty; that baseball was beautiful; that politicians were connivers; that ballplayers had the hearts of children; that [the] smoke-filled caucus room was the hellish furnace of democracy and that a sunny ballpark was its shrine and reward.[2]

The difficulty of analyzing sports is increased by a pervasive "folk understanding" of American sports that has generated numerous self-proclaimed seers and journalistic experts. An interesting and nonobvious point often will bring a "Well, sure, everyone knows that" response from the involved fan. It only becomes obvious, however, after it gets articulated. Tackling such a subject is risky because everyone feels like an expert, and a major insight is as valued as a two-day-old box score.

This popular folk belief—what I call the "I-played-second-base-in-high-school syndrome"—is abetted by academic hostility toward sports. On many college campuses the football or basketball team carries more prestige than any academic subject or academician. Historically, coaches and physical educators have struggled with professors and deans over the alleged overemphasis of intercollegiate sports. Additionally, coaches often are anti-intellectual, which strikes a responsive chord in the American public. Not to be outdone, intellectuals have exhibited an equally potent snobbery and disdain. As a result, the study of sports has been left mainly to physical educators, who have been disinclined to examine its larger political and social implications.

The creation of this sports (trivial) and politics (serious) dichotomy has been one of the most persistent obstacles to the serious examination of American sports. It is one thing to study societies with ministries of physical culture whose aims unblushingly reflect those of the ruling political party. It is quite a different task to analyze sports in a society where political and ideological purpose is often disguised and where socialization frequently is accomplished "through the back door."

The exaltation of sports above politics was severely challenged during the upheavals of the 1960s. Each protest movement had its own sports section. The New Left criticized the "fascist," "antilife," and "dehumanizing" aspects of sports. Black militants became enraged at quota systems and racial stereotypes. Women, during the latter part of the decade, began challenging sexual discrimination and supermasculinity.

These critiques, attacking the rose-colored view that sports were untainted by political purpose, were aimed at two of SportsWorld's weaknesses. Initially, the attackers enthusiastically exposed SportsWorld's hypocrisy. After uncovering weaknesses of SportsWorld itself, the critical thrust went on to reveal how SportsWorld promoted the purposes of the larger political and social system.

If the defenders of sport pointed out the beauty and joy of play, critics charged that sport "perverts" play in a joyless spectacle. If sport was glorified as an arena of mobility and equality, critics dramatized the elitism, racism, and inequality of SportsWorld. If the athlete was portrayed as a creative worker, a craftsman, then the critics exposed the dehumanization of the jock, the strapping of the athlete into a rigidly stereotyped role.[3]

The critical onslaught was relentless and exhaustive. If the world of sports valued discipline and authority, the critics gleefully attacked the Vince Lombardis and Woody Hayeses as lifeless martinets who subordinated all human relationships to the all-consuming goal of winning. If athletes were portrayed in the media as innocents, and their relationships with one another as the ultimate in spiritual camaraderie, critics detailed the money-grubbing, the sexual hypocrisy, the general mean-spiritedness of the players, and the shallowness of a locker-room scene that promised intimacy but rarely delivered.

After taking on SportsWorld itself, the critics further described how they felt sports served the established power structure of the larger political system. The critics energetically red-dogged the "above politics" notion of SportsWorld. While its defenders saw sports as separate from everyday reality, the critics zeroed in on sports as an "opiate" or "emotional Disneyland."

A primary target of the critical anger was sports' screening people from accurately assessing the harmful realities of the political and economic system. While defenders saw sports as providing for the therapeutic release of pent-up hostility and aggression, the critics revealed how often this emotional release prevented the causes of aggression and hostility from ever being creatively tackled.

The critical offensive clearly caught SportsWorld offguard. But the radical attack soon provoked an equally emotional defense of sports as integral to the "American way of life." This counterattack helped illuminate how sports had been put to ideological uses in the past. Only when athletic elites and their journalistic allies defended previously unexamined SportsWorld premises could these premises be linked to the structures and norms of the larger society.

The attacks and counterattacks lifted sport out of its sacred and unexamined playground. Within the space of a few years, sport had become a significant social fact. Yet confusion remained, stemming partly from the critical assault on sport itself.

The critics were harshly, unavoidably "realistic." Legends must be demystified—in coaches' jargon, "They put their uniforms on one leg at a time, just like we do"—so players are not blinded by the aura of an opponent's reputation. This belittling strategy contains danger, though. "Cutting them down to size" runs the risk of seriously underestimating the opponent's real strengths.

The critics lack sensitivity to sport itself. Detailing all the "perversions" of SportsWorld does not explain the seductive allure that sport has for its millions of emotionally involved fans. The critical devaluation makes it almost impossible to understand how any sensible individual could be taken in by SportsWorld's sleight of hand. In order to understand SportsWorld we need to identify with the straining athletes and the cheering crowd. We must be alive to the real drama, rich symbolism, and emotional strength of sport before we can begin to see clearly its important links to the larger political and social system.

SportsWorld creates an extremely meaningful world for those who inhabit its arenas. As Neal Offen has observed: "Sport is life to the nth degree. It is life in extremis: every season you are born and you die, every sixty minutes or nine innings, you win and you lose. Every play encompasses an eternity."[4]

SportsWorld is a lived world, like those of literature and the theater, that is highly charged with human meaning. As a dramatic and symbolic world SportsWorld has its own plots, scenes, characters, and settings. The game itself is the ritual hub of the sports universe; the team provides social structure; sports language gives the world cohesion; fans play the game vicariously through the athletes. Underneath and penetrating all the dramatic appeals is the powerful symbolism of play. The success of SportsWorld rests on its ability to build its symbolic structure on the memory of play, on the illusion of play, and, finally, on the fantasy of play.

The political and social importance of SportsWorld rests on its rich symbolism and dramatic structure. The dramatic power of sport pulls people out of their everyday worlds. As in the theater, sport encourages the willing suspension of disbelief, which enables the plots and characterizations from the larger society to be inculcated "through the back door." In this way SportsWorld enacts the dominant values of the larger society, while cultivating fan appreciation at the same time. Because we are transported to a playful world "above politics," we unwittingly permit values to make an "end run" around our conscious defenses.

SportsWorld not only has acted and continues to act "through the back door" as a socializer of dominant values. It creates its own reality, an apparent autonomy from the mundane aspects of "real" life. This is a second source of its larger political and social impact.

Life may be dull, frustrating, and largely insignificant, but SportsWorld is a world of feeling where *values* are still adhered to. Neal Offen again dramatizes the point:

> There is a theory quite prevalent among analysts . . . that sports is a microcosm of life. It isn't. . . . Sports is a world speeded up and a world of absolutes. There is good and bad, black and white, right and wrong. It's not gray and tentative like the real world. It's hyperlife under glass.[5]

This "hyperlife under glass" contrasts sharply with a world of widespread alienation, a world in which people long for close individual and communal ties to overcome the impersonality and coldness of American life. Sport acts as the "magic elixir" that nourishes; the rest of the world merely drains.

SportsWorld becomes a cultic movement that compensates for the deficiencies of the world surrounding it. James Reston captures how sport compensates for the world's deficiencies: "The world of sports has everything the world of politics lacks and *longs for.* They have more pageantry and even more dignity than most occasions in American life, more teamwork, more unity and more certainty at the end than most things."[6] SportsWorld exquisitely provides the aesthetic form and supposed ethical content that for many Americans contrasts with a political and social world lacking either drama or ideals.

SportsWorld not only creates an ethical realm, it also creates a bond that unites individuals. SportsWorld is a more "personal," more "concrete," and more "intense" world than the rest of society. This intensity enables sports to become a refuge. Lipsyte dramatizes this theme: "Sport is a sweaty Oz you'll never find in a geography book . . . an ultimate sanctuary, a university for the body, a community for the spirit, a place to hide that glows with that time of innocence when we believed that rules and boundaries were honored."[7]

Sport provides a "utopia of escape" that refreshes the partisan crowds and allows them to return with renewed vigor to their places in the political and social system. Analogously, SportsWorld generates a diffuse "rain or shine" attachment to the ongoing political system.

If sport does act as a utopia of escape, it may also forestall real projects of reconstruction. On an individual level, SportsWorld provides for the "sweet closure of anxiety," but the possibilities for personal growth and political change—two closely related themes—are effectively stalled.[8]

Any analysis of SportsWorld must proceed sympathetically, yet critically, inside the boundaries of the world itself. We must move beyond naïve theories that depict sport as a "mirror of American life," but also beyond the radical arguments that see sport purely as an escape—an "opiate of the people"—without seeing at the same time how sport acts as the "heart of a heartless world."

Through an understanding of SportsWorld we can glimpse something of the structural malaise of American politics and society. SportsWorld's rich symbolism echoes the deficiencies of the larger environment within which it is absorbed. However, can we not press for more satisfying remedies for these deficiencies? We must remember that when we return to our private lives from an emotionally uplifting game somebody else is cheerfully counting the receipts.

Notes

1. See Robert Lipsyte, *SportsWorld: An American Dreamland* (New York: Quadrangle, 1976). Lipsyte coined the word *SportsWorld,* and I use it because it captures the way in which sport becomes a vivid alternative reality for sports fans.

2. Ibid., 40.

3. Paul Hoch, *Rip Off the Big Game* (Garden City, N. Y.: Doubleday, 1972). Athletic "alienation" is discussed in Chip Oliver and Ron Rapoport, eds., *High for the Game* (New York: Morrow, 1971), and Dave Meggyesy, *Out of Their League* (Berkeley, Calif.: Ramparts Press, 1970).

4. Neil Offen, *God Save the Players* (Chicago: Playboy Press, 1974), 9.

5. Ibid., 9.

6. James Reston, "Sports and Politics in America," *New York Times,* 12 September 1969.

7. See Robert Lipsyte, *SportsWorld;* Ann Leider, "The National Football League and American Life," *New York Times,* 18 January 1976, Sec. 5. As Michael Novak has observed in *The Joy of Sports:* "Sports are deeper than politics—deeper than any single political system and deeper in the human heart than political authority. Sports lie at the

very root of liberty . . . in the free play of intelligence and imagination. . . . (In Heaven, it is rumored, the angels play in the presence of great love and light. Sports yield our metaphors for paradise.) Who imagines that the completely good life would entail *working*, pursuing means towards ends? . . . Sports constitute the place in life where the revolution is already *here.*" The point that Novak doesn't make is that the sports utopia is integrated within a larger, much less utopian environment and functions to support that environment. (New York: Basic Books, 1976), 216.

8. "Sweet closure of anxiety." See H. L. Niebeurg, *Culture Storms: Politics and the Ritual Order* (New York: St. Martin's Press, 1973).

4

Where Have You Gone, Frank Merriwell? The Decline of the American Sports Hero

RICHARD C. CREPEAU

Sport, in one of its functions, serves as a vehicle for social myth, primarily through its projection of a heroic type who embodies particular aspects of the myth. This heroic type illustrates the myth's reality by parading before society its highest potentials. As Henry Fairlie points out, "A hero is not just someone whom we admire. He is someone whom we idealize. The hero has some very definite attributes of his own, but it is we who give a special significance to them. The process is two-way. We choose the hero. He is fit to be chosen. To talk of heroes is to talk of ourselves, of our own aspirations and our endeavors to realize them, of what we expect of ourselves and of our times."[1] In other words, the hero shows us what we ought to be, and we make him a hero because we wish to be what he is. He calls us beyond ourselves, toward the ideal.

In the past, such sporting heroes, both real and fictional, played a prominent role in American popular culture. Jack Dempsey, Babe Ruth, Knute Rockne, Joe Louis, Lou Gehrig, Joe DiMaggio, as well as the mythical Frank Merriwell, were all portrayed as embodying various positive qualities of the American character. (In some cases, especially that of Babe Ruth, less

76

attractive traits were withheld from public display and adjudged as not worthy of emulation by American youth.)

In recent times there has been an increasing number of social analysts such as Britain's Henry Fairlie, a keen observer of the American scene, who have commented on the death of heroes in America. One reason we have no heroes, says Fairlie, is that "we have no shared values to inspire us in common effort," and as a result we are no longer capable of imagining the "selflessly disinterested hero" who would "give himself for a cause."[2] We no longer have causes because we feel no need for them in an age of "grossly distorted individualism," whose motto might well be "get what you can now before it runs out."[3] This view was certainly reinforced by the sudden rise of baseball pitcher Fernando Valenzuela as a hero. During Valenzuela's first year in Los Angeles, "Fernandomania," especially in the Mexican-American community, was a powerful force. It appeared that here was a case where a sports hero could again represent a group within society who shared common values, and that Fernando himself, playing out his rookie contract while giving the heroic appearance of the highly talented but unassuming young man, just might be a refreshing variation of the "selflessly disinterested hero." But Fernando's holdout in the spring of 1982, with its clear-cut demand for "megabucks," quickly dispelled any such illusion. Clearly, Fernando was also of the new order which dictates to "get what you can now before it runs out." And quickly the Los Angeles Mexican-American community displayed its disillusionment, a reaction that may reveal an inherent but frustrated longing for a return of the traditional sort of hero.

Fairlie goes on to say that the hero has been replaced by the anti-hero—"someone who says that he does not need other people. The nonhero is someone who says that he does not even care much to need himself. Our novels are the literature of the artful dodger in a meaningless and fretful present."[4] Furthermore, Fairlie observes that a world without heroes is a world without beliefs, a world that has lost confidence in itself and the ability to believe in anything. Hero worship reinforces our resistance to fatalism and determinism and resists the feeling that we have lost control of our lives and our destinies.[5] This may be the result of our present-day commitment to empiricism, which has led to an all-pervasive obsession with facticity and data and the consequent overexamination of the objective world.

Categorizing personalities, especially the heroic type, as part of the factual world demands public examination in the full glare of the spotlight from all angles. The public figure, it seems, is continually being probed from within and without, and often what should be self-evident is divined for underlying, hidden meanings. No one can survive this sort of scrutiny without finally being trivialized. The sheer volume of such treatment becomes overwhelming, and the world of imagination, where heroes are born and where they live and move freely, is ultimately denied expression and buried in a blizzard of data. Then it is that cynicism is bred. Ironically, we probably know as little about sports heroes today as we knew about them in earlier times. The difference is only in what kinds of things we know. What has revelatory journalism really revealed beyond titillation for a voyeuristic age? The myth of the flawed, perhaps.

Baseball star Steve Garvey offers an excellent example of this journalistic overexposure and of the change in the public's attitude toward sports heroes. One newspaper story on Steve Garvey goes so far as to describe him as an ironic example of extreme social deviance. Garvey has short hair, polite manners, a pleasant smile, a twinkle in his eye. He loves baseball, family, and has probably never even seen marijuana. Garvey takes pride in his commitment to Christianity and he even worries about being a proper example for youth. He also takes pride in maintaining dignity under stress and adversity. He plays in All-Star games injured. The only time he has ever expressed anger in public was to defend the honor of his wife and family. When asked if all of this was merely image, Garvey said, "I don't believe in images . . . An image is something you work on, like a politician. I am what I am.[6]

In days gone by, this latter-day Frank Merriwell would have been a hero of enormous stature, in sports and perhaps beyond. In the age of Marshall McLuhan's three-year-old cynics, though, he invokes in many people feelings of discomfort, disbelief, or nostalgia. In others he provokes a search for a press agent. He is a relic; there is no other word. He speaks to an age and a time long since past. He has only limited appeal. Steve Garvey calls us to something which many no longer believe in, or maybe even care about. He is a hero of myths past, operating in a society where the sophisticated have dismissed heroes of this type for the new myths of the scientific, the literal, and/or the flawed. Although a hero to some, he has not survived the trivialization of

the new journalism, and has become a prototype of the myth of
the flawed.

In the course of his lament on the death of heroes, Fairlie says
that heroes have been replaced by celebrities. He sees the celebrity as a product of press agents and media-hype who are sold to
the public, rather than being chosen by the public for their heroic
qualities. In looking back to Joe Louis and Babe Ruth as sports
heroes, Fairlie contrasts them with Joe Namath and Muhammad
Ali, whom he dubs celebrities. These contrasting heroic types
illustrate for Fairlie three fundamental changes in the nature of
sport and reflect similar changes in society. First, in an earlier age
sports were more "vivid," not seen merely as ways of getting out
of the ghettoes and immigrant slums. Second, sports embodied
the belief that individual skill and effort were the best way to
improve one's lot against all odds. Third, sports crowds were
participants, not merely spectators. The crowd was the embodiment of community life that called forth fierce allegiances. There
was a sense of community, an identity. Today, David Riesman's
"lonely crowd" is to be found in the bleachers—the kind of
"people who believe that to some extent they have made it, and
that they no longer need community with others represented and
idealized in a common hero."[7] The personal stories coming out
of the bleachers at Yankee Stadium and Wrigley Field point to
this anomie of the hard pines.

One might argue with Fairlie whether all conventional sports
heroes are really gone. First, Steve Garvey is still here. While it
is true that many cannot react to Garvey, still others can, and not
just for his baseball ability, but more importantly, for his life-
style. A second quarrel with Fairlie centers around his failure to
recognize the social fragmentation that has occurred within
American society. No longer is it possible or necessary to have
heroes who appeal to all classifications of people. Now, heroes
have only partial appeal to certain segments of society. As there
is no unified system of values, there are no universal heroes.
Each hero has his own constituency. Garvey appeals to those
who hold to what once was regarded as the traditional mainstream values, whereas Namath appealed to the new urban
sophisticates. In addition there are the purely ethnic heroes, and
there are the small cults who follow a certain player who appeals
to their particular sense of values. This could indicate greater
security of identity for Americans as a people, and therefore a
willingness to accept differences and reject the bygone preju-

dices of one-hundred-percent Americanism. Then, there are the modern throwbacks who combine the traditional values with modern business acumen. Surely someone like Pete Rose embodies the rugged individualism of the self-made capitalist, even if in a new package. As Wilfred Sheed recently observed of Rose: "Racing from city to city this winter, sliding into tax shelters and beer distributorships as if they were so many pot-bellied catchers, one had to wonder what he hustles for, and whom."[8] In addition there is the Pete Rose who talks openly of his personal life complete with broken marriage, paternity suits, and live-in girl friend, to say nothing of "greenies" in the clubhouse.[9] Is he still a hero? Certainly he is to some people. But not the sort of hero Henry Fairlie has in mind. There is nothing "selflessly disinterested" about Pete Rose.

Another of the new sports heroes is the owner whose economic success has been sufficient to allow him to buy a team or teams. Having produced the bread, he buys the circus and becomes an important heroic type—the successful capitalist who makes his own world and his own rules. In the late nineteenth century this role was played by the American rich whose activities in New York and Newport were daily reported in the New York and national press. Their extravagance, waste, and eccentricity were followed assiduously in the society news. Certainly, George Steinbrenner and Ted Turner fit that model. Both of these men speak and act in no less than seven figures as they scatter their money about with reckless abandon. More importantly, they are men who have established fascinating public images of making their own rules and living by their own styles. George Steinbrenner's antics with the Yankees—buying and selling players, hiring and firing managers, issuing public apologies for the team's failure—seem both whimsical and awesome. Ted Turner, appearing as the Atlanta Braves bat-boy on national television after the Commissioner of Baseball tells him he cannot appoint himself manager for a day, plays out fantasies that countless Americans have had. And best of all, both men's antics get blanket coverage in the media worthy of a head of state. To an extent, though, both of these men *are* heroes. They may be envied, but they are not resented in playing out a role that the rich have historically played in modern America. Both demonstrate the American dream of acquisition of vast wealth which brings with it power and even more importantly the ability to do whatever you want to do, no matter what others say or think. They are the heroes of totally unfettered individualism. While sports fans complain that players make too much money, no one ever suggests the same of a Steinbrenner, a Turner, or any other owner.

In addition, sports heroes now come in alternative types displaying varied traits for emulation. The acceptance of new social roles and life-styles within bourgeois culture is one factor in this change. Another is the confusion over standards which has opened new role possibilities. The proliferation of hero types has been further enhanced by the growth of the mass media, with its penchant for the new and the unusual. Another factor is the inability of the sports establishment to dictate control of the athlete's image, despite the efforts of vast public relations budgets. Beyond all this, expansion of media coverage as well as the number of teams has led to sensory overload. Too many teams, too many players, too many events, and too much coverage have produced two extremes, the blandness of the mass and a preoccupation with the unusual or bizarre. It has also led to celebrity proliferation, an important commodity in American consumer culture.

The distinction Fairlie makes between celebrity and hero may be an important one. However, while celebrities may convey values in much the same way as heroes, the distinction between the two categories may be a function more of Fairlie's rejection of the new values and styles than anything else. The celebrity is a media product, the result of a process which involves what Daniel Boorstin has called being known for your "well-knownness." What these celebrities reflect may be as depressing as anything Fairlie suggests, being superficial and disposable. Such vacuous qualities as being "a winner" or "number one" are increasingly cited in discussions of both celebrities and athletes and with ominous spillover to the larger society. It may be that rather than hero worship, this envy of celebrity is all that remains for a society that has lost its sense of shared values.

Notes

1. Henry Fairlie, "Too Rich for Heroes," *Harper's* 257 (November 1978): 36–37.
2. Ibid., 43.
3. Ibid., 97.
4. Ibid.

5. Ibid., 98.

6. Shelby Strother, "For Goodness Sake, It's Steve Garvey," *Today* (Cocoa, Florida), 13 April 1979, 10.

7. Fairlie, "Too Rich for Heroes," 97.

8. Wilfred Sheed, "Pete Rose: The Swell Smell of Success," *Family Weekly,* 6 May 1979.

9. Roger Director, "The Devil and Charlie Hustle," *Inside Sports* 4 (May 1982): 27–35; Maury Z. Levy, "Interview with Pete Rose," *Playboy* 26 (September 1979): 77ff.

5

American Televised Sport: Business as Usual

JOAN CHANDLER

Roger Angell is far from alone in his conviction that the quality of baseball is inexorably declining, while the meaning of the game has been lost, because the owners and commissioner have decided to place the interests of television viewers before those of fans in the stadium.[1] It is now conventional wisdom that TV has trivialized whatever sport it has touched, by altering rules to make the sport more exciting to casual viewers, by changing schedules and extending seasons so that players are exhausted and game rhythms disrupted, by substituting artificial for natural surfaces which makes a sport visually more attractive but changes its pace and induces player injury, and by making so much money available that sport has become not merely show business, but an activity in which agents, lawyers, and union officials have become as important as players. This perception of TV's effect on sport, however, appears to me quite wrong. TV has not changed sport; rather, the societal values which sport epitomized have changed in the last thirty years, and TV has reflected those changes. In castigating TV, we are simply ordering the execution of the messenger with unwelcome tidings; it may make us feel better, but it does not help us much in dealing with the reported situation.

The fact of the matter is that we know very little about the relationship of TV and viewer even in those fields such as news and violence which have been studied most assiduously.[2] The relationship between TV and sport has been taken for granted but studied hardly at all.[3] The subject is enormously complicated, not least because it rests on philosophical premises which are rarely mentioned, much less explicated. This is not the place to explore the huge corpus of literature concerning the changes which the industrial revolution is asserted to have wrought in human habits, perceptions, and aspirations.[4] Television critics of the "cultural wasteland" persuasion are, however, working out of the tradition which postulates that the spread of literacy and then of broadcasting progressively debased popular taste. Writers such as Hoggart, Leavis and Thompson, Rosenberg and White, and Gans set "high culture" against "popular culture"; popular culture always represents a falling away of standards set by the critics themselves.[5] Barnouw takes this argument a step further; whether television deals with "high" or "popular" culture is to Barnouw irrelevant because both are simply a conduit for commercials.[6] Whether or not one accepts this pessimistic and fundamentally contemptuous view of human beings, it is easy to relate it to much of the criticism of televised sports. The stadium fan's attachment to the game in itself has, according to this view, been replaced by the TV viewer's concern for result rather than process, for entertainment rather than catharsis.

Apart from postulating a division between "high" and "popular" culture, a fundamental suspicion of technology betrays itself in the attitudes of those critics who view the very act of watching TV as unhealthy. To writers such as Goldsen and Winn,[7] TV is sensually overwhelming and renders its viewers helpless by substituting vicarious for real experience, thereby making viewers incapable of distinguishing between them. To such critics, television viewers are literally watching the shadows in Plato's cave. None of these writers specifically addresses the issue of sports; but whether or not one accepts the premise that TV overwhelms a viewer by its very nature, it is quite true that the sporting event watched in the stadium is not the event watched on television. A TV viewer sees only what the camera crews show him, and while he may have a close view of some segments of the game, he cannot see the position and flow of all the players on the field in a team sport, or even know where individuals on a tennis court are placed. He sees some plays over and over again, often from different angles, and his attention is directed by the commentary to certain players and aspects of the game.[8] What he is watching is a technological translation of the event itself into another, two-dimensional language, and into a different cultural setting, the living room. In this act of translation, certain liberties may be taken. Commentators, for instance, always seek to persuade the viewer that he is watching a splendid game, when his eyes tell him he is not, or camera crews will focus on cheerleaders rather than on an injured player. Nevertheless, TV is not providing a wholly new text; rather, TV is simply recasting the original in terms which make it accessible to its audience.

Other TV critics have argued that the American television industry reflects the economic structure of American society, and operates simply to legitimatize the status quo. Tuchmann believes that TV audiences are sold to advertisers; she postulates that changes are not made in program content in response to the demands of an enlightened audience, but represent merely cosmetic alterations designed to co-opt viewers so that economic, political, and social power will remain with the powerful.[9] As Chesterton quipped, the English could not be brought to consider the equality of man, because they were so interested in the inequality of horses; but, unlike Chesterton, TV critics of this persuasion assume that their audiences are essentially without strong likes and dislikes and therefore easy prey for manipulators. Unless, however, one presupposes that the manipulators are very small in number and equally in control of all channels of information about sport, it is hard to explain why televised football is so popular and televised hockey so unsuccessful. As Swingewood points out, the "upper classes," as well as "the masses," thoroughly enjoy cultural products designed for the hoi polloi.[10] It is, I suppose, only in Dallas that football scores are announced in the intervals at the opera, but it is palpably clear that all the people who watch televised sport are far from sharing similar political views or occupying similar positions in the American power structure.

Common to all these criticisms of television is the assumption that it represents the total cultural life of most of its viewers, and that all viewers, however much or little they watch, however diverse their intelligence, attitudes, and cultural baggage, are affected similarly by the medium. Not only is this unlikely, but observation of any group of viewers demonstrates that people do not even watch a show in the same manner, much less react to it similarly. I am aware of only one study in which the actual behavior of viewers was documented; as one would expect, the degree of attention paid to any program varied enormously.[11] It is also clear that viewers are perfectly capable of distinguishing between sports programs. To admit, however, that people know full well what they are doing when they watch TV is much less comforting than to believe that "the wasteland" has somehow been foisted on a helpless but aspiring public.[12] Similarly, to blame television for the existence of the commercialized entertainment industry which professional sport now so clearly is, preserves one from two uncomfortable thoughts. The first is that spectators have always determined the nature of American professional sport—the greater their numbers, the more power they possess; the second is that, given the societal changes of the last thirty years, the sports industry would have changed fundamentally, with or without television.

Whether, however, the sports industry would have assumed quite its present shape without television is another matter. Nevertheless, what has altered sports more than anything else is the presence of huge sums of money. Because television has been the conduit through which millions of dollars have flowed, this medium has been used as a scapegoat for all the ills which the sports industry now seems heir to. On the contrary, it is love of money, not love of television, which remains the root of all evil.

The perception that the "ideals of the game" took precedence over the profit motive until the advent of television is historically inaccurate. From its inception as a professional sport, baseball has been treated by its promoters as a marketable product. The very rules of the game were experimented with until they had settled into a form which would guarantee the maximum possible spectator interest. Throughout the 1880s substantial rule changes were made which transformed the original "gentleman's game."[13] Sidearm pitching was accepted in 1883, although overarm pitching was banned, only to be allowed in 1885. This gave pitchers such an advantage that their movements in the box were restricted the following year. By 1887, batters could no longer request a high or low strike zone, but could have four instead of three strikes; in 1888, the three-strike rule was restored. In 1889, one substitute was allowed, the thin end of the specialist wedge. These wholesale experiments ceased when promoters were satisfied that the game was as exciting (i.e., unpredictable) as they could make it.

Further, the search for dollars led baseball promoters to challenge the sanctity of the Sabbath. As Catholic immigrants from Southern Europe poured into cities like Cincinnati and St. Louis, baseball promoters prepared to do battle with the Protestant notion that the Sabbath should be kept free of worldly pursuits. As Protestant trans-Mississippi immigrants had often left their churchgoing habits behind, professional baseball found a ready market on Sundays there, while Easterners were still refusing to allow it. The fight lasted bitterly into the twentieth century, but it was the promoters of "the national game" who were branded as perverting morality rather than upholding it.

Baseball promoters, however, were clearly in search of dollars rather than accolades. Experiments were made with night baseball as early as 1883; it may not be "natural" to play in artificial light, but if technological progress could enable baseball games to be played at a time when working people were free to watch them, promoters were willing to fool Mother Nature. Promoters also took advantage of changing business practices by improving ball parks and having them run by specialists. This early twentieth-century investment in stadiums built of steel and concrete tended in itself to stabilize franchises. To move to another city meant abandoning one investment while financing another. The post–World War II demographic changes left many ballparks in areas of actual or potential urban blight; with or without the lure of television markets, owners who wanted to attract the middle-class entertainment dollar would have been forced to look at new sites and cities for profit.

When television executives became willing to pay large sums to broadcast baseball, promoters simply continued their lifelong practice of adapting rules, schedules, and parks to the needs of those who purchased their product. Yet the pre–World War II product was labeled a sport. Early twentieth-century fans might be tempted to the ballpark by pleasant seating, food, and beer, but what they had really come for was to take part in a ritual. The 1919 World Series scandal was devastating precisely because professional baseball players had been carefully marketed as symbols of incorruptibility in a corrupt world. The players' punishment was correspondingly severe. If professional baseball was to continue to be profitable, fans had to be convinced that the erring White Sox players were an aberration, and that the mythic American values of honesty and reward for individual striving under rules of fair competition were indeed being upheld.

At the same time, the actual amount of money a baseball

player could make was carefully controlled. The first version of the reserve clause was introduced in September 1879; under it, owners agreed that none of them could offer a better salary to any of five designated players in each Boston National League club. By the mid-1880s, all baseball players had a reserve clause in their contracts.[14] As Riess has so convincingly shown, baseball in the Progressive Era was marketed as a democratic sport run by public benefactors, when it was nothing of the sort.[15] Yet so successful were the mythmakers that baseball still retains its antitrust exemption, although thirty years ago the Celler Report demonstrated that baseball was admittedly an interstate enterprise.[16] Well before the advent of television, baseball promoters, like owners of other industries, were concerned to get what they could. In doing so, they persuaded themselves, as well as the fans, that they were marketing not a game but a way of life.

The huge sums of money TV poured into sport made it easier to pursue the profit motive. Nevertheless, the precise relationship between televised sport and the money it provides is hard to untangle, not only because the subject is complicated, but because owners, TV executives, and even players are extremely reluctant to disclose their financial affairs.[17] What is clear is that money obtained from sale of TV rights differs from sport to sport[18] and has affected players and owners differently in different sports.

TV has made it possible for athletes whose faces are well known to secure much more lucrative commercials and endorsement contracts than the print media could ever provide. Larger salaries and payments for playing the game itself relate less, however, to TV as a medium than to the commercial structure of the American TV and sports industries. Tennis and golf are televised less than football; but top professionals in these sports collect more money than their counterparts in football and baseball. The NFL Players Association has charged not only that football players are underpaid but that owners have no reason to pay their best players well or vie for their services because whether a team wins or loses, its revenue remains about the same. Money had a different effect on basketball. Halberstam suggests it changed from a business in which franchise owners made or lost real money according to attendance at stadiums to one which multimillionaires took up like a new toy, writing off their basketball losses against their other businesses.[19] Seeking instant glory, these newcomers gave players no-cut contracts and a schedule of games designed to exhaust them. Fans therefore learned to watch only the play-offs; the college game, in which money figured less, became higher rated on television. Baseball owners have reacted differently again to the presence of big money. Operating as individuals in their time-honored fashion, they used their increased affluence to outbid each other for free agents, and have been publicly miffed when their attempts to "buy the pennant" were unsuccessful.

The effect of money on sport can be seen most clearly in tennis, because the sport itself has no history to speak of as a spectator attraction in the United States either at professional or college levels.[20] Although small bands of professionals tried from 1926 on to wring a living from tennis, it was not until 1968 that Wimbledon ended "shamateurism" by allowing professionals to compete in a tournament sanctioned by the International Lawn Tennis Association. In 1970, Lamar Hunt signed contracts with thirty-two of the top male players in the world; in 1971 the World Championship of Tennis demanded $24,000 expense money for sending its players to Wimbledon. In 1972, Wimbledon refused to pay, and WCT players, under contract year-round, did not play. In the negotiations which followed, Hunt was reasonable; but as a businessman, he had reminded the authority which had set international tennis standards for eighty years that he who pays the piper calls the tune.[21]

Hunt had accurately gauged his market. In the United States of the 1970s there were plenty of young, affluent men and women caught up in a burgeoning fitness movement and ready to watch a game they could play themselves, which was cerebral, bisexual, and individual. Hunt was not alone in preparing to attract spectators by supporting the introduction of colored clothing and balls, tiebreaks, acceptance of behavior by players which broke tension as it raised eyebrows, and play on specially prepared indoor surfaces. Gladys Heldman and Billie Jean King helped make women's liberation a reality for women tennis players.

Lawn tennis was thus metamorphosed, not primarily for television, but in ways which made the game visually more exciting and less time-consuming and thus more suitable for the medium. Seeding was continued, a practice which tended to make finals unpredictable and hence "good"; the court was small enough for the action to be transferred to a small screen. Each point started in the same way, so the cameras could safely provide close-ups which would enhance rather than detract from the overall pattern of the play.

Nevertheless, tennis failed to pull in the ratings. The kind of people who play tennis and go to tournaments are not among the groups that watch TV most.[22] Most adult Americans have never played tennis; there is no team with which they can identify,[23] nor clearly defined season from which one team emerges a winner. Computer rankings matter to players; they evoke no emotion in the breasts of spectators for whom a pennant race has meaning. Nor are Americans used to watching a sport during which they keep quiet; the roar of the crowd behind the football or baseball commentator is in comforting contrast to the eerie sound of ball on strings. As ratings dropped, so did television exposure.

Tennis players, however, show no signs of being on the breadline. Just as television did not cause the changes in the game which have transformed it from a patrician to a plebeian sport, neither will lack of television ratings bring about its demise. While television exposure, particularly on cable, may help convince sponsors that they should provide cash for tournaments, with or without much television professional tennis will thrive.[24] Television money has not, and will not, bring the squabbling factions which now make up international tennis together. Only when live audiences tire of watching injured teenagers[25] and petulance will professional tennis wither.

Neither money nor television, nor their symbiotic relationship, caused the fundamental economic and social changes in the United States since World War II. These changes alone would have altered professional sports. Better air and road transportation made nationwide scheduling possible; the possession of a car took fans from local parks to towns. The armed forces integrated during the war; the civil rights movement guaranteed not merely that blacks could move into professional sports, but that younger, affluent fans would not cease to buy tickets when blacks were more than token players. As workers' rights to a safe and healthy workplace became increasingly taken for granted, the assumption that a professional athlete was lucky to be able to accept whatever working conditions his owners were pleased to provide was challenged. In a period of concern for human rights, the chattel status of many athletes became abhorrent. Young lawyers attempted social engineering through the courts in a variety of causes; whatever the size of their salaries, athletes would have appeared in court in the seventies and eighties.

Further, the social schisms made evident by the Vietnam war and the counterculture made the values of the prewar sports hero passé. While the phenomenon of "letting it all hang out" could be variously regarded as *The Greening of America* or *The Culture of Narcissism*,[26] Joe Namath rather than Babe Ruth epitomized the postwar sports hero. Namath still had to choose between playing a professional sport and owning a club gamblers frequented; but the public image he personally projected was entirely different from the carefully sanitized picture of Babe Ruth. Like the prewar public, postwar fans had to be assured that the event they were watching was as safe from illegal manipulation as official scrutiny could make it, not least so that the fans could gamble on the result;[27] but the players themselves no longer had to epitomize the public values of a bygone age.

Television alone was not responsible for these changing values. Nor did television cause the increased violence among players and spectators at professional sporting events.[28] Even tennis, that most mannerly of sports, was affected. Nastase, Connors, and McEnroe would speedily have improved their court behavior had the public boycotted matches in which they played; rather, their presence sold tournament tickets. While the Men's International Pro Tennis Council increased penalties for "aggravated behavior" in the 1982 season, its members also refused to allow Borg to play at Wimbledon (because he had entered only seven out of the required ten Grand Prix tournaments) unless he played in the qualifying matches. Borg is the consummate gentleman and five times Wimbledon champion; had the professionals been serious about restoring courtesy to a game which now sadly lacks it, a means of allowing Borg to play could easily have been found. Television cannot be held responsible for such a failure of vision.

Nor is television to blame for the cynical treatment of athletes who have been lured to college to play ball rather than to study. "Saturday's Children" exist only in the United States, where colleges have undertaken to provide public entertainment through their athletic programs. Complaints about the effect of spectators on college athletics were heard long before the advent of television. In 1928, Jay Nash pointed out in the *North American Review* that "the earmarks of bad athletics . . . will always center around intensive coaching of a few, neglect of the many, spectators, gate receipts, State and National Championships. Such activities are not educational. They exist to give publicity to the coach, the principal of the school, the president of the university, the alumni, some local newspapers, the town boosters' club, and the players."[29]

The postwar expansion of colleges, however, compounded the problem. A large number of colleges and universities in the United States were, except in the eyes of their alumni, equally undistinguished. The "Big Game" was the only established Ivy League tradition which was publicly understood and could be copied fast; it survived even the growing popularity of professional sport in the 1950s. Just at a time when Ivy League colleges decided to stop conferring athletic scholarships, status-seeking institutions began to develop expertise in buying up high-school athletic talent.[30] Gary Shaw's account of his experiences as a student athlete was one of the first signs that scholarship holders themselves had begun to wonder what their "education" consisted of;[31] by the 1980s students had taken to the courts. As U.S. District Judge Lord pointed out in ordering the University of Minnesota to enroll Mark Hall in a degree-granting program, "The plaintiff . . . was recruited to come to the University of Minnesota to be a basketball player and not a scholar. His academic record reflects that he has lived up to those expectations, as do the academic records of many of the athletes presented to this Court. . . ."[32]

The College Football Association is now making belated efforts to restore some credibility to its athletic programs; yet two of its members have gone to court to claim rights to their own television revenues, which is to say that they regard their athletic programs in reality as marketable products.* Few students who are practicing and playing with the level of intensity nationally competitive college teams now require can be expected to possess the additional energy necessary to complete a challenging academic program. It was not television which produced this demand that a student serve two masters, but the frenetic scramble to be a "winner." Even the fact that the Dallas Cowboys used

---

*[Ed. note] Since this writing, the United States Supreme Court, on 27 June 1984, declared that football contracts negotiated exclusively with the NCAA violate antitrust law. The two institutions referred to here thus won their cases. It will indeed be interesting to observe the effect this latest ruling will have on the winning obsession which pervades contemporary intercollegiate sports.

their second 1982 draft choice for a Yale player is not likely to stem the tide. Colleges seeking prestige through sport cannot afford to worry too much about the fate of players once they have left college, or their activities off the field while they are there. Neither the NCAA nor individual colleges have expressed much interest in the modest proposals presented by the newly formed Center for Athlete's Rights and Education. One of CARE's suggestions is to place some of the NCAA television revenues in a trust fund to help students finish their degrees after their eligibility is over. Thus far, this simple way of helping athletes make their lives more manageable and productive has fallen on deaf ears.

The scandals in college athletics have not gone unremarked. Nor have the contract negotiations of professional players, and court battles by owners. While baseball players were "working stiffs," powerful only on the field, where they exemplified rule-governed and godlike skill, fans could believe Judge Landis when he said, "Baseball is something more than a game to an American boy; it is his training field for life work."[33] In the 1970s, fans became uneasily aware that sports were not games, as they had been led to believe, but a product, just like any other. They began to understand that Seymour was right when he wrote, ". . .professional baseball is not a sport. It is a commercialized amusement business."[34]

Television unwittingly ripped the mask off the sports industry, and in so doing, unmasked spectators as well. But this puts us all in a difficult position. When one cannot overlook the fact that spectator sports always have been, are, and must be, industries, one can no longer believe that sports per se possess inherent values which have somehow been perverted by commercialism. This realization leads to awkward questions about athletic programs at all levels. If, for instance, the art of "team play" is something children should learn, why can they not learn it by playing in a band or orchestra, singing in a choir, or dancing a ballet?[35] If "leadership" is to be learned through sports, why cannot students organize practices and schedule matches, and why do schools persist in spending money on sports in which coaches tell children precisely what to do?

Yet this realization can be immensely productive. When I watch a sporting event, I am engaging in exactly the same order of activity as watching an opera or play.[36] I can stop worrying about what "ought" to be happening on the field unless events hinder and diminish the action. McEnroe's temper tantrums then are not unsportsmanlike and hence to be deplored, but delays in the game and therefore the more deplorable. I can stop yearning for a golden age; instead, I can start thinking about what separates spectator from participatory sports. Little League will no longer automatically be regarded as a valuable experience for any child, but as a marvelous opportunity for well-coordinated, competitive children with the appropriate temperament. I can start to think about the nature of competitive activity, physical skill, and prowess, the values children need to acquire and which educational institutions ought to exemplify. I can also take sport in American society seriously, because I shall be considering it on its own terms.

Television gives a viewer the best seat in the stadium, at a time when he can usually be at home to occupy it, provides commentators to instruct and entertain (whom he can tune out if he wishes), and helps the stupidest among us to begin to apprehend the superlative skill, courage, and abilities of star players. In telecasting sports, TV provides a common interest for its heterogeneous audience. TV has also made clear to us that what we are watching is a spectacle, organized primarily for profit. If we are unable to discard our illusions, but prefer to bewail their loss, the problem does not lie with television or with the sports industries; it lies with ourselves.

Notes

1. Roger Angell, *Five Seasons* (New York: Popular Library, 1978), 406–9.

2. See George Comstock's *Television and Human Behavior: The Key Studies* (Santa Monica, Calif.: The Rand Corporation, 1975) for an analysis of the flood of literature devoted to the relationship between television and behavior. George Comstock et al. later published a different volume called *Television and Human Behavior* (New York: Columbia University Press, 1978). A newer approach can be found in Ronald Frank and Marshall Greenburg, *The Public's Use of Television: Who Watches and Why* (Beverly Hills, Calif.: Sage Publications, 1980).

3. I know of no booklength treatment of the subject, and only one dissertation, Donald Parente's "A History of Television and Sports" (Ann Arbor, 1975). Theoretical articles, such as "Media Sport: Hot and Cool" by Susan Birell and John Long, *International Review of Sport Sociology* 14 (1979): 5–19, are few and far between.

4. Jacques Ellul's *Propaganda* (New York: Knopf, 1966) and *The Technological Society* (New York: Knopf, 1970) provide a useful introduction to the topic.

5. See Richard Hoggart, *The Uses of Literacy* (London: Penguin Books, 1958), F. R. Leavis and Denys Thompson, *Culture and Environment* (London: Chatto and Windus,

1937); and Bernard Rosenberg and David M. White, eds., *Mass Culture: The Popular Arts in America* (Glencoe, Ill.: Free Press, 1957). Herbert Gans, in *Popular Culture and High Culture* (New York: Basic Books, 1974), presents a robust critique of this position.

6. Eric Barnouw, *The Sponsor: Notes on a Modern Potentate* (New York: Oxford University Press, 1978).

7. Rose Goldsen, *The Show and Tell Machine: How Television Works and Works You Over* (New York: Dial Press, 1977); Marie Winn, *The Plug-In Drug* (New York: Viking Press, 1977).

8. Paul Comisky, Jennings Bryant, and Dolf Zillman demonstrated that viewers who saw taped segments of hockey games without commentary regarded the games as less violent than viewers who saw the segments and heard the commentary as well. The commentary, in other words, determined what viewers thought they saw. This article is one of the very few to deal with sports commentary per se. "Commentary as a Substitute for Action," *Journal of Communication* 27 (Summer 1977): 150–53.

9. Gage Tuchmann, ed., *The TV Establishment: Programming for Power and Profit* (Englewood Cliffs, N.J.: Prentice-Hall, 1978). Martin Seiden, in *Who Controls the Mass Media? Popular Myths and Economic Realities* (New York: Basic Books, 1974), presents precisely the opposite viewpoint. To his mind, the audience, not the media, control the marketplace.

10. A. Swingewood, *The Myth of Mass Culture* (London: Macmillan, 1977).

11. R. B. Bechtel, C. Archelpohl, and R. Akers. "Correlates Between Observed Behavior and Questionnaire Responses on Television Viewing," in E. A. Rubenstein, G. A. Comstock, and J. P. Murray, eds., *Television and Social Behavior* (Washington, D.C.: Government Printing Office, 1972), 274–344.

12. See Sally Bedell, *Up the Tube: Prime-Time TV and the Silverman Years* (New York: Viking Press, 1981).

13. What follows is taken from David Voigt, *American Baseball: From Gentleman's Sport to the Commissioner System* (Norman: University of Oklahoma Press, 1966), 206-7.

14. Lee Lowenfish and Tony Lupien, *The Imperfect Diamond: The Story of Baseball's Reserve System and the Men Who Fought to Change It* (New York: Stein and Day, 1980), 18.

15. Steven Riess, *Touching Base: Professional Baseball and American Culture in the Progressive Era* (Westport, Conn.: Greenwood Press, 1980).

16. U.S. Congress, House Judiciary Committee. *Organized Baseball.* Report of the Subcommittee on the Study of Monopoly Power of the Committee of the Judiciary Pursuant to Res. #95. (Washington, D.C.: Government Printing Office, 1952).

17. It is, for instance, quite impossible to discover what tax arrangements have been made by individuals and corporations without having access to information only the IRS possesses. The NFL owners have adamantly refused to open their books to the players' union, while disputing the union's figures. *New York Times,* 25 Feb. 1982, B19. The disclosure of Dallas Cowboy salaries and a few comparative salaries from other teams caused public gnashing of teeth by the management. *Dallas Morning News,* 23 Feb. 1982, B1, 24 Feb. 1982, B1, 6.

18. According to Waggoner, TV and radio revenues now amount to 54% of football's total revenues, 30% of baseball's total, and 27% of basketball's total. "Money Games," *Esquire,* June 1982, 53.

19. David Halberstam, *The Breaks of the Game* (New York: Knopf, 1981), pp. 12–14.

20. In 1958, a Boston cop arrived at a party held by the Australian Davis Cup Team to

stop the noise. When told who the partygoers were, he asked, "Now what in hell is the Australian Davis Cup team?" Rod Laver, with Bud Collins, *The Education of a Tennis Player* (New York: Simon & Schuster, 1971), 113.

21. Material in this and the following paragraph is derived chiefly from Rich Koster, *The Tennis Bubble: Big Money Tennis: How It Grew and Where It's Going* (New York: Quadrangle/New York Times Book, 1976)

22. Frank and Greenburg, *Public's Use of Television,* divided audiences into fourteen groups based on a combination of factors, including sex, age, and interests. The groups who watched television most were older females, mothers at home, adolescents interested in "indoor games and social activities," and the poor. The people labeled "Cosmopolitan Self-Enrichment" were among those most likely to play tennis themselves; they watched TV less than any of the other groups.

23. Team Tennis has had a checkered career; the fundamental problem with the concept is that once a match starts, no one can replace any of the players. So a game has to stop if a player stops.

24. In 1982, Hunt persuaded five multinational corporations to sponsor the whole tournament schedule, instead of using a single sponsor for each separate tournament. The tournament format has been changed for 1983, and Hunt has recently announced his own computer rankings. *Dallas Morning News,* 11 Oct. 1981, B20; 27 June 1982, B11.

25. In the Avon of Dallas Tournament, in March 1982, the following injuries were reported: five pulled groins, one shoulder pull, one thigh strain, and one heel problem. *Dallas Morning News,* 15 March 1983, B8.

26. Charles A. Reich, *The Greening of America: How the Youth Revolution Is Trying to Make America Liveable* (New York: Random House, 1973); Christopher Lasch, *The Culture of Narcissism: American Life in an Age of Diminishing Expectations,* (New York: Norton, 1979).

27. A well-documented account of the relationship between gambling and sport is H. Roy Kaplan's "The Convergence of Work, Sport, and Gambling in America," *The Annals of the American Academy of Political and Social Science: Contemporary Issues in Sport,* 445 (September 1979): 24–38. [Ed. note] See Neil Isaacs's essay in this chapter.

28. This is a worldwide phenomenon. See Robert Yeager, *Seasons of Shame: The New Violence in Sports* (New York: McGraw-Hill, 1979). John Underwood writes specifically on football in *Death of an American Game* (Boston: Little, Brown and Co., 1979). Reviewers castigated Jack Tatum for his frankness in *They Call Me Assassin* (New York: Everest House, 1979), but few discussed the suggestions he made for rule changes which would make football safer.

29. Quoted in Ellen Gerber, "The Controlled Development of Collegiate Sport for Women, 1923–1936," *Journal of Sport History* 2(1)(Spring 1975):20. The Carnegie Corporation sponsored a report on college athletics published in 1929; the American Council on Education made inquiries in 1951–52. Neither had any effect. Howard J. Savage et al., *American College Athletics,* Bulletin No. 23 (New York: The Carnegie Foundation for the Advancement of Teaching, 1979); "Report of the Special Committee on Athletic Policy," *Educational Record* 33 (April 1952): 246–55. Another documented and futile work was Reed Harris, *King Football: The Vulgarization of the American College* (New York: Vanguard, 1932).

30. The best account of the process is John F. Rooney's *The Recruiting Game: Toward a New System of Intercollegiate Sports* (Lincoln: University of Nebraska Press, 1980).

31. Gary Shaw, *Meat on the Hoof,* (New York: St. Martin's Press, 1972).

32. *Chronicle of Higher Education,* 13 January 1982, 5.

33. Quoted in Lowenfish and Lupien, *The Imperfect Diamond,* 204.

34. Harold Seymour, *Baseball: The Early Years* (New York: Oxford University Press, 1960), p. 3.

35. The changing concept of masculinity in the United States no longer requires a man to demonstrate his physical toughness, or eschew pursuits regarded as "pantywaisted."

36. Much of what Michael Novak has to say about sports can be applied to opera and theater; Covent Garden and Drury Lane, for instance, are as much "sacred spaces" as any stadium. See Michael Novak, *The Joy of Sports* (New York: Basic Books, 1976).

6

Rotten Apples of Gold: Gambling in American Sports

NEIL D. ISAACS

Ordinarily I deposit polls and questionnaires in the handiest circular file, but I was recently challenged by a "Form for Ranking the Ten Greatest Sports Figures in American History." A number of names occurred to me: Arnold Palmer, who made golf a major attraction; Jack Kramer, who initiated the modern era of tennis as a player and then made it commercially viable as a promoter; Billie Jean King, the hero of all equity-seeking women athletes; Branch Rickey, who changed the face of baseball; Bill Russell, who lifted the face of basketball to new heights and horizons; Pete Rozelle, who operated on the commercial face of football to implant the TV eye; and Renee Richards, who changed more than a face.

But when I began to consider what really matters in American sports today, the names of union organizers like Alan Eagleson and agents like Donald Dell flashed by, until I moved on to the heart of this jockocracy's focus on sports, where the money is, the real money, the big money. And then my list took final form: Billy Hecht, Leo Hirschfield, Max Stein, Petey Cohen, Karl Ersin, Arnold Rothstein, Jack Molinas, Joe Hacken, James Snyder, and Bob Martin.

The issue, of course, is gambling. Sports may be big business, but sports gambling dwarfs it in financial terms at least tenfold, perhaps fiftyfold. I begin, on this issue, from the point that there is nothing inherently, intrinsically wrong with gambling. But I end with a warning that gambling presents a clear and present danger to American sports in general and intercollegiate sports in particular.

It is a long way to go from innocence to apocalypse in the space of a few pages, but several observations from a cultural-history perspective will help. It may be useful to observe, at the outset, that in every other culture that we know anything about, where sports and games are significant, there are intimate associations of stakes and spectator involvement.

The aberrant attempt to separate gambling and sports in our culture has a curious background. It begins in the Middle Ages when the Catholic Church generalized from negative associations of particular types of gambling (*e.g.,* dicing, with reference to the Roman soldiers disposing the personal effects of Jesus after crucifixion) to moral condemnation of all types. In their quest for orderly hierarchies and a symmetry of fear in all earthly things, the medieval Fathers assigned gambling to the most understaffed of the Seven Deadly Sins. Sloth (which some called a vice with virtue because it militates against committing the other deadlies) was established as the rubric under which gambling was classified. Then the moral guilt of sloth was further condemned by association with sister categories of Gluttony, Avarice, and Lust.

Though the early Puritan communities in the New World usually had their own institutionalized lotteries, it was a congenial notion for Puritan America to condemn gambling on the bum charge of seeking profit without work. The next step was inevitable: legislate the sin into crime. Antigambling laws, however, have traditionally been honored in the breach. When newspapers and magazines in this century began regularly to report on sporting events, they openly recorded betting, including not only odds but the size of individual bets. Betting on college football was institutionalized by printed "tickets," the ancestors of parlay slips or cards.

Sports betting took a quantum leap forward in the late twenties with the invention of the point spread. Its origin is traditionally associated with the Gorham Press in Minneapolis. The first five names on my list of "Ten Greatest" are the legendary gambler who was the proprietor and the staff of that outfit, publishers of a Green Sheet and other sporting information primarily for gamblers. With a point spread, every football or basketball game is theoretically a good fifty-fifty sporting proposition. But along with the advantages of that development came a concomitant risk: the opportunities for corruption were multiplied.

The sixth name on my list should always serve to remind us of the potential for corruption in our sports. Arnold Rothstein was able to fix the World Series in 1919, though F. Scott Fitzgerald (who called him Meyer Wolfsheim in *The Great Gatsby*) wondered how one man could play with the faith of fifty million people. In the forties, when basketball fixes began to surface, such naïve wonderment persisted, until in 1951, thirty players at seven schools were found guilty of fixing games in twenty cities in seventeen states. Such widespread corruption was widely thought to be merely the visible tip of a monstrous submerged leviathan.

Reactions ranged from the hypocrisy of Adolph Rupp, who thought the phenomenon limited to New York City, and that of Columbia's athletic director, who said it happened only in public arenas and not campus field houses, to the chagrin of Nat Holman, who lamented the increased pressure to win in front of growing audiences, and the bitterness of Clair Bee, who was bewildered by his own and other coaches' naïve ignorance. The clearest voice on the subject, strangely enough, was that of J. Edgar Hoover, who spoke of all the "hypocrisy and sham;" blamed colleges for violating their own athletic codes in practices of workless jobs, outright gifts, and summer jobs for the express purpose of playing basketball; and said that the colleges were simply not creating the proper atmosphere for rejecting bids from gamblers.

But no one heard. The fixing went on, right through scandals and arrests and trials and convictions. And it grew. Throughout the fifties, college basketball and football games were so involved that sometimes both sides had players trying to dump or shave points. In 1957, Jack Molinas, who had been banned from the NBA for betting and had then become a lawyer, went back into business with Joe Hacken (the seventh and eighth names on my list). Hacken had once paid Molinas to fix games in college and then made him a partner in his bookmaking business during his senior year. But now they operated on a much larger scale. At the peak of their activities they had as many as four college basketball games in one day set up for point shaving (though two of those fixed teams covered the spread anyway), and they were interested in college and professional football as well.

When the new round of scandals came to light, with indictments and trials in North Carolina as well as New York, it was simply a rerun of a decade earlier. The revelations were widespread but touched only a fraction of the action. Hacken and some of his associates pleaded guilty and went to prison; Molinas was tried and found guilty and sent to prison. But no serious attempts were made to defend against recurrence; a few protuberances were excised, but the cancer grew toward metastasis.

In the twenty years since Molinas, the so-called "master fixer," went to Attica, a number of changes have taken place in public attitudes toward sports gambling. The fixing of horse races, both thoroughbred and standardbred, by a variety of means, has become so commonplace that new scandals barely make wire-service news stories. More and more newspapers, general and specialized periodicals, and even TV networks openly discuss odds, point spreads, and betting lines for all sports, but especially pro football. The NFL's extraordinary success as commercial entertainment owes less to the inherent beauty of the game as the NFL plays it than to its TV packaging, its PR media-blitz programming, and its universal acceptance as a vehicle for betting.

The ninth name on my list, that of Jimmy the Greek, is meant as a token of this success. Neither a handicapper nor a linesmaker, Snyder has been so good a promoter of sports betting that he has been accepted by the public at large as the ubiquitous symbol of a national activity, what Larry Merchant has called the "National Football Lottery." It may be illegal in every state but Nevada and New Jersey, but it's OK. It is not coincidental that NFL football has risen to preeminence among American sports just as it has become preeminent as a betting vehicle, and the highest TV ratings for Super Bowls and Monday Night Football coincide with the heaviest gambling handle. The NFL acknowledges this by the monitoring of point-spread fluctuations through Las Vegas contacts and by the supervised publication of injury reports.

The enormous rise of betting on pro football has carried over to other sports. It is less a trickle-down effect than a Niagara Falls of chips. And as has always been the case, where there has been a lot of gambling action and a lot of deliberate ignoring of the situation, there has been corruption. Ostriches make neither good judges nor good policemen, not to mention reporters.

Ironically, the one case that has come to light recently, the fixing of basketball games at Boston College, was an isolated one, a freakish by-product of a criminal investigation. The heaviest irony involved was that the publicity attendant on that one little case of point shaving effectively undercut at least two ongoing investigations of point-shaving scandals of major proportions involving schools in at least two major conferences that may now never be satisfactorily exposed.

It is not, then, from a position of naïveté or of moralistic horror that I view with alarm the present state of affairs. I know that gambling is part and parcel of the commercialization of sports in our jockocracy. What I want to make clear is that in dollar terms it is by far the biggest part. Recent headlines bannered the sensational report of a five-year TV deal by the NFL with the networks amounting to $1.9 billion. But by the most conservative estimate, more than that is bet *each year* on pro football. More than *ten times* that much is closer to the reality. College football attracts the second biggest handle, college basketball the third and fastest growing, thanks to successful TV packaging in the last two years.

The intimate connection between TV and gambling is well established. Any bookmaker can demonstrate a direct correlation between televised games and betting action; any fan can testify he'd rather bet on what he can watch and that a bet makes the watching more exciting, more involving. And the networks know, too: they can sell commercials at the end of games, no matter how early the winners have been determined, because the point spread keeps the gambling results in doubt and the betting public in their seats in front of their sets.

I used to think that all the ills of intercollegiate athletics stem from recruiting. I now believe that recruiting is just one finger of the hand that's on the throats of our college sports, threatening to choke them to death. The other fingers are boosterism, drugs, TV, and gambling. And they are all related, interrelated, and interlocked in the prevailing atmosphere of commercialized exploitation.

How can it be stopped? The gambling cannot be (I won't argue here whether it should be); the corruption should be. Most law enforcement agencies say that sports betting should be legalized, that illegal gambling contributes mightily to the subversion and corruption of the criminal justice system. The FBI, however, opposes that move, and so does the NCAA, taking their stand with most organized religious groups in this country as if their position were a matter of moral principle. It seems to me, however, to be more nearly a matter of vested interest and expediency.

Some insight may be gained by referring back to the Boston College case. How did it surface? As part of the meticulous, routine investigation of the great airport robbery. As a general practice, the Organized Crime Task Forces use gambling as a way to get at other criminal activities—loan sharking, narcotics, pornography, the taking over of legitimate businesses, the manipulation of union pension funds, et al. Gambling is the easy way in; it's an easy mark, visible and detectable, and because of all the victimless crimes it is the most nearly acceptable to the citizenry at large and most readily accessible to legitimate clientele. It is in the interest of the FBI, then, to keep it illegal; otherwise they couldn't use it in their war against crime.

And why does the NCAA share this position? Surely the answer is not so simple as pointing out that their investigative staff consists mainly of former FBI personnel. Nor is it so simplistic as the PR virtues of a Bobby Knight and his devoted followers haranguing against the gamblers as a way of deflecting attention from the other ills and evils in the way they play their games. No, I'm afraid it's more a matter of pragmatic capacity. The NCAA is ill-equipped and grossly understaffed for effective policing and control of those offenses it actually attends to. The NCAA is uninterested in acknowleging the gambling problem (or the drug problem) because unprepared to cope with it. (Of the others I have mentioned, the NCAA is part of, or party to, the problems.)

The NCAA's ignorance of gambling is legendary. For example, when, belatedly, official eyebrows were raised because of a radical adjustment in the line on a college football game, appropriate oracles in Nevada were consulted. The game, of course, as all bettors knew, had been published as the "lock of the year" by one of the more popular tout services. "Well, good," said the NCAA, "then everything's all right." But the NCAA should have been aware of the extent and influence of the sports-gambling information industry, should regularly examine the products of that industry, and should be checking out every detail of that information.

Here is where Bob Martin, the tenth name on my list, comes in. Dubbed "The Head Linesman" by columnist Gerald Strine

because he has for many years set the most influential point
spreads in Las Vegas, Martin stands four-square for the integrity
of linesmaker and bookmaker. He does not predict; he sets a
number which he anticipates will attract equal interest on both
sides. The free market may then adjust it, but very few NFL
games move more than a point in the six days until kickoff. But
the point here is that *more than anyone involved,* the gambling
industry relies on honest sporting events.

Martin and his co-workers in Nevada, abetted by the bookmakers around the country who rely on their astuteness and
acumen, are in the best position to detect the slightest hints of
chicanery. Properly employed, they would be the best bulwark
against corruption. And they would be pleased to make common
cause with institutions and officials in the interest of the integrity
of sports.

Legalization of sports betting, I believe, is the answer. Get it
out in the open where it can be observed and subject to oversight, and fixes become virtually impossible. Truth and knowledge will free our sports from one of their more persistent ills
and one of our gravest fears for them. And the way to do it, I
think, is to license bookmakers (as in England) and tax their
profits (not the individual winners), setting aside the largely
phony issue of morality. On this issue institutional integrity is
clearcut, like the ethics of gambling; its morality or immorality is
at best problematical, at worst a distraction from significant action.

But if we persist in our inaction, if we continue down the road
we're on now, we will see that stranglehold I have described
tighten and stifle the life out of organized competitive sports.
And since sports and games, as we know, both reflect and teach
the value systems of the whole culture, down that road of total
corruption lies the decay of our civilization as we know it. And
all those frantic displays of "We're number one" will be replaced
by the universal acknowledgment that we are all zero.

PART II
The Individualized Experience

We [Texas football candidates] were eighteen-year-old high school heroes lost in a new world and daily being stripped of dignity and any past identity.

—Gary Shaw,
Meat on the Hoof: The Hidden World of Texas Football (1972)

Quarterbacking had provided me with a great education. I had found a way of being me and being in the world that I value very much. It's one reason I finally learned to love football, and love it now.

—John Brodie,
Open Field (1974)

Issues and Contentions

Our system of intercollegiate athletics, especially as it is exemplified today in NCAA Division I football, typifies what has happened in our society to the athlete's role within the context of athletics at large. Big-time college football, having evolved from prototypal activities that once concerned only the extracurricular interests of students, now represents a multimillion-dollar business involving a wide variety of interrelated concerns in an undertaking of gigantic proportions. In *The Big Game: College Sports and American Life* (1978), Edwin H. Cady has comprehensively described the complexity of this operation as it relates in particular to the preparation for a football weekend at a large collegiate institution. Clearly, though, the thing that stands out overall as most critical to perpetuating the success of any institution within this system is the extent to which an athletic department devotes its energies to the recruitment of promising players. Unfortunately, this part of the Revenue Sport System, as Jack Hutslar labels it, also stands out as the most abused and corrupt with respect to the proper treatment of athletes within the system. As a result, the schizophrenic role of today's college athlete is characterized by two counterattitudes.

In 1972, Gary Shaw, a former member of the University of Texas football team, startled the sports world with his candid revelations of what a scholarship player must endure to make it in a system that espouses an all-winning philosophy. However, the negative opinions set forth in *Meat on the Hoof: The Hidden World of Texas Football* were sharply countered by John Brodie's intensely personal feelings about his long involvement with football in school, college, and the professional ranks. In fact, his autobiographical *Open Field* (1974) comes across to the reader in such positive fashion that its outlook appears to offset any bad times the author might have encountered in the system of organized athletics. For Brodie the act of participating in athletics becomes an intensive learning experience, heightened at times by unaccountable insights into being and self. It is this same kind of individualized experience that informs a work like George Leonard's *The Ultimate Athlete* (1975), whose thesis contends that, at heart, any athletic endeavor is only worth what it can teach the participant about his or her self. But even while agreeing with Brodie's special feeling for the transcendental or spiritual side of sports experience, Leonard, in the vein of Gary Shaw, can vehemently criticize the delimiting effects of traditional team sports on the individual.

So for every John Brodie the system has produced, we have to wonder how many Gary Shaws have come along, who, naturally enamored at first with the self-expressive possibilities of athletics, have had their love for them undermined and destroyed in the end by an oversystematized approach. In the initial essay of this section ("Varsity Syndrome: The Unkindest Cut"), CBS sports analyst Robert Lipsyte goes right to the core of what may be wrong with organized sports in America. His dissection of the evils of sexism, elitism, and commercialism in athletics is intended to show us the necessity for recovering "the natural birthright of our bodies," apparently lost to us now, he affirms, through the manipulation and distortion by these forces of sport's original purpose. His thoughts lead naturally into the well-informed comments of former Notre Dame football player Allen Sack, whose platform defending athletes' rights not only describes how commercialization and exploitation have infiltrated intercollegiate athletics but also makes some realistic suggestions for reform ("The Amateur Myth: The Rights and Responsibilities of College Athletes").

Complementing the above concerns, Jack Hutslar's candid piece dealing with the conflict between the academic concerns of the college professor and the athletic goals of the college coach traces the reason for this antagonism to the powerful sway held today by the Revenue Sport System in intercollegiate sports. However, the paradox implicit in Hutslar's analysis precipitates a degree of ambivalence concerning the extent of criticism or praise we may direct at either side of this confrontation for carrying out its self-perceived sense of mission: either the professor who advances the cause of his discipline through attracting and turning out superior students or the coach who publicizes the name of his school through recruiting talented athletes and producing a successful athletic team. Obviously, both parties are conditioned to a universal understanding that in today's society the bottom line is quality performance. Within the ironic ramifications of the academic-athletic conflict, the role of an influential teacher today is becoming as competitive and demanding as that of an effective coach, it would appear.

If the black experience in American sports has taken an unduly long time to find itself, William H. Wiggins's comparison of two all-American basketball players' reactions to the recruiting system of professional basketball dramatically points out the excesses that have developed in the short time since the black athlete has been accepted into the mainstream of American athletics—both collegiate and professional. In comparing and contrasting the social backgrounds and cultural attitudes of superathletes Ralph Simpson and Ralph Sampson, Wiggins not only exposes the powerful system which identifies and seeks to control the athletic talent produced by our schools and colleges, he also shows how it can plant false dreams of material success in the minds of many black athletes. In sacrificing the opportunity for an education to the more immediate and powerful lure of earning big bucks in professional sports, the black athlete frequently discovers too late the error of his ways.

The basic problem facing the woman athlete in this country has been not so much that of her right to participate in athletics as that resulting from the kind of role she is expected to perform in the act of participating. In a traditionally male-dominated area of experience, American women have been conventionally conditioned to perform as women and not as athletes. This ironic predicament pervades John Bridges's "Women's Professional Football and the Changing Role of the Woman Athlete," a piece dealing in part with the social repercussions within the sports establishment when women athletes break the boundaries of their prescribed sphere of activity. We have to wonder, though, if the rise of the woman athlete will indeed win her a new aura of prestige and respect or if the defects of the system will create a new breed of female Gary Shaws.

In closing out this section, Jeffrey H. Goldstein discusses the relatively new field of sports psychology, whose main concerns relate to the experiential perceptions and reactions of both athlete and spectator. His central focus here is the need to rid ourselves of the "misplaced emphases, fallacies, and foibles in the field" in order to develop more of a humanistic understanding of athletic performance, spectator behavior, and the interrelated areas of aggression/violence and socialization. Goldstein's opinion that "sports should be viewed as integral to a society and as reflective of the values of that society" pervades a thoroughly documented overview of this field's developing theories and how they compare with conventional thinking about the respective roles of athlete and spectator in American society. Because sports psychology is naturally sensitive to a number of ills pervading the contemporary sports scene (e.g., drug abuse, violence, gambling, etc.), an understanding of the interrelationship of the athlete's and spectator's complementary roles may reveal more to us about the humanistic conflict in American sport than any other subject area covered in this collection.

7

Varsity Syndrome: The Unkindest Cut

ROBERT LIPSYTE

Americans must win back the natural birthright of their bodies, a birthright which has been distorted and manipulated by political and commercial forces that have used sports and physical education for purposes that often negate the incredible potential for individual and community progress that is inherent in sports—the one human activity that offers health, fun, and cooperation with the chance to combine physical, mental, and emotional energy.

Sport is the single most influential currency of mass communication in the world. Unlike so many other activities—music, art, literature—sport easily hurdles the barriers of age, education, language, gender, and social and economic status that tend to divide a population.

Sport has the potential to bring us together, but the evidence suggests it rarely does. In fact, it often further divides communities by promoting overzealous competition, violence, specialization, professionalization, and an attitude of "win at all costs" that spills over into other aspects of daily life.

Over the years there have been changes, hopeful changes, in sport. The emergence of the black athlete, the emergence of the woman athlete, the proliferation of serious academic studies of athletes and of their impact on our culture are examples. Yet, there has been no real breakthrough in the attempt to reduce the effects of a pervasive pattern of emphasis and expectations which keeps us from realizing the intensive pleasures of sport. I call that pattern the "varsity syndrome."

We experience the effects of the varsity syndrome in childhood and its influence is lifelong. It begins in kindergarten with "organized games" and culminates each year when more than eighty million Americans watch perhaps eighty men act out our fantasies—the Super Bowl, a celebration, we are conditioned to believe, of manliness, courage, fruitful labor, pain, endurance, strength and achievement, all characteristics to which every man would aspire to some degree.

Varsity Syndrome—Sexism

Confrontation with the varsity syndrome starts early for boys in any neighborhood; the killer word is "fag." Call a boy a fag and he will have to fight or slink away. The homosexual connotation of the word is implicit, though not primary. Since we were taught that homosexuals were unmanly, somehow "feminine," the word really meant to us that a boy was "girlish," unfit for the company of men. We all "knew" that girls were smaller, weaker, less physically skilled. They had no place or future in the big leagues of life. Sports taught us that.

A boy tried very hard to avoid being labeled a fag. He might play games in which he found no pleasure; he might root for teams that bored him; he paid constant lip service to sports. In my day it was, "Who you like better, fella, Mantle or Mays?" You could answer anyway you wanted to, you could even say "Duke Snider," just so long as you didn't say, "who cares?" The schoolyard—that no-woman's-land—was a male sanctuary, and the first of many arenas in which a man would be tested for his ability to perform under stress, with skill and with the ruthlessness that passes for pragmatism.

Sport was the first great separator of the sexes. Sometime after kindergarten, a girl was handed (symbolically or literally) the majorette's baton and told to go in the corner and twirl. Her athletic moment was over. She now existed only as an encourager of males. There were, of course, girls who dropped the baton and picked up the bat and beat males at their own games. However, the culture had prepared a way to combat this seeming inconsistency. Athletically superior boys might be considered supermen, but athletically superior women were something less than real women. They were locker-room jokes. Boys would tell each other, she's playing because she can't get a date; she's a tomboy; or, most devastatingly, she's a dyke. And if she turned out to be worldclass, the world was quick to suspect her chromosomes.

Reading about Babe Didrikson in Paul Gallico's popular 1938 book, *Farewell to Sport,* I had no reason to disbelieve his statement that she became one of the greatest of all American athletes merely as an "escape, a compensation."[1] Gallico wrote that Didrikson "would not or could not compete with women at their own best game . . . man-snatching."[2] Most sportswriters, observers, and participants accepted Gallico's statement as fact, or at the least as a manifestation of routine sexism. After all, women were barred from press boxes, locker rooms, and anything other than cheerleader positions in sport. Only recently, while researching a book, I came across an even simpler explanation for Gallico's slur. A fine and vain athlete himself, Gallico once raced Didrikson across a golf course. She ran him into the ground. And he never again wrote about her without mentioning her prominent Adam's apple, or the down on her upper lip. I assume his rationalization was traditional: A woman can't beat a man unless he's a fag or she's not really a woman.

The usual justification for restricting women from sports competition—the very first manifestation of the varsity syndrome—was that their delicate bodies needed protection from physical harm. More realistically, I believe, women were rejected to protect the delicate egos of men who have been taught that their manhood depends on the presence of an underclass. James Michener, a respected writer and an avid sports fan and participant, recently published a book called *Sports in America,* which contained a concept that I feel is very dangerous because it is so widely held.[3] Michener wrote that between the ages of about eleven and twenty-two, men and women should not compete against each other in sports because of the possible damage to the male's ego should he lose.[4] No consideration is given to the ego of the young female who is striving to exhibit and stretch to the outer limits her own talents and skills.

The sexism of the varsity syndrome transcends sports. Athletics give youngsters an opportunity to learn the positive values of leadership, of cooperation and dedication and sacrifice for a goal. Games are a source of skill development, whether it be physical, mental, or social. Many women have been stunted in their growth toward full citizenship because they were denied an opportunity routinely afforded to every male. The woman who does succeed in American sports does so at a certain cost. I recall one afternoon in the middle sixties, coming off a tennis court after a victory, sweaty, rackets under her arm, Billie Jean King was intercepted by a male spectator from the stands who asked, "Hey, Billie Jean, when are you going to have children?" Billie Jean answered, "I'm not ready yet." The man continued, "Why aren't you at home?" Billie Jean snapped right back "Why don't you go ask Rod Laver why *he* isn't at home?"

Varsity Syndrome—Elite Deference

Another component of the varsity syndrome, learned on the streets and reinforced throughout school, is elitism. Special privileges are afforded athletes, including a special psychological aura or deference that ultimately proves to harm the athlete as well as the nonathlete. This aspect of the varsity syndrome is so pernicious it finds its supporters at both poles of the playing field, from Neanderthal coaches on the right, whose authoritarian methods squeeze joy out of sports, to so-called sports revolutionaries on the left who see athletes as a higher order of human beings.

Traditionally, soon after 51 percent of the potential athletes—the women—are cut from the team, the process of winnowing the boys begins. This process, which George Sauer, the former New York Jets wide receiver, has called a form of social Darwinism, has many ramifications.[5] First of all, it separates boys into worthy and unworthy classes just at a time in their lives when they are most confused about their bodies and their relationships with their peers. Those anointed as athletes often drop away from other social and intellectual pursuits, and it becomes harder and harder for them to catch up when they, too, are eventually cut from the team. It happens to everyone eventually, and no matter the age or level of competition, the cut is hard to take. Those who are marked as failures at critical times in their lives often seem to spend the rest of their lives measuring up. Those who measure up early and last for awhile become jocks.

In our society the jock is often the male equivalent of the stereotyped female, the broad.

The jock and the broad are selected and rewarded for beauty and performing skills. They are used to satisfy others and to define themselves by the quantity and quality of that satisfaction whether it be as a Heisman Trophy winner or as Miss America, rookie of the year or starlet, all-American or prom queen. When they grow too old to please they are discarded.

One of the cruelest ramifications of the elitist component of the varsity syndrome is the way it has been used to turn black athletes into a gladiator legion in American sports. Contrary to prevailing opinion, sports success has probably been detrimental to black progress. By publicizing the material success of a few hundred athletes, thousands, perhaps millions of bright young blacks have been swept toward sports when they should have been guided toward careers in medicine or engineering or business. For every black who escaped the ghetto behind his jump shot, a thousand of his little brothers were neutralized, kept busy shooting baskets, until it was too late for them to qualify beyond marginal work.[6]

Those who do make it big, white or black, male or female, are generally lionized out of all proportion to their intrinsic worth, or to their importance to society. The athlete is damaged by the exaggerated adulation and the rest of us are given a pantheon of heroes on a nest of false laurels. An example from my own experience illustrates this point. When I was about twenty-one, a brand-new reporter at the *New York Times,* I was sent to Yankee Stadium to interview Mickey Mantle. Several nights earlier, a fan jumped out of the stands and traded some punches with Mantle. This was years before the advent of what psychiatrists now call "recreational violence," and it was quite unusual. Apparently Mantle had gotten the worst of the scuffle; he couldn't chew very well for a day or two. No one had dared interview him about the incident. I was sent because I was expendable as a cub reporter and I asked him about it because I didn't know any better. So, in my most polite reportorial tones I asked Mickey if his jaw still hurt. Mickey looked at me contemptuously and made an obscene and physically impossible suggestion. Somehow, after years of reading about Mantle in newspapers and magazines and books, I was not exactly prepared for his answer. So I rephrased it and tried again. He then signaled to

Yogi Berra, another all-star charmer, and they began throwing a baseball back and forth an inch over my head. I sensed that the interview was over.

I don't want to make too much of this because I think a celebrity has the right (within limits that apply to us all) to act any way he or she wants. But I also think the rest of us have a right not to be deceived. That little incident at Yankee Stadium was a real consciousness-raiser for me. If this was the real Mickey Mantle, I thought, then we haven't been getting the right information. Like so many athletes in our culture, Mantle had been isolated early by virtue of the varsity syndrome, given privileges denied the rest of us. Those privileges begin with favors and gifts in grade school, little presents in high school such as an unearned diploma, perhaps a college scholarship. Athletes are waved, as it were, through the tollbooths of life. And then, as celebrities, they are given a whole new identity as heroes.

Of course, to publicize any frailties in athletic character structure is to bring down a wave of criticism and often categorical rejection. When Jim Bouton's book *Ball Four* came out a few years ago, the big rap against the book wasn't its stories or that major league shenanigans were untrue, but that kids shouldn't hear them—that the false image of athletes as somehow a super-race apart, must be retained, even at the price of truth.[7] Why is it so important that kids look up to false heroes as models of behavior? Why not know the truth and learn to separate what people do from what they are; to appreciate athletes as dedicated specialists, as entertainers, but not as gods.

Varsity Syndrome—Athletes as Salesmen

There are, of course, so many components of the varsity syndrome we could never even touch them all in this limited space. But there is one other significant dimension that deserves mention—the use of athletics and athletes to sell a product. In its lowest form, athletes sell shoes or panty hose, breakfast cereals or underarm deodorant. They sell colleges that have four books in the library but a multimillion-dollar fieldhouse. Athletes sell cities which mortgage their futures to build ball parks in order to be plunged into a national entertainment network which is valuable for tourism and investment. And, on the highest and perhaps most grotesque level, athletes are used to sell ways of life, ideologies.

This is the most distorted level, not only because world-class athletic competitions, like the Olympic Games, are such major events, but because they would not be possible without the varsity syndrome, that careful and calculated selection process that starts in kindergarten. This narrow elitism makes most of us failed athletes long before we've had the chance to really feel the sensuous delights of the wind in our hair while running, or the water lapping at our bodies while swimming, or the almost orgasmic pleasures of that one perfect shot or catch or leap that comes to everyone involved in sport. Sport is the best thing you can do with your body in public.

The Olympic Games are grotesque in themselves. As is probably known, the modern Olympics were the brainstorm of a French baron from a military family who never got over France's defeat in the Franco-Prussian War. Baron de Coubertin wanted a rematch, and he thought French youth could get in shape for the rematch through sports. That kind of nationalistic taint has never been removed from the games. In 1968 we saw the spectacle of black athletes, who raised their fists in protest against racism in America, thrown off the team even though theirs was an individual gesture in a context that is supposed to exist for individualistic expression. In 1972 the hideous extension of de Coubertin's nationalism—the use of the Olympics as a showcase for the strength of democracy or the goodness of socialism or the love of the Junta—resulted in the murder of a team of competitors from Israel. In 1976, the various machinations over China and South Africa reinforced the Olympics as *Politics in a Sweatshirt.*

The Olympics not only represent a major political event, they also are a significant entertainment and commercial event. The most poignant lesson, to me, came at a press conference prior to the 1976 games. The president of ABC sports at the time, Roone Arledge, a very powerful man in international sports, was asked by an idealistic journalist why the opening event of the Games, the ceremonial parade of athletes, couldn't be run for its full hour or more without commercial interruptions. Arledge replied quite amiably that it wouldn't be commercially feasible . . . "after all, sponsors pay for telecasts."

But the questioner continued . . . "Many countries which use the Olympics as a showcase or as a statement of identity, might never be seen except in that opening parade. After all, many countries win no medals at all. And some sports, like field hockey, water polo, and volleyball, are not well covered. So some countries, lost in a commercial, might never get on the world television feed at all."

"That's true," said Arledge.

"How do you pick candidates for obscurity?" asked the journalist.

"Well," said Arledge, "we have to make judgments. Suppose we've just had two little South American countries, and its time for a commercial, and here comes a third South American country . . . sooooooo, sorry about that, Chile."

That third little South American country, or that little Midwestern college, betting its identity on the ephemeral possibility of national or international exposure, is putting a kind of graffiti on the windows of the world, shouting, "I'm here, we're alive."

They are in the trap of the varsity syndrome. The payoff can be great, but the price to pay is also great and, for most, rarely worth the gain. The struggle to success may be stalemated prematurely by the whim of a television producer or the vagaries of the system itself. Win or lose, the country and the college invariably sell their souls cheap to a system that uses them up and moves on.

This is a system in which, for the past hundred years or so, most Americans have been taught to believe that playing and watching competitive games are not only healthful activities, but exert a positive force on our national psyche. Through sports, they have been led to believe, children will learn courage and self-control; old people will find blissful nostalgia; families will discover nonthreatening ways to communicate among themselves, immigrants will find shortcuts to recognition as Americans, and, rich and poor, black and white, educated and unskilled, we will all find a unifying language with democratization the result: The melting pot may be a myth in real life, but in the ballpark or on the playing field we are one community, unified in common purpose. Even for ball games, these values, with their implicit definitions of courage and success and manhood, are not necessarily in the individual's best interests. But for daily life they tend to support a web of ethics and attitudes, part of that amorphous infrastructure called *SportsWorld,* that acts to contain our energies, divert our passions, and socialize us for work or war or depression.

In 1928, the Columbia University historian John Krout wrote: "During depressions, with thousands out of work, sports help refocus our attention on the great American values and ideals and also help us to remember that life does not begin and end with the dollar."[8] This infrastructure, SportsWorld, is neither an American nor a modern phenomenon. The Olympics of ancient Greece were manipulated for political and commercial purposes. SportsWorld is no classic conspiracy, but rather an expression of a community of interest. In the Soviet Union and East Germany, for example, where world-class athletes are the diplomat-soldiers of ideology, and where factory workers exercise to reduce fatigue and increase production, it is simple to see that the entire athletic apparatus is part of government.

In this country, SportsWorld's power is less visible, but no less real. In America, banks decide which arenas and recreational facilities will be built; television networks decide which sports shall be sponsored and viewed; the press decides which individuals and teams will be celebrated; municipal governments decide which clubs will be subsidized through the building of stadiums; state legislatures decide which universities, and which aspects of their athletic programs, will prosper; and the federal government, through favorable tax rulings and exemptions from law, helps develop and maintain sports entertainment as a currency of communication that surpasses patriotism and piety while exploiting them both.

Educators and journalists are at fault for their support of this system. And we are often in the position of being the fall guys. It sometimes seems as though we are in what the play-by-play announcers call a no-win situation. By working within the rules of the system, preparing athletes and teachers to function smoothly in SportsWorld and to prosper with the varsity syndrome, we are perpetuating a pattern that is basically antisports, that denies the joy of healthy play and competition to the society as a whole. By trying to beat the system by de-emphasizing big-time sports and cutting back on the massive construction of arenas that are wasteful in terms of human use, in favor of some broad-based physical education programs, we are often in danger of jeopardizing the financial health of our institutions and discriminating against the really talented athletes who deserve the chance to develop to their limits just as surely as do the young people in the English department or the student engineers. Educators and journalists are the fall guys because when things go wrong they are often blamed, and sometimes fired— even though the ultimate decision-making power in SportsWorld is never theirs.

Sport is, has always been, and will always be, a reflection of the mainstream culture or the society. Those who claim that we could or should keep sport free of politics, or free of commercialism, or free of ideology are fools. If sport were not such a reflection, it would be nothing more than an isolated sanctuary, an irrelevant little circus, and hardly worth considering. But sport is, as I firmly believe it should be, a critical part of the lives of every man, woman, and child in the country and in the world. Furthermore, it should be accessible, inexpensive, and fun.

Activists have always seen sports as a tool to change or direct society, and they have been criticized for it. Yet when establishment politicians and coaches talk about sports as preparation for life or about football as a way of training young men for war or for corporate positions, they are using sports as a tool just as surely as is anyone who calls for a boycott of an all-white South African rugby team. The answer, of course, is that society must be changed before sports can be changed. But that, too, can sometimes be a self-defeating answer. It allows too many of us to sit back and throw up our hands. Changing society seems like an incomprehensible, much less possible, task.

However, things are happening in sports, exciting things, some progressive, some reactionary, some scary. First, there's a growing awareness of the importance of sports in our lives. Second, the increasing academic interest in sports is a hopeful sign. Institutes, both independent and on campuses, are being created with the explicit goal of investigating, analyzing, and understanding the role of sport in society. Third, there are new laws to help end the systematic exclusion of women. (But care must be taken that the varsity syndrome does not permeate the organization of women's sport.) Fourth, there's a growing body of work exposing the so-called Lombardi ethic of "Winning isn't the Most Important Thing, it's the Only Thing" (a phrase, by the way, which Lombardi didn't invent) as appropriate for the professional Green Bay Packers, but a crippler, physically and psychologically, when applied to youngsters just starting in sports.

Despite the enormous amount to be accomplished, there are

little contests each of us can engage in that will win for us all: one little community recreation program for older people; one totally nonsexist grade-school sports program; one high-school program which involves every student regardless of skill level; a girls' team that doesn't use the JV's leftover shoes and the gym at dinner time; a college pool that doesn't discriminate against nonvarsity swimmers; a little league that defuses the pressures of joyless competition; and a university classroom that openly approaches the possibility of new games, new methods, and fresh concepts in sport studies. Each victory will shed some light on sports and will help shape our lives through its cultural impact. Each victory will help dispel the darkness of SportsWorld, the varsity syndrome, and a system that separates people by calling some athletes and some nonathletes. When this beautiful and good thing we call sports allows each person to be an athlete forever, then it will have been true to its original purposes.

Notes

1. Paul Gallico, *Farewell to Sports* (New York: Alfred A. Knopf, 1945), 229.
2. Ibid., 229.
3. James Michener, *Sports in America* (New York: Random House, 1976).
4. Ibid., 129.
5. Robert Lipsyte, *SportsWorld* (New York: Quadrangle, 1975), 51.
6. Rick Telander, *Heaven Is a Playground* (New York: Grosset and Dunlap, 1976).
7. Jim Bouton, *Ball Four* (New York: World, 1970).
8. John Krout, "Some Reflections on the Rise of American Sport," Proceedings of the Association of History, #26 (1929). Reprinted in *The Sporting Set,* ed. Leon Stern (New York: Arno Press, 1975), 84–93.

8

The Amateur Myth:
The Rights and Responsibilities of
College Athletes

ALLEN L. SACK

Several years ago, the Center for Athletes Rights and Education (CARE) gained a degree of national prominence by presenting an "athletes' bill of rights" at a Washington press conference. "College athletes are students and workers," the preamble declared. "Their time and sweat bring in millions of dollars from ticket sales, TV contracts, and contributions. As students, they are entitled to an education similar in quality to other students. As workers they are entitled to safe working conditions and fair compensation for the money they generate." The bill went on to assert the right of college athletes to form unions and to bargain collectively on all issues affecting financial aid and working conditions.

The reaction of the college sports establishment was predictable. Joab L. Thomas, president of the University of Alabama, said simply, "You've got to be kidding," then added that the proposals would turn college athletes into "gladiators" and would "move college sport away from amateurism." Cas Myslinski, athletic director at the University of Pittsburgh, called the bill "a lot of baloney" and insisted that athletes are not laborers. Tom Hansen, assistant executive director of the National Collegiate Athletic Association, argued that collective bargaining would be "contrary to the entire spirit of college athletics."

The notion that big-time college athletes are mere amateurs engaged in playful extracurricular activities is deeply ingrained in the American consciousness. As the above statements make clear, it is also the dominant ideology of key decision-makers in the sports establishment.

The fact, however, is that scholarship athletes are really professionals, and the imposition of an amateur label on them robs them of important forms of medical, legal, and academic protection. Furthermore, the myth of amateurism is the root cause of the most pernicious form of athletic abuse in college sport today.

No clear distinction exists between the responsibilities of scholarship athletes and those of other employees in the American work force. The decisions in numerous court cases support this contention. In *Taylor v. Wake Forest University,* for instance, the courts ruled in 1972 that an athletic scholarship is a binding contract and that scholarship aid can be withdrawn if an athlete decides to give up sports.

The regulations of the NCAA also suggest that scholarship athletes are hired guns. Under current regulations, a scholarship athlete who decides to quit sports is entitled to scholarship aid only until the end of the semester. An athlete who is injured or is not performing to a coach's expectations can lose aid at the end of one year. The one-year scholarship or contract gives college coaches the flexibility to hire and retain highly skilled athletic personnel. But it also transforms athletes into wage laborers whose compensation is solely determined by athletic performance. For some athletes, loss of a scholarship can mean returning to a ghetto with no education, no job, and no prospects. For them, college sport is not a game but a livelihood.

A number of cases which have been handled recently by CARE clearly illustrate the contractual nature of an athletic scholarship. A University of Massachusetts athlete, for instance, was told by the school's scholarship committee that his scholarship would not be renewed because he was "not a basketball player of sufficient calibre to play intercollegiate basketball" for that university. The committee based its decision entirely on "the athletic department's evaluation of [the player's] athletic ability." In this case financial aid was contingent solely on athletic performance; classroom performance was not considered.

When the athlete failed to meet his employer's expectations, he was "fired."

A University of Maryland basketball player also contacted CARE after his scholarship was revoked. In this instance the athlete argued that the demands of his academic major necessitated that he give up sports during his senior year. The University's position was unequivocal: If the player could not continue in his sport, the University had no legal obligation to provide financial aid. The athlete was told to adjust his academic schedule to meet the demands of basketball or to look elsewhere for financial aid. In both the Maryland and Massachusetts cases, the universities clearly were treating athletes like employees under contract.

Because coaches and athletic departments can unilaterally determine who is deserving of financial aid, it is not surprising that they have considerable control over an athlete's behavior. Like any employer, college coaches can control the time, manner, and discharge of their worker's duties. They can insist, as a condition for continued financial aid, that an athlete play while injured or engage in other activities that pose a threat to his long-term health. A truly amateur athlete can freely decide the extent to which he is willing to take such risks. A scholarship athlete, like a professional, has far less discretion.

A scholarship athlete's responsibilities to his sport can also obstruct his academic progress. Attending practice, taking long road trips, and meeting the many other demands imposed by coaches are conditions for continued financial aid, and as a consequence many athletes find themselves taking academic shortcuts. Some cheat, others cut classes, and a few even accept credit for classes they never attended. The alternative is to take academic life seriously, thereby risking the loss of a competitive edge on the playing field and, possibly, the loss of a scholarship.

Clearly, when it comes to outlining responsibilities, universities and courts have not hesitated to treat athletes as employees under contract. Unlike professional athletes, however, scholarship athletes are denied a wide range of rights and protections that are taken for granted in this country by other employees. When it comes to responsibilities, universities treat athletes like employees; when it comes to rights, they treat them like amateurs. This practice is not only hypocritical, it is dangerous and exploitative.

Few occupations have a higher injury rate than professional sports such as football and basketball. The average career of players in the National Football League lasts about four or five years, and few escape some form of permanent injury. In order to cushion the blow of the more debilitating injuries, professional athletes have a right to state workmen's compensation. Such athletes also are covered by the Fair Labor Standards Act, the Occupational Safety and Health Act, and the National Labor Relations Acts.

Scholarship athletes—whose responsibilities are indistinguishable from the pros—are denied these protections on the grounds that they are amateurs. The financial exploitation that results is obvious. Scholarship athletes help to generate for their universities millions of dollars in revenue. By insisting that these athletes are amateurs, universities can pay them only a minimum wage of room, board, tuition, and books. This may be a shrewd way of cutting costs, but it is nonetheless an exploitative practice.

Several years ago Jackie Sherrill was offered a $1.7 million contract to coach at Texas A & M University. Recently a number of football powers made close to $1 million dollars each from a single bowl appearance. What legal or moral justification can there be for denying the athletes whose sweat and sacrifice make such salaries and revenues possible a right to bargain over what constitutes a fair economic return on their investment? Big-time college athletes are among the few employees in America who are denied the right to sell their skills at their market value.

The amateur myth has also served to deny scholarship athletes the educational opportunities they have been promised. By insisting that college sport is an extracurricular activity, the special problems of being a professional athlete and a student at the same time can be ignored.

Many college students work full time while pursuing their degrees. Because they work, universities encourage these students to take fewer courses each semester even if this delays graduation. Graduate students who are working as teaching or research assistants also are encouraged to take a reduced course load.

Scholarship athletes, on the other hand, must take the same number of credits as other students if they expect to graduate before their scholarship money runs out. Schools make this demand even though scholarship athletes, in effect, are working their way through school by engaging in one of the most physically and emotionally demanding jobs there is, professional sports.

Not only is this treatment of athletes educationally unsound, but it may also constitute a breach of contract. By creating conditions which obstruct academic opportunities for scholarship athletes, universities are failing to uphold their end of scholarship agreements.

Truly amateur athletes, who have control over the nature and extent of their athletic involvement, have no need for the rights and protections I have outlined. The unionization of Ivy League athletes, for instance, would be inappropriate and unnecessary. The truly amateur athlete can avoid physical and academic sacrifice simply by walking off the field. This may hurt his pride, but it will not affect his livelihood.

Although the myth that even big-time college sport is an amateur enterprise is alive and well, a number of court cases have begun to challenge it. In a case that ultimately went to the Indiana Supreme Court, a Court of Appeals judge ruled that a student attending college on a sports scholarship is entitled to worker's compensation for injuries received on the playing field. Fred Rensing, the plaintiff, was a varsity football player at Indiana State University when he was rendered a quadriplegic by a head injury sustained during football practice. According to the ruling of Judge Stanley Miller, "the benefits received by Rensing were conditioned upon his athletic ability and team participation. Consequently, the scholarship constituted a contract for hire and created an employee-employer relationship."

Although Judge Miller's ruling was overturned by the Indiana Supreme Court, the logic of his argument remains extremely compelling. The fact that several other workman's compensation cases have emerged in other states during the past year suggests that the Rensing case was an opening salvo rather than the final round on this issue.

Whether college athletes will organize to defend their rights in this new legal climate is difficult to say. The guess here is that unionization of college athletes is unlikely even if the courts rule that it is legal. More likely, individual athletes will begin to press court cases to challenge rules which deny them a share of sports revenues. Just as individual universities are challenging the NCAA cartel, individual athletes are bound to begin challenging rules which restrict their economic freedom.

In the end, those who want to restore a modicum of integrity to college sport have two choices. The first is to impose the Ivy League model on every athletic program in the country by eliminating scholarships based solely on athletic ability. This would allow athletes to give greater priority to education than to sports without fearing the loss of financial aid. In this model, athletes are students first and foremost. Sports truly are an extracurricular activity, not a way of paying for an education.

Although fine in theory, imposing the amateur model across the board is not a practical alternative. Institutions such as Nebraska, Oklahoma, Penn State, and Notre Dame have athletic programs whose primary goals are winning games and producing revenue. It is unlikely that such schools would abandon aggressive recruiting and the athletic scholarships it requires.

Given this reality, higher education can best be served by acknowledging that an athlete at such schools has responsibilities both as a worker and as a student. Steps could then be taken to insure that the demands of his sport do not obstruct his opportunity for an education.

One reform that would go a long way toward helping scholarship athletes reconcile their contradictory roles would be the addition of a fifth year of scholarship aid beyond athletic eligibility. Although this may seem like a modest proposal, it has been fought by both college presidents and NCAA officials. The major reason for opposing this reform is that it assumes that scholarship athletes make greater sacrifices in time and energy to get their education than do other students. Such an admission is unlikely from people who would have us believe that big-time college sport differs little, if at all, from a friendly game of intramural frisbee.

The fact of the matter is that college sport is a big business which employs highly skilled athletes to attract revenue. The rights of the athletic work force will sooner or later have to be acknowledged. Until this is done, the hypocrisy and subterfuge which are becoming the hallmark of sport in American higher education will continue unabated. Institutions which are supposed to represent knowledge, enlightenment, and transcendent ideals will continue to support practices which encourage illiteracy and inspire little more than cynicism from the American public. The time for forthright action is long overdue.

9

The Revenue Sport System and the Academic-Athletic Conflict

JACK HUTSLAR

In his book *Gamesman* (1978), Michael Macoby notes that we tend to type people according to our situation in life and our perception of social behavior. Thus, police type people as dishonest and honest. Doctors type people as sick and well. Coaches type people as losers and winners, and teachers see things in terms of dull and bright or dumb and smart.

The counter perspectives of coaches and teachers point to a long standing problem that appears to be taking on renewed prominence with the increased emphasis on winning in college athletics. The battle lines which divide sport and education have traditionally derived from a basic conflict between the unfettered idealism of coaches who feel that skilled athletes should also be naturally good students and the high expectations of college professors who are compelled to tolerate academic washouts sent to them by the athletic department. More recently, the familiar scenario of college sport that has been portrayed in literature and film as well as in real life has introduced a "villain" increasingly responsible for the widespread antagonism between coach and professor—what I refer to here as the Revenue Sport System.

College athletes who participate in Revenue Sport (i.e., sport structured around million-dollar gate receipts, lucrative television contracts, rampant boosterism, all-out recruiting, and winning at all costs) can be placed in either of two distinctive and perhaps mutually exclusive academic categories—students or nonstudents. Those athletes who take the classroom seriously through interacting with other students seem to present no particular problems, and in fact, are as compatible in the educational setting as any other students. The only potential problem here lies with those professors who are known to make it rough on athletes and other athletic types (e.g., physical education majors) just for being who they are. However, those athletes who are basically nonstudents present a peculiar set of problems to the higher educational system.

The dilemma, according to former Cleveland Browns' quarterback Frank Ryan, stems from the fact that for most athletes who participate in Division I athletic programs it is difficult to excel at both sport and studies. The paradox, says Ryan, who is athletic director at Yale as well as a member of its mathematics faculty, is that the coach and the professor each set high goals of excellence for his or her sphere of influence, and while excellence is a worthy end, it appears that athletic and academic goals are generally incompatible in the Revenue Sport System. Further irony is apparent in the coach's overall unwillingness to consider nonathletes as varsity material, while the professor is routinely expected to pass nonstudents through their programs in order to keep athletes eligible for intercollegiate competition. While some professors reluctantly comply, others bow to internal pressures, usually brought on by external forces, as for example, the alumni. Coaches, on the other hand, may pay lip service to academic excellence, but in the long run their main concern, of course, is to improve athletic performance in order to maintain competitive superiority.

Ryan, that rare individual who is both an athlete and a Ph.D., brings a refreshing point of view to sport and education. However, in the Ivy League, where young adults are expected to be students first and perform other roles like that of an athlete, second, Ryan can freely practice his credo that athletics should not impinge on the primacy of education. Accordingly, many successful coaches must have held this view at one time. However, attaining lofty position in the Revenue Sport System may have brought them to the posture, whether correct or incorrect, that the Big Game is significantly much more important than the classroom and academic performance. Actually, such a coaching perspective is quite justifiable in the context of the Big Game as opposed to that of academics. After all, a coach gets paid for winning games, not turning out scholars. Even so, the supposed conflict between coach and professor or the presumed incompatibility of sport and education is highly ironic, for in many cases it is the coach who is most vociferous about the virtues of the student-athlete. Nonetheless, given the current entrenchment level of Revenue Sport in this country and the popular support it has achieved, it would not now seem possible that many athletes in this system could be successful in both sport and scholarship. Calvin Hill, a former Yale star and NFL running back, has pointed out the difficulty in making it in professional football. Nevertheless, he, along with others like Alan Page, found college ball to be just as demanding as the professional game. In fact, Hill questions whether athletes could ever give scholarship the serious attention it requires while playing college ball, for the time and physical demands of Revenue Sport make study difficult, if not impossible. Consequently, the studies of college athletes suffer even when the motivation to do well is present.

Unfortunately, the Revenue Sport System allows bright young sport stars to excel on the athletic fields and courts with little or no effort in class, and evidence of the following scenario abounds. A young star, popularly known as a blue-chipper, is recruited to play college ball. Then, after four years and the end of his playing eligibility, he usually finds himself still one to two years away from qualifying for a degree. To keep players eligible during this time, many coaches use the players' present standing on the team and their future earning potential as levers to obtain compliance. In other words, athletes who wish to qualify for the professional draft must do as they are told or they will quickly become outsiders. In fact, both the coach's official and his informal methods of communication will ensure that those who do not comply may never play again in the System. The acknowledged player goal of a high-paying professional contract, so prevalent since the emergence of televised sport in the 1960s, is perhaps the same goal that has irreversibly transformed sport and education into strange and incompatible partners. When the future earning potential of a college athlete is tied directly to his performance in the Big Game and not in the classroom, it becomes quite clear what he must do to go high in the pro draft. When we realize that this emphasis extends from youth sports through high school on to college without the proper concern for educational achievement, the magnitude of the Revenue Sport System's influence begins to manifest itself.

Unfortunately, attending to the proper balance between mind and body extolled by Greek culture during the fifth and fourth centuries B.C. has never been a real concern of the Revenue Sport System. It should be obvious, however, that more attention needs to be directed toward achieving a healthy balance in the entire system of American sports. In youth sport, for example, there are far too many youngsters being prepared for Revenue Sport by parents and coaches who show very little concern for classroom performance, even when there is little chance that any youngster will land one of the thirty thousand Revenue Sport jobs available in the United States and Canada.

Who cares then? Apparently, the fans and boosters care very little about an athlete's problems in the classroom. Their primary concern is to win the Big Game and improve their team's national ranking, so in the main they are as unconcerned about classroom performance as they are about theoretical constructs. The payoff for fans, of course, is to have the psyche massaged through another victory by the orange and white, the gold and blue, or the scarlet and gray—a normal and expected reaction from fans.

Who cares? Athletes should care, but the System places them directly under the influence and control of the coaches and their benefactors who see to it that they don't have to care. Why should they care when the living conditions for most young athletes are so good? Many drive new cars and dress well, thanks to under-the-table payoffs from their personal benefactors. In fact, Calvin Hill and other professional athletes have noted ironically that college athletes sometimes are forced to reduce their standard of living when they move up from college ball to the professional ranks.

Paradoxically, the System could probably be made more honest if players were given a living wage, beginning the first year of college. They could then play for four years under escalating terms, using the money to pay for tuition and expenses. That way, the Revenue Sport System could be aboveboard. (This proposal may not be as far fetched as it sounds. It has been reported that a reputable Southwestern university is even exploring the feasibility of purchasing a professional sport franchise to increase visibility of the institution, among other things.) Athletes should care, then, but they are caught in a system in which making waves or blowing the whistle will cause lasting harm to their future earning potential.

Who cares? It would seem that both college coaches and college presidents should care. However, Notre Dame basketball coach Digger Phelps's disclosure a few years ago that some coaches at other schools have been allowing under-the-table payments to players did not meet with magnanimous support from his coaching peers. Perhaps Coach Phelps's timing was bad, as he did not decide to bring the complaint before the public until *after* he suffered through one of his most inglorious seasons. College presidents, who should be in control of what happens in their institutions, often allow to happen what they are pressured to let happen. In their defense, though, it may be that the Revenue Sport System has become so powerful it cannot be controlled. The System, after all, is moving under a momentum that has developed out of the lure of television contracts and big money. Originally, faculty representatives kept collegiate athletics in the academic setting in order to exert absolute control, but after a hundred years a great deal of control has come to exist outside the educational system in the hands of alumni, boosters, gamblers, and those who have something to gain beyond the concerns of the classroom.

Who else might care? Most college professors care, but mainly when they have something personal at stake in their classroom. A few professors actually try to teach athletes who have neglected their studies, while others just cry foul. College senates, presumably the seat of decision making in university life, have become merely forums where academicians can posture and pontificate rather than places where action can be directed at such things as athletic abuses. At the same time, sport has never been too serious a topic among most college professors nor have the sport preparation programs of recreation and physical education departments been held in too high academic esteem. The mind-body dichotomy still exerts a strong following in academic circles, a vestige of the Middle Ages that may never die. Perhaps the suspicion of sport and its relationship to education has been covertly manufactured by the scholars themselves to protect their academic image. From a popular point of view, the teaching and study of academic subject matter are small-time and insignificant in comparison to the social impact of the Big Game. College teachers who are tough on athletes could be subconsciously getting back at their coaching peers by putting obstacles in the way of a successful athletic program.

Who cares? An organization like the North American Youth Sport Institute cares. It wants youngsters to play sport, have fun in a healthy sport scene, and pursue their studies. It wants youngsters to develop into well-rounded individuals in the sense of the classical Greek ideal, particularly since so few will ever succeed in playing college, much less pro ball.

Who cares? Obviously, the Center for Athletes' Rights and Education (CARE) cares in more than just name. With the cooperation of the National Football League Players Association, the National Council of Black Lawyers, and several operating grants, this organization, directed by a former Notre Dame football player, is beginning to develop a national network to help athletes obtain those things colleges and their recruiters have promised but frequently fail to deliver. CARE's "Athletes' Bill of Rights" highlights some of the System's abuses—race and sex discrimination, absence of due process in disputes, dangerous coaching methods and training systems, funneling players into "mickey mouse" curricula where prospects for a degree are nonexistent, and inadequate compensation for services rendered and provided. Through such a service, fortunately, CARE could ultimately bring normalcy and sanity to Revenue Sport in the high schools and colleges.

Who cares? Academicians like Clemson historian Joseph Arbena care. Through the generosity of Clemson University's Athletic Fund, Professor Arbena has founded and conducted the annual Clemson University Conference on Sport and Society.[1] The 1982 conference, which focused on Sport and Education, was attended mainly by that small body of professors who study their discipline intensively and freely recognize, at the same time, that sport exists not only to play but to study. Through such gatherings sponsored by the academic community, the climate for change and understanding may be fostered more effectively than any other way.

Obviously, very little good or positive change will come to the players in the Revenue Sport System if academicians continue to look the other way and refuse to get involved. Likewise, coaches who do not come forward and support a revelation like that of Digger Phelps contribute nothing to bettering the system, particularly when it is commonly known, from high-school players being recruited in small towns to the gamblers in Las Vegas, that the system of Revenue Sport as it applies to academics and athletics is schizophrenic. Those who have been trained in sport, recreation, and physical education have always held the Greek ideal of balance between mind and body in high regard. Now the opportunity is at hand to match words with deeds.

Note

1. The Division I NCAA football champion for 1981 was Clemson University, but after a lengthy investigation by the NCAA, the school was found guilty of recruiting violations and placed on probation. The fact that such a thing could happen to an institution that has done so much to build a closer relationship between academia and athletics is not only ironic, it substantiates my stand here on the evils inherent in the Revenue Sport System.

10

Ralph Sampson and Ralph Simpson: Two Case Studies of Professional Basketball's Hardship Draft and the American Dream

WILLIAM H. WIGGINS, JR.

The black athlete has had a significant impact upon Afro-American history and culture. In a number of instances the black American community's push for social recognition in this century can best be symbolized by the heroic athletic deeds of some black champion. Jack Johnson's winning of the heavyweight boxing crown at the dawn of this century[1] and Jackie Robinson's integration of organized baseball as this century waxed toward its noontime[2] are two watershed events which have had considerable psychological and sociological impact upon America's black and white communities. These were essentially athletic endeavors that separated the country along racial lines. Johnson's success gave rise to the call for a "great white hope" to wrest the title away from this upstart black champion. (Faint reverberations of this racial cry were even heard recently during the prefight hype of the Larry Holmes–Gerry Cooney fight.) And racially motivated harassments of Robinson through players' threatened strikes, knockdown pitches, brutal bench jockeying, and the like have all been well publicized.

During the 1930s, Joe Louis and Jesse Owens united these

warring factions of the American population as they had never been before, except in time of war. Today, Jesse Owens's sterling Berlin Olympic performance is considered a part of American legend. Black and white Americans still tell the story of how this superb athlete embarrassed the German leader Adolf Hitler by handily defeating his supposedly superior athletes.[3] We also recall the story of how Hitler opted to leave the stadium rather than to stay and pay homage to Owens as champion. Joe Louis's dramatic knockout of Max Schmeling was another repudiation of Hitler's "master race" theory that has since become a part of American folklore. Once again a poor black youth was allowed to step out of his racial group and represent all of his countrymen.[4] Since this time, record-setting performances, like Henry Aaron surpassing Babe Ruth's career home-run record and Maury Wills initially breaking Ty Cobb's season stolen-base record, have helped undermine the myth of white supremacy in sport.

The black athlete's accomplishments have also had tremendous influence on Afro-American and American popular culture. Even his sayings, like Leroy ("Satchel") Paige's "Don't look back, something might be gaining on you" and Joe Louis's "He can run, but he sure can't hide," have become American aphorisms. The showmanship of Muhammad Ali's shuffle and Julius Erving's graceful and gravity-defying dunks are looked upon as exquisite athletic expressions of black dance. Such dramatic exploits as Jackie Robinson's and Jack Johnson's achievements have inspired both the American playwright and the theater-going audience. And the images of Henry Aaron's Atlanta Stadium statue and Jackie Robinson's memorial postage stamp graphically attest to the acceptance of the black athlete in our society.

It is because of this rich and pervasive athletic legacy that a large number of contemporary black youth have turned to sports as their primary means of realizing the American dream of fame, wealth, and success. Sports exist as the major means for many black youngsters to acquire a college education, pursue a lucrative professional career, financially assist their families, and become objects of community and national adulation. In short, sports are the most viable means to many black youths for becoming "somebody" in our increasingly specialized society. Unfortunately, few make it to professional sports stardom, while all too many fail. Hence, for every O. J. Simpson or Sugar Ray

Leonard, there are thousands of frustrated, rejected black athletes who fall by the wayside in their bids to latch on to the brass ring of success. All too often they flounder like bits of societal flotsam and jetsam, singled out in the nation's newspapers or media broadcasts as criminal types and drugs/alcohol abusers. Many discover they are functional illiterates who, in reversing the ride from rags to riches, wind up trying to live on the meager earnings from menial jobs perennially assigned to minorities.

Over the last two decades, the NBA hardship draft has contributed a great deal to black youth's marked tendency toward overdependence on sports as an avenue to success. Supporters of the measure point to an elite corps who were successful in their jump from either high school (e.g., Moses Malone and Darryl Dawkins) or college (e.g., "Magic" Johnson, Julius Erving, George McGinnis, Mark Aguirre, Isiah Thomas, and Buck Williams). Detractors, however, are quick to point out the numerous failures—the young black basketball players in particular who are cut from the teams that drafted them as well as from their athletic scholarships. They are the unfortunate ones whose shattered dreams make them prime candidates for the newspaper crime reports or the unemployment rolls.[5]

The basketball careers of Ralph Sampson, the highly publicized University of Virginia all-American, and Ralph Simpson, a high-scoring Michigan State University basketball player who opted for the ABA hardship draft in the early 1970s by casting his lot with the Denver Nuggets,[6] are contrasting examples of the hardship dilemma confronting many black athletes today. Their athletic careers illustrate many of the humanistic issues and concerns surrounding the controversial role of sports in American society in general and on our nation's college and university campuses in particular. Why did Sampson elect to resist the hardship draft and finish college before signing a professional contract while Simpson decided to leave college after his sophomore year?

To answer this question, several psychological and sociological factors about these athletes' backgrounds must be considered. First, one observes that they are geographical opposites. Sampson was born and reared in a primarily rural area of the American South, the original region of the country in which the African slaves lived and worked, the place that many blacks longingly refer to as "down home" and to which they annually return for festive "homecomings" and family reunions, Simpson, on the other hand, was born and reared in an urban area of the American North, the region referred to as "up the country," to which masses of blacks migrated during the first quarter of this century in search of work in the proliferating factories and steel mills. Although originally viewed with pride and hope, these urban black communities have taken on pejorative aspects over the years, having deteriorated into "the ghetto," a place from which most blacks now hope to one day escape.[7] From a sociological point of view, then, Sampson's conservative milieu undoubtedly conditioned him to respect and pursue enduring values like the worth of a college education as an end in itself, while Simpson's disoriented background must have contributed to his perception of a basketball contract as having more immediate and tangible worth than a college education.

Another factor to consider is that the social achievements of both Sampson and Simpson symbolize the racial progress that black Americans have made through collegiate athletics. Although Simpson's Big Ten Conference has a long tradition of allowing blacks to play varsity football (e.g., early stars like Indiana University's George Taliaferro and the University of Iowa's "Duke" Slater), it wasn't until the late 1940s that Indiana University's all-American center Bill Garrett broke that conference's "gentleman's agreement" to keep blacks off the conference's varsity basketball teams.[8] Ralph Sampson's success is representative of the dramatic social changes that have occurred in Southern collegiate athletics since the 1954 Supreme Court decision on desegregation and the tragicomedy of Governor George Wallace's symbolic stand in the University of Alabama classroom door. Sampson is a part of a new black collegiate legacy, inspiring numerous other outstanding Southern black athletes to attend their home state universities.

Third, on a more personal basis, Sampson and Simpson were exposed to excessive public attention and pampering long before they enrolled in college. Sampson's exceptional height, with all of its latent potential, and Simpson's prodigious jumping ability, which was dramatically evident at a young age, set them aside as future basketball stars. Simpson's father recalls discovering his son's superior jumping ability: "I remember when Ralph was 13 . . . I got home one day and he said, 'Come on out, I've got something to show you.' He had started dunking the ball."[9] By the time he entered college, Simpson could palm two balls and dunk them in one leap. He scored a game high 43 points in

Pershing High School's championship victory over Flint Central. He played in the Dapper Dan High School All-Star game and held his own in a one-on-one contest with the Pistons' Dave Bing in a summer camp confrontation. Simpson's basketball brilliance continued at Michigan State. A national sports writer assessed his collegiate playing in this laudatory manner:

> Ralph Simpson is a gifted sophomore on an otherwise mediocre Michigan State team. He lives basketball and, scoring 30 points a game, he probably is the best rookie in the country today.[10]

Sports analysts made similar evaluations of Ralph Sampson when he was at Virginia.

However, these two highly gifted basketball players differ radically in their assessments of the college experience. Ralph Simpson perceived his college career as a launching pad into the glamorous life of professional basketball. As a result, he chose to isolate himself from the larger campus experience of lectures, concerts, plays, films, museums, and libraries, and spend all of his spare time in the university's gym, further refining his already considerable basketball skills. Connie Hawkins of the University of Iowa and "Fly" Williams of Austin Peay State University were two other talented collegiate basketball players who saw their college careers only as a professional proving ground and not as a golden opportunity to acquire an education that would serve them long after their playing days were over.

Unfortunately, some colleges and universities make no attempt to counsel such athletes—many of whom are the first of their families to attend college—about the value of a college education or enrolling in degree-granting programs. In far too many cases the objective of the college counselor is simply to keep the player eligible. Harry Edwards[11] and Jack Olson[12] were two of the earlier voices to address this issue. A recent salvo was fired by Fordham University professor Mark D. Naison, whose paper "Scenario for Scandal: Sports in the Political Economy of Higher Education" carries this ringing indictment:

> The major problem in college sports is not commercialism. . . . It is the exploitation of athletes and the proliferation of illicit patterns of action which dilute educational standards. Many universities are currently deriving substantial benefits from sports programs that depend on the efforts of athletes

drawn from the poorest and blackest segments of America's population.[13]

Ralph Sampson came to see his college career not only as a time for playing basketball and achieving fame, but also as a time for study, reflection, and intellectual growth. As a result, the efforts of Red Auerbach of the Boston Celtics to coax him into the NBA hardship draft proved unsuccessful.* Critics of Sampson's decision to stay in school tend to argue that Ralph was either being exploited by his university or wasting his time playing college ball when he could have been making big money in the NBA. Arthur Ashe, a friend and advisor of Sampson, answered these criticisms with this line of reasoning:

> Professional sports' front-office people often underestimate the maturity one gains in four years of college. . . . While improving as a student, Sampson is also rubbing shoulders with the greatest mixture of people he'll ever get to know. . . . He is not being used. It would have been well worth it to him to borrow money to attend a school like the University of Virginia. If anyone is "using" someone, Sampson is using the University. . . . He decided to "use" Virginia to market his basketball skills while attending classes. And as his price at contract time is liable only to go up, the University of Virginia can hardly be charged with exploitation. . . .[14]

Ralph Sampson's University of Virginia world was much broader than Ralph Simpson's Michigan State University gym. He involved himself in a variety of extracurricular activities ranging from outdoor social events to concerts and other activities which took him far from the school gym. Sampson matured academically, because he was motivated by more than just the goal of "staying eligible." During his senior year he earned the right to live on the Lawn, an honor reserved for the truly exceptional Virginia student. In this regard, Sampson was emulating the college careers of such black scholar-athletes as Bernie Casey, the Bowling Green University football player, who expanded his considerable talents as an actor, painter, and poet while earning his undergraduate degree, and Bill Russell, who, thirty years later, still recalls the joys of learning that he

---

*Upon graduation, Sampson signed a long-term contract with the Houston Rockets.

experienced as an undergraduate student at the University of San Francisco.[15]

On the face of the evidence, Ralph Sampson's decision seems to be the proper one. Ralph Simpson, because of poor counsel or lack of understanding, was unable to operate successfully off the court. In 1971 his mother complained that her son had signed a contract with such long deferment pay schedules, he was not able to send her any money. And despite making several ABA All-Star teams,[16] Ralph Simpson was eventually waived from the league in the late 1970s, a bitter and disillusioned man. He had neither the athletic fundamentals nor the intellectual training to successfully cope with the myriad psychological and sociological problems that routinely confront the professional basketball player. In this day and age, black athletes, as well as their white counterparts, must come to realize that to cope, they must be educated. Athletic talent alone isn't enough.

Notes

1. William H. Wiggins, Jr., "Jack Johnson as Bad Nigger: The Folklore of His Life," in Robert Chrisman and Nathan Hare, eds., *Contemporary Black Thought: The Best from the Black Scholar* (Indianapolis, Inc.: Bobbs-Merrill, 1973), 53–70.

2. William G. Kelly, "Jackie Robinson and the Press," *Journalism Quarterly* 53 (1976): 137–40.

3. R. D. Mandell, "Sportsmanship and Nazi Olympism," in B. Lowe et al., eds., *Sport and International Relations* (Champaign, Ill.: Stipes 1972), 135–52.

4. Anthony O. Edmonds, "The Second Louis-Schmeling Fight: Sport, Symbol, and Culture," *Journal of Popular Culture* 7 (1973): 42–50.

5. For a case study of an athlete, see Barry Beckham, *Double Dunk* (Los Angeles: Holloway House Publishing Co., 1980).

6. J. Jares, "Ex-doughboy Who Can Shoot with the Best: Ralph Simpson of Michigan State," *Sports Illustrated,* 19 January 1970, 44.

7. For a discussion of this issue see Stanley Sanders, "I'll Never Escape the Ghetto," in Abraham Chapman, ed., *Black Voices: An Anthology of Afro-American Literature* (New York: New American Library, 1968), 347–53.

8. Herman B. Wells, *Being Lucky: Reminiscences and Reflections* (Bloomington: Indiana University Press, 1980), 217–18.

9. Jares, "Ex-doughboy," 44.

10. Ibid.

11. Harry Edwards, *The Revolt of the Black Athlete* (New York: Free Press, 1969).

12. For a discussion of Mr. Olsen's views, see James A. Michener, *Sports in America* (New York: Random House, 1976).

13. Quoted in Paul Desruisseaux, "College Accused of Exploiting Student Athletes: Historian Proposes that Players with Scholarships Get Additional Benefits—Perhaps Even Salaries," *Chronicle of Higher Education,* 14 April 1982, 6.

14. C. Kirkpatrick, "Hello, America, We Came Back," *Sports Illustrated,* 1 December 1980, 37.

15. Bill Russell and Taylor Branch, *Second Wind: The Memoirs of an Opinionated Man* (New York: Random House, 1979), 51–92.

16. "Ralph Simpson Named to ABA West All-Star Team," *Washington Post,* 19 January 1973, 5, sec. D.

11

Women's Professional Football and the Changing Role of the Woman Athlete

JOHN BRIDGES

At the close of the 1970s, one of the primary areas of interest to the sports community was the growth and emerging professionalization of women's athletics. Title IX of the Education Amendments of 1972 was a major reason for the gains made in women's collegiate programs by this time. Accordingly, the Association of Intercollegiate Athletics for Women (AIAW) estimated more than one hundred thousand women to be participating nationwide in the thirteen championship sports sanctioned by the AIAW. While athletic budgets have not reached parity, the AIAW has begun to generate television money by obtaining national exposure for its championship basketball game.* In high schools between 1971 and 1978, female athletic participants increased from 294,000 to more than 2 million even though enrollments began to decline.[1]

On the professional level, women have managed to achieve some celebrity—if not equal compensation—for achievements of individual merit in a variety of sports such as tennis, golf, track, swimming, and auto racing. The opportunities for women's professional team sports, however, have been ex-

*In 1982, the AIAW ceased operation, bringing suit against the National Collegiate Athletic Association, who, it is charged, illegally lured AIAW members away through the attractive resources of the highly successful NCAA men's program. The AIAW statistics are nevertheless still revealing for the purposes of this study.

143

tremely limited. Alternative structures have begun to emerge in recent years to meet the professional needs of this portion of our population. The Women's Professional Basketball League (WBL) was created in 1978, and 1980 salaries reportedly ranged from $3,000 to $50,000 annually with an average salary of about $11,000.[2] Although experiencing some financial difficulty, the WBL opened its third season (1980–81) with nine franchises in operation. Unfortunately, it folded the following year due to lack of fan support. The National Women's Football League (NWFL), although less well organized and financed than the WBL, has existed since 1965 with teams in Ohio, Texas, and Oklahoma. Other professional women's football teams are in operation in Arizona, California, Washington, and Pennsylvania.[3]

Because athletic participation has traditionally been regarded as inconsistent with commonly accepted female stereotypes, this particular study focuses upon the NWFL through investigation of two important areas of interest. First, it will examine ideological or humanistic considerations which may emerge as women athletes attempt to resolve the potential conflicts between athletic competition and the "feminine" role as defined by American society; secondly, with regard to socialization into the role of player, this inquiry seeks to determine how participants came to be involved in the sport and how they acquired requisite skills when nonprofessional opportunities for participation are so severely limited. In this concern, football may certainly be considered quite removed from the concept of "femininity" and the "feminine role."

Data for this analysis were collected through in-depth interviews with members of the Ohio NWFL franchise in the spring of 1980.* The franchise chosen has been particularly successful on the playing field, compiling a record of better than 90 percent victories through some sixty games. Home attendance for this franchise averages approximately three thousand per game. However, the NWFL itself cannot be considered an established professional sports league. League management and operating regulations are minimal, with each franchise operating autono-

*Interviews ranged from one to one-and-a-half hours in length and normally involved two players at each interview session. The respondents were between the ages of 18 and 35 and consisted of both black and white Americans, one German, and one Mexican-American. Occupations of the respondents ranged from computer operator, surgical technician, and National Guard administrative technician to beautician, restaurant waitress, and housewife. Players arrived for their interviews in clothing ranging from modish feminine styles to jeans and motorcycle helmets.

mously. The range of salaries, or even the decision to pay salaries, is left to the discretion of the franchise operator. In most cases players have been paid salaries, although rising expenses and small gate receipts have frequently forced a reduction in compensation of meal money, payment of insurance premiums, and chartered buses for away games. Considering this absence of adequate financial support and formal structures, the NWFL may be considered professional in name only—perhaps the term *semiprofessional* is more accurate in describing the league and its franchises.

Publications of the early to mid 1970s represent a somewhat critical period of analysis for American sport (Bridges 1979). While some analysts focused on functions served by the institution of sport, others presented various ideological reformulations of a humanistic or, even more radically, of an "antiprofessional" nature. Edwards (1973, 103–30) defined the "Dominant American Sports Creed" as it reinforced American themes such as achievement, discipline, competition, character development, physical fitness, and nationalism. Scott (1973) contrasted the American sport ethic with alternative "countercultural" and "radical" sport ethics of his own conceptualization. Schafer (1971) considered the uses of sport in socializing the young into the larger social system. Although these and other works noted the marginal position of women in relation to the system, only Jan Felshin (1974, 1976) presented a set of specific, contrasting ideological postures that women, as participants, would find compatible with their personal views of sport. As an analytical device, Felshin's typology forms the basis for my discussion at this point.

Felshin's first position is labeled the "apologetic." The female athlete, in manifesting an apologetic demeanor, "frequently denies the importance of her athletic endeavors and avows the importance of her appearance and the desire to be attractive and to marry and raise a family as the overriding motivations of her life" (Felshin 1976, 432). It is not difficult to see how such a posture would develop, considering the stance taken by the more conservative elements of the male sports bastion. The remarks of former Ohio State football coach Woody Hayes serve as a reminder of the extremist position. Speaking of Jack Scott's egalitarian efforts at Oberlin College, Hayes remarked:

I hear they're even letting w-o-m-e-n in their sports program now. That's your Women's Liberation, boy—bunch of god-

damn lesbians. . . . Man has to dominate. There's just no other
way. . . . The best way to treat a woman . . . is to knock her up
and hide her shoes. . . . (Vare 1974, 38)

Del Rey (1978), in attempting to test Felshin's apologetic empirically, describes the emphasis on traditional femininity as
"dressing in sex-appropriate ways, not taking sports seriously,
pursuing the so-called more acceptable sports, or in any way
reaffirming the feminine values of the society" (1978, 107).

As a group, the members of the Ohio football team in this
sample cannot be characterized as adopting an apologetic position. There is no indication that the players are not taking the
sport seriously (one player allegedly committed the "unladylike"
act of striking a game official), and certainly football is not a
"more acceptable" feminine sport. The aggressive, physical nature of women's football as a contact sport was evident in such
injuries as dislocated shoulders, bruised and broken ribs, broken
fingers, pinched nerves, bad knees and ankles, spinal fractures,
and tendonitis, which players discussed in the interviews. The
injuries were frequently described as nagging "little hurts" that
gave rise to considerations of quitting but have not yet ended the
careers of those interviewed. In addition, the impressive won-
lost record cited above may have contributed to giving team
members a sense of pride and accomplishment that counter-
balances any potential denial of the importance of their endeavors.

Participants felt it was possible to play the game "as it was
meant to be played" and then to walk off the field and be "soft
and feminine." One respondent, a middle linebacker, described
her feelings about femininity and aggressiveness:

Some women are just not aggressive enough to play our game
and they shouldn't even try to do it. I like to hit people—to
really do some damage. Especially when I get a blindside shot
at a runner. . . .

The same player also discussed being "physical" in a somewhat
different context:

I don't think of myself as being unfeminine at all . . . we're
probably *better* lovers than most girls because we're in
shape. . . .

Still other players felt the conditions which would necessitate an apologetic demeanor were "old and forgotten-about" attitudes. "More people," one explained, "now think it's neat that we're football players and want to know when and where the next game is." The assertion of traditional femininity did not appear to be a dominant, central concern of any of the athletes.

The "forensic" position in Felshin's typology parallels the politico-judicial wing of the feminist movement. Kanter has pointed out that

> Since women and blacks have legal remedies that disadvantaged white men may lack, the levers are at hand, via [the] issue, to encourage policy-makers to reconsider organizational design; equal . . . opportunity is a stated policy of the United States government and practically all major organizations. (Kanter 1977, 266)

Women's rights are emphasized in the context, and sport is an important *visible* area. "The forensic position demands women's rights to equal protection under the law" (Felshin 1976, 433). Women should be equal to men and the concept of "women's sport" would cease to exist. As Felshin has also noted, sport contributes to a stronger feminist image:

> Feminism seeks to establish a concept of woman as strong, physical, and bodily competent. One of the strongest attacks of the women's movement has been on the stereotype of woman as weak, passive, unable, and a decorative "sex object." (1974, 198)

The majority of the respondents in the present sample disavow any direct identification with the feminist movement, especially as activists. The following statements are typical:

> I play sports for the fun of it, I'm not making any statement for women's sports. If it helped, it would be okay—but that's not why I'm doing it.

> I don't care about that stuff [feminism] . . . it's sports that matter, not who plays them.

> Women's lib has been taken much too far. . . . I play the sport because I love it, and not just football but all sports.

Only one respondent said she felt like a "pioneer" in women's athletics and hoped that her daughter or nieces would be able to compete professionally as a result of her efforts.

While football may lead to an implicit statement of the female as "strong, physical, and bodily competent," there is no identification with the more political or legalistic components of the forensic position. The end result, an elimination of the distinction between men's and women's sport and the celebration of sport for sport's sake, may be considered desirable, however, in both the case of the forensic position and the present sample.

The last of Felshin's concepts is the "dialectic." Firestone's *The Dialectic of Sex* (1970) theorizes that the "class analysis" done by Marx and Engels is "limited" as it fails to evaluate the sexual substratum in its own right (1970, 5). Analysis should include sex and "opposites yet inseparable and interpenetrating" (Firestone 1970, 3). In the same fashion, Felshin's dialectic involves the

> social view of women *in* sport . . . a dialectic of woman *and* sport. Both sport and woman must be understood in relation to society, and the clarification of each concept contributes to understanding the relationship between them. (Felshin 1974, 179)

This position, according to Felshin, also maintains that gender is irrelevant to sport and is based on the assumption that "sexism, like racism, is social and that the disease should not contaminate the relationship between ethical and actual structures of sport . . ." (1976, 434). The dialectic should serve to broaden participation in sport while not disturbing the present system: "Carried to its logical conclusion, this view supports the status quo of sport except that it includes women" (1976, 435). Felshin has also suggested, however, that the dialectic sees "the model of sport developed by men . . . objectionable for all human persons, the possibilities for new conceptions of sport emerge as alternative options" (1976, 435).

An area of overlap with the forensic position may be seen in the allusion here to the more androgynous or genderless view. However, while the forensic position seeks structural revision and equality, the dialectic seeks inclusion—although changes in the nature of sport itself may be suggested, supposedly without disturbing the status quo.

The women in the present sample do not want to compete

directly with men, but simply seek the opportunity to play the sport professionally. Nor do they believe the women's game will reach the level of the men's:

> I know I'll never be rich or famous for playing football. Women's football could never equal the men's game. Our team is about at the level of the male high-school team—a good high-school team but a high-school team.

Most players are, of course, in favor of the women's game gaining the necessary exposure to "catch on," but also fear that, at the same time, money and further formalization could ruin their game:

> I'd like to see more money brought into our game, but I also think that's what ruined the [male] game.

> Money would definitely change our game, you'd have to be more competitive—try a lot harder all the time . . . a lot of the players on our club would probably lose their jobs to the better players that money would bring out.

> There's already too much football on TV. There's no room for women's football. But it would be nice to get enough money to pay expenses and medical bills.

There were also respondents, less oriented toward an "amateur" ideology perhaps, who felt that money would not create any real problems or affect their participation significantly:

> The money wouldn't change anything for me, I'd take it but I would also play for nothing. . . . I have a lot of experience and I know I could make any women's team.

On the other hand, most players felt that increased formalization would help the most in improving management and training facilities:

> The league has to be losing money; they don't publicize or promote the teams right . . . we've got it together on the field but the office-thing is a different story.

> The fact that we don't have good facilities or weights to work with causes more injuries. . . . Most of the injuries are knees and ankles, some elbows and shoulders, but joints that could be stronger with better training.

Better financial management carries perhaps much greater weight for these team members because of the difficult in-season workload the players are required to maintain. Since no salaries are paid by this franchise, most of the players have full-time jobs. Added to job demands are five nights of football practice averaging two hours a night plus the weekly game and bus travel on road trips.

In summary, Felshin's typology does not seem to adequately define the athletes in the present sample. Although asserting their femininity, the athletes are not in any way apologetic in demeanor or attitude. The forensic position seems to suggest greater utility for "school" athletic inequities, as well as other more "institutionalized" areas, rather than direct application to professional or semiprofessional women's team sports. The dialectic provides an inclusion for women in the large system without disturbing the status quo, but brings with it the fears and potential dangers of "overprofessionalization" which is often lamented in the male sport. The more reformist or humanistic concerns that Felshin sought to incorporate into the dialectic were not in evidence in the present research. This emphasis is of great importance to some observers. As Hoch has noted:

> . . . the fight against sexism in sports, or in society generally, is *not* won by fitting a few females into the slots of the same repressive system. . . . The apparent incongruity will be resolved only if the mass participation of women in sports is geared to changing the distorted, ultra-macho character of the sports themselves. What we don't need is a new generation of *female* gladiators. (Hoch 1972, 161)

While the Felshin typology may not adequately characterize the views of athletes in the present research, application of the "American Sports Creed" does appear tenable. The values expressed by the players and the "lessons" cited, which, to some extent, are the result of their participation, mirror the "standard" sport values cited by such writers as Edwards (1973) and Eitzen and Sage (1978). The themes most commonly addressed are competition, discipline, character development, teamwork, and cooperation.

The competitive nature of the sport, as in athletics in general, is thought to foster the development of competitiveness, motivation, courage, perseverance, and self-reliance. Participation in sport prepares one "to meet the challenges of day-to-day problem solving" (Edwards 1973, 117) and to be a self-made, hard working "winner" (Eitzen & Sage 1978, 60, 63, 67):

> I've learned to be competitive. I used to have really low self-esteem. I've learned that I could make it on my own. It's the greatest thing I've ever done on my own.

Sport's emphasis on discipline, according to Edwards, "helps to support the assumption that sports participation enculturates athletes with a high regard for self-discipline and with a healthy respect for the necessity of social control . . . any advocacy of relaxation in discipline . . is seen as endangering the whole of American society" (1973, 115–16):

> I'm a disciplined ballplayer. When my coach tells me to run, I run. A person needs to learn discipline.

With regard to character development, mental and physical fitness, and an appreciation for a physically healthy body (Edwards 1973, 103, 119–20), the women verbalized important component themes such as responding to challenges, developing self-confidence, and becoming self-actualized:

> Before I came out I was *really* overweight; my parents used to worry a lot about me. But football enables me to lose a lot of weight and get in shape. It really changed my whole life.

> I always wanted to play sports; it used to be soccer when I was little. I just enjoy the challenges. . . . I wanted to experience the challenge of playing quarterback for this team.

> You just feel better, you know? It's better than just sitting around. You feel so much better when you're physically fit. You feel healthy, alert.

The importance of teamwork and cooperation may be observed in the following comments:

> I just enjoy sports more in a big group. I like the teamwork when everybody works together.

> When I was in the Army, we had 60 girls living together that were disorganized, lacked teamwork, couldn't cooperate. . . . They could have learned some lessons from football.

There were also other extrinsic considerations. Some players enjoyed the travel opportunities; the championship game in the Texas Stadium home of the Dallas Cowboys; appearing on the Phil Donahue television show; the trophies and awards, such as "Rookie of the Year," which were presented at team banquets.

One player summed it up by describing the thrill of game-day as a kind of weekly "rush" she always looked forward to:

> There's just no feeling like it. You dress-out and do your warm-ups; the adrenalin starts to build and you're introduced [on the public address system] as the "World Famous [name of team]." As you run out on the field there's just nothing like it . . . then you make a good hit that you just know was solid and get [congratulations] from your teammates. . . .

It is thus suggested that players in the present sample have begun to express the values of the American Sports Creed and, apparently, to seek assimilation through harmony: integration into the sport establishment via the path of least resistance. The values of sport which are seen as acceptable for males would be defended as also appropriate for females. The adoption of these values also implies a rejection of the positions found in Felshin's typology.

While these emergent values and roles may mirror the male game, the ways in which the athletes were socialized into participation in sports do not. The second concern of the present research focuses on the ways in which these individuals were socialized into participation, and specifically, into their roles as semiprofessional football players.

Previous research done by Greendorfer (1978) on the socialization of female athletes and by Spreitzer and Snyder (1976) on the sport socialization process suggest numerous useful areas of interest for researchers. At present, this study's findings may be grouped into two general areas: the athlete's previous participation in sport; and the role of influential factors or significant others upon the athlete's career.

The members of the team are strikingly similar in two important areas concerning their participation in sport at the high-school or college level. First, the girls all reported being much more interested in team sports than "individual-centered" activities. While some players reported experience in track, especially running backs and wide receivers, all reported being involved in team sports. Those figuring most prominently were basketball, softball, and volleyball. Despite the fact that school programs offered most of their activities in more traditionally "acceptable" sports such as swimming, diving, tennis, gymnastics, or even golf and bowling, the athletes in this study chose primarily team sports or "less desirable" events such as track and field.[4]

Second, lacking skills necessary for specific positions in football, all of the athletes reported learning skills on their own after graduation from high school. Some of the players reported learning to play through "sandlot football" or "neighborhood" experiences, but that no formal instruction had been received prior to coming out for their present team. For the players' view, it is significant to note that lack of skills and experience did not inhibit their interest in participating. At the same time, of course, lack of skills in their positions overall retards the caliber of play in women's football, which in turn limits the efficiency of the coaching staff by requiring that the "finer points" of the game be ignored, while more time is spent on fundamentals.

Even though the opportunities for females to learn specific football skills are minimal, the members of the team interviewed felt at least "comfortable" at their position. A large portion of their self-confidence may be derived in part from the impressive won-lost record noted earlier. The veterans on the club who have begun to master the skills needed to play specific positions are self-assured enough to face tougher challenges from any high-caliber newcomers that further professionalization might bring into the game. The veterans with the most experience feel they are easily "better than most" at their position.

Some of the respondents sought to minimize high school athletic participation as contributing to their development, preferring to emphasize self-reliance instead:

My high school only had P.E. classes; I never had much opportunity to play sports.

In high school we had no athletic program, no chance to develop. . . . I've learned to do everything on my own.

A majority of the football players continue to participate in amateur sports programs in the off season. In their locality, both basketball and women's civic softball programs are also in operation. Many of the players have friends playing in one or both of the other leagues, and the "better" athletes are often recruited between leagues. Some of the respondents reported that they did not participate in *any* high school sports and were not seriously involved in any sports until beginning to play football. These individuals also now find community programs valuable.

Significant Others

In the majority of instances the players in this study reported that their mothers were frequently opposed to their participation in football, fearing the injury problem. Most often the father was supportive in these circumstances and convinced the mother to attend a home game, after which both parents took the initiative—to the point of clipping "try out" announcements from the newspaper for their daughters. Only one player reported that both parents opposed her participation, and she indicated she would probably quit at the end of her second season.

Although teachers and coaches are undoubtedly an influential factor in a large number of cases, no player in the present study could remember being greatly influenced by any teacher or coach.

Very few of the respondents identified any role models, either in or out of the sport, that were influential. In this regard, one player described the lack of female role models in this fashion:

> I can't remember any female in sport who influenced me or anyone that I ever watched on TV. I'd probably be more into it [women's sports] if there had been more females [active].

Once candidates become members of the team, models appear to develop in both the male sport and among other team members. Several players said that because they regularly watched pro football on Sunday afternoons, names like Brian Sipe, Lynn Swann, and others became "football hero-models." Two particular team members were identified as role models by other players, especially younger players. One running back, a veteran of eight successful seasons, had received a great deal of publicity, and teammates admired both her athletic ability and success. The second individual was a housewife and mother in her early thirties who possessed considerable athletic skill. A teammate stated:

I really admire [her]. She has so much athletic ability. She's really healthy, really fit. She's a hard worker [and is] raising a family. She's certainly not masculinized at all.

A number of the players are married and raising families. In those instances, husbands and children often attend home games. Husbands and boyfriends frequently attend practice sessions, bringing beer and socializing while watching practice from vans parked at the edge of the practice field. Only one player reported nearly losing her husband as a result of her participation in football.

In summary, women players who become involved with football appear to do so as a result of self-interest, parental encouragement, or recruitment by peers. Further, they become involved despite any lack of specific athletic skills, direct experience with the sport, or relevant role models. Most of the players have been active in team sports and community athletic programs. Community programs are seen by respondents as more important than school programs. After a relatively brief period during which players acquire basic skills and playing experience, the athletes develop a strong sense of self-confidence and faith in their abilities.

This study has sought to provide an overview of women's changing athletic roles through their participation in a particular professional and/or semiprofessional team sport. A specific objective has been to consider participants' attitudes and self-concepts, while also seeking to determine how women athletes become involved with football.

It is suggested that the increasing formalization of women's athletics has led to an embracing of the American Sports Creed as defined by certain sport sociologists (such as Edwards 1973, Eitzen & Sage 1978, and others), and which embodies such values as competition, discipline, teamwork, and so on. The implication is that women's sports may continue to develop along the lines of the professionalized male sports world, without the "alternative options" which some writers have seen as preferable for sport. Parallels may be seen, to an extent, in Kanter's (1977) work with women and corporations, which points out that the unique qualities of individuals are "distorted to fit" existing structures.

Women's sports, at virtually all levels, most frequently lack funding, facilities and equipment, coaching, medical and training

facilities, travel expenses, media coverage, and adequate opportunities for participation (Coakley 1978, 255–59). Obviously, the
lack of women's football programs in high schools and colleges
results in no available talent pool for professional teams, such as
exists in the male game. The development of professional
women's sports will continue to lag as long as talent at the lower
levels is afforded no increased opportunity to develop; thus
women's potential for a bright professional sports career appears dim. As Rossi (1965) has pointed out, support and encouragement must be given to women in the early stages of life—
particularly in secondary education as preparation for college—
in order to achieve entry into such careers as engineering,
medicine, or science. Likewise support and encouragement in
athletics may be recognized as important to a potential athletic
career. Writers such as Pogrebin (1980) have suggested that a
reorientation toward sport as a component of childhood socialization is necessary:

> . . . play situations are patriarchal power relationships in mi-
> crocosm, and patterns established in sports and games carry
> into adult life. (1980, 341)

Critics among sport sociologists as well as scoffers in general
feel that the women's movement in sport is overestimated in
terms of significance; that professional leagues such as the
NWFL and WBL are noteworthy only because the athletes are
women and the idea is still somewhat novel; that the role of
professional sport as mass entertainment cannot be enlarged
widely enough to include women's athletics. Nevertheless, the
perpetuation and visibility of sport as a sex-segregated, male-
dominated institution is likely to warrant continued attempts at
reform.

Notes

1. Figures released by the Department of Health, Education, and Welfare, published
in the *Toledo Blade,* 16 December 1979, sec. D.

2. "Women Are No Longer Stuck with Half a Court," *Chicago Tribune,* 27 January
1980, 1, sec. 12.

3. Personal communication from the NWFL Information Center, Columbus, Ohio, 18
March 1980.

4. The classification of "desirable" or "less desirable" sports for female competitors is
based on a study by Sherrif, cited in Eitzen and Sage (1978, 277).

References

Bridges, John. 1979, "Criticism and Intercollegiate Athletics: A Content Analysis of Sport Biographies." Paper presented at the Joint Meeting of the Midwest Popular Culture and American Culture Association, Bowling Green, Ohio.

Coakley, Jay J. 1978. *Sport in Society: Issues and Controversies.* St. Louis, Mo.: C. V. Mosby.

Del Rey, Patricia. 1978. "The Apologetic and Women in Sport." In *Women and Sport: From Myth to Reality,* ed. Carol A. Oglesby, 107–11. Philadelphia: Lea and Febiger.

Edwards, Harry. 1973. *The Sociology of Sport.* Homewood, Ill.: Dorsey Press.

Eitzen, D. Stanley, and George H. Sage. 1978. *Sociology of American Sport.* Dubuque, Iowa: William C. Brown Co.

Epstein, Cynthia Fuchs. 1970. *Woman's Place: Options and Limits in Professional Careers.* Berkeley: University of California Press.

Felshin, Jan. 1974. "The Dialectics of Woman and Sport." In *The American Woman in Sport,* ed. Ellen W. Gerber, Jan Felshin, Pearl Berlin, and Waneen Wyrick, 179–210. Reading, Mass.: Addison-Wesley Publishing Co.

———. 1976. "The Triple Option . . . for Women in Sport." In *Sport in the Sociocultural Process,* ed. Marie Hart, 2d 3d., 431–37. Dubuque, Iowa: William C. Brown Co.

Firestone, Shulamith. 1970. *The Dialectic of Sex.* New York: Morrow Quill Paperbacks.

Greendorfer, Susan L. 1978. "Socialization into Sport." In *Women and Sport: From Myth to Reality,* ed. Carole A. Oglesby, 115–40. Philadelphia: Lea and Febiger.

Hoch, Paul. 1972. *Rip Off the Big Game.* Garden City, N.Y.: Doubleday-Anchor Books.

Kanter, Rosebeth Moss. 1977. *Men and Women of the Corporation.* New York: Basic Books.

Pogrebin, Letty Cotton. 1980. *Growing Up Free: Raising Your Child in the '80's.* New York: McGraw-Hill.

Rossi, Alice S. 1965. "Barriers to the Career Choice of Engineering, Medicine, or Science Among American Women." In *Women and the Scientific Professions,* ed. Jacquelyn A. Mattfeld and Carol S. Van Aken. Cambridge, Mass.: M.I.T. Press.

Schafer, Walter. 1971. "Sport and Youth Counterculture: Contrasting Socialization Themes." Unpublished paper presented at the Conference on Sport and Social Deviancy, State University of New York, Brockport, 19 December 1971.

Scott, Jack. 1973. "Sport and the Radical Ethic." *Quest* 19 (January): 71–77.

Spreitzer, Elmer, and Eldon Snyder. 1976. "Socialization into Sport: An Exploratory Path Analysis." *Research Quarterly* 47 (2): 238–45.

Vare, Robert. 1974. *Buckeye: A Study of Coach Woody Hayes and the Ohio State Football Machine.* New York: Popular Library.

12

Athletic Performance and Spectator Behavior: The Humanistic Concerns of Sports Psychology

JEFFREY H. GOLDSTEIN

Before beginning a discussion of specific areas of sports psychology, let me first dispense with what I see as a number of generally misplaced emphases, fallacies, and foibles in the field. Then I will provide what may ultimately turn out to be a different set of uninformed opinions, covering such areas as psychology and sports performance, aggression and sport, and the psychology of the spectator.

Fads and Foibles in Sports Psychology

Theory in Sports Psychology

Of the many theoretical points of view in contemporary psychology, two seem to be favored by sports psychologists—the very same two that are, philosophically speaking, most heavily laden with errors of proof and disproof: radical behaviorism and psychoanalytic theory. These two points of view suffer from such an abundance of problems and ambiguities as to be almost useless to the serious scientist. And yet they find their way into the mainstream of the newly developed field of sports psychology.

Of American football, Dundes (1978), for example, notes in a series of psychoanalytic observations bordering on the ludicrous that football is analogous to "male verbal dueling," and finds Freudian significance in the terms "end," "down," "penetration of the end zone," "split end," "tight end," and so on. Of course, as a parlor game, psychoanalytic interpretation of common events is an interesting and often amusing diversion. One can always interpret some phraseology and behavior in such terms. For example, in education we "crack the books," "bone up for exams," and "take gut courses." This no more proves the relevance, to say nothing of the validity, of psychoanalytic theory than saying that "one participates in a sport because of past reinforcements" proves the validity of behaviorism. I suspect that both theories find some measure of popularity because they can be interpreted as relevant to *any* conceivable situation, always seeming to imply some action on the part of the training and coaching staff; they are simple to get the hang of and require little serious study and even less sensitivity of perception on the part of the practitioner; and they are commonly accepted as valid and are unlikely to be suspect among management and administration. They are, in short, the simplest and most popular that psychology has to offer.

Sports psychology seems to be entering the second of what may be seen as three developmental stages. First, the sports psychologist shares the concerns of management with productivity and performance, and applies more or less current theories and tests from psychology to the improvement of performance. In the second stage, concern is shown with the well-being of participants (athletes) and, to a lesser extent, consumers (spectators). In the final stage, management, participants, and consumers are seen as having common, or at least complementary, interests, the satisfaction of one set of goals leading to the fulfillment of others. This is a rudimentary scheme and not one to be taken too literally. However, it does point to what I see as some of the current deficits of sports psychology as we progress through the second decade of its prominence; namely, an overconcern with maximizing player productivity, often at the expense of the athlete's own well-being, and a de-emphasis of the humanistic or spiritual and nonmaterial rewards of sport.

Sport as Metaphor

A related issue is one in which the sports psychologist views sports as a metaphor for other areas of functioning. The analogical view of sports is often carried to absurd limits, viewing sports as anything from a reenactment of the Oedipus complex (see Dundes 1978; Ginsberg 1980; Whitman 1969) to warfare (Lorenz 1966) to a microcosm of society (Snyder & Spreitzer 1979; see also Hardaway 1979; Balbus 1979).

The primary objection to the sport-as-social-microcosm metaphor is the disservice it does to sport as an avenue of psychological, emotional, and physical growth. The most common of these metaphors discusses as the relevant sports, football, boxing, and other "combative" sports. Tennis and racquet sports, gymnastics, and track and field, to name a few, are less often seen as possessing the necessary point of contact with society to permit the metaphor to stand. In other words, sports are *selectively* chosen as analogical models of society, which implies that there already exist some fairly fixed notions of the nature of society and sports. In December 1980, for example, the *Miami Herald* ran a letter concerning an earlier news story about high-school football. The letter noted that the goal of "real life" is winning, though losing, too, is a part of life; that society involves a contest of survival; that life is often unfair; that there are rules to be followed, lest a penalty be exacted; and so on. It is the familiar litany of social Darwinism.

I will not take time here to recite the flaws inherent in this argument from the viewpoint of society; Hofstadter (1955) has done an admirable job of that. I will, however, discuss the weakness in this metaphor from the point of view of sports.

What seems to me to be the most often overlooked characteristic of sports is that, while competition may be inherent in some form in nearly any game or sport (though that is not a necessary component), this is inherently built into the structure of the game. For competitive sports, the desire to best one's opponent is pretty much a *rule*—albeit an implicit one—and not a functional characteristic. Likewise, cooperation within teams is also a necessary feature of team sports (Lüschen 1970). *Cooperation is the Yin to competition's Yang.* In fact, one's opponent must also cooperate with his competitor in the sense of sharing the same view, adopting the same set of rules, and generally sharing the same *definition of the situation,* to use a phrase from symbolic interactionism.

The metaphor of sports-as-social-microcosm breaks down when it is assumed that the primary if not the sole function of all games and sports is victory. It is incumbent on a team or athlete to play one's best. This goes without saying. But it is not the

raison d'être of sports and games. Cooperation is equally necessary to athletics. This, too, goes without saying. Whatever is the
primary function of sports and games, it cannot be either competition or cooperation, as these are implicit structural features of
most such pastimes. Among the functions of sports are with-
drawal from the day-to-day concerns of the workaday world; to
provide humanistic enrichment in a variety of realms, from the
purely physical to the purely spiritual; to permit the smooth
interfunctioning of mind and body; to impart a set of values to
the youth of a culture (Lowe 1977). *Sports and games should
perhaps be seen, not as metaphors for society, but as integral
parts of a society which serve a variety of personal and collective (i.e., social) functions.*

Sports and the Psychology of Performance

Since so much attention has been devoted to the study and
improvement of performance, it seems reasonable, if not altogether desirable, to begin with such a topic.

Personality

Some years ago, Walter Kroll (1970) noted: "The amount of
research data concerning personality and athletics is not very
extensive, but it is admittedly confusing. The amount of research data concerning personality in general is, of course, both
extensive and confusing. Thus, we [sports psychologists] are
only behind in one phase of our work." Well, I am pleased to
report that sports psychologists have at last filled the gap: There
is now extensive research on sports and personality; but it is still
confusing. (For reviews of this literature, see Cooper 1969; King
& Chi 1979; Ogilvie 1968, 1979; Ostrow 1974; Rushall 1972,
1978; Sage 1972).

As a general rule, studies of personality and sports performance—either individual or team—find either few statistically
significant relationships or else contradictory and inconsistent
ones. The reasons for this lack of consistency and relationship
are legion. First, our conception of personality is both primitive
and vague. Not only can personality be defined in a vast number
of ways, but controversy has arisen in recent years over whether
the concept of personality itself is even useful any longer. The

notion that people have a single set of traits that is more or less stable across situations and time is more and more rejected in favor of a situationally variable set of traits, subject to change from moment to moment. Thus, personality may not relate to sports participation or performance in any consistent fashion because personality itself is not consistent. Second, even if we were to agree on a reasonable definition of personality as a stable entity, its measurement would still be fraught with difficulty and error. Many of the personality measures used in sports psychology were designed exclusively for use with abnormal populations; and their use to differentiate, say, football players from squash players, is a misuse of the test and is bound to lead to erroneous conclusions. Third, we do not have very good measures of sports participation or level of achievement with which to correlate our measures of personality. These and similar problems are discussed in detail by Fisher (1976) and Martens (1975).

In order to begin to deal with these methodological and conceptual problems, Rushall (1978) has developed a situation-specific instrument designed to measure relevant behaviors for specific sports. Jones and Williamson (1976) have developed an attitude inventory related to athletic performance, rather than a personality inventory, assuming that attitudes, if not personality, are relatively stable across time. In other words, researchers are beginning to examine personality traits, not merely as a function of the individual, but also as a function of particular sports and nonsports situations. Given this growing sophistication among sports psychologists, it should soon be possible to predict athletes' behavior at least some of the time.

Structural Variables and Performance

The growing sensitivity to situational and structural variables in performance has also led some sports psychologists to examine the relationship between the structure of a team and its performance. Such variables as team leadership, group structure, cohesion, attitudes of and toward the coaching staff, and the presence or absence of cliques or subgroups within a team have been examined and, once again, have resulted in inconsistent findings.

Only a very few structural variables have yet been studied, and a great many additional ones remain to be explored. To date, those studies employing Fiedler's contingency model of leadership and its bearing on team performance have been promising but, again, inconsistent both in their findings and in the measures used to determine interpersonal attitudes.

Research and theory on problem solving and task performance in psychology suggest that, not only must one examine structural characteristics of the group, such as leadership, peer relations, the existence and nature of subgroups, and group homogeneity, but also the nature of the task at hand; whether it has a unique solution, whether one action precludes another, whether the task is simple or complex. Furthermore, one should perhaps examine feelings of equity among athletes, the exchange of interpersonal resources, such as status and affection, and other socio-emotional and cognitive factors.

Some Alternative Psychological Approaches to Performance

If psychoanalytic theory and radical behaviorism are inadequate ways of improving or studying performance, what are the alternatives? As I have already mentioned, there is a variety of theories in psychology, ranging from neo-Freudian views, such as those of Alfred Adler, Erik Erikson, and Harry Stack Sullivan, to cognitive views of motivation and performance, such as those of Atkinson (1957) and Feather (1968), that may prove relevant to sports. A few of these approaches that have already been applied to athletic performance will be reviewed briefly.

Perhaps the best-known and most central of these is the ideational-behavioral theory developed by Richard Suinn. Called Visual-Motor Behavior Rehearsal, the technique is based on "imaginary," "covert," or "ideational" practice under conditions of relaxation (Fensterheim 1980; Suinn 1976). VMBR is used for practicing basic skills, correcting performance errors and deficiencies, and learning to manage performance anxiety. The technique has been employed by Suinn with Olympic ski and track and field teams, and in a study by Kolonay (1977, in Fensterheim 1980), it was found that foul shooting improved among college basketball teams using the technique.

Cognitive dissonance theory and one of its variants, equity theory, have both been applied to the study of motor performance. In all these cases, the theory refers to performance at Time 2 based on prior performance and ego involvement at Time 1. Equity theory maintains that individuals rely on social comparisons to gauge the fairness of their outcome/input ratios. If outcomes are low relative to inputs, in comparison with similar others, then a state of inequity results. Inequity is an uncomfortable tension state that motivates the person to attempt to restore equity, often by reducing inputs or increasing outcomes.

"Peak Performance" and "Flow"

One approach to athletic performance, whether of an individual or team, concentrates upon successful athletes and attempts to examine those factors that contribute to peak performance. When asked to describe their greatest moments in sports, athletes frequently point to the ability to execute basic skills effortlessly, without thought; a total immersion in the movements of the sport; a transcendence of self; and an almost mystical perception of the universe as integrated and unified (Ravizza 1977; see also Murphy 1977; Csikszentmihalyi 1976; Murphy & White 1978; Adler & Adler 1978). This temporary state of peak performance, called "flow" by Csikszentmihalyi, was well described by the British golfer Tony Jacklin:

> It's not like playing golf in a dream or anything like that. Quite the opposite. When I'm in this state everything is pure, vividly clear. . . . I'm living *fully* in the present, not moving out of it. [This state] comes and goes, and the pure fact that you go out on the first tee of a tournament and say, "I must concentrate today," is no good. It won't work. It has to already be there. (In Doust 1973).

What is to me most remarkable about these descriptions is the similarity they bear to reports of creativity by artists, musicians, and writers. In a famous but disputed letter, Mozart wrote that he never sat down with a piece of blank paper with the intention of writing music. He would suddenly hear a completely composed piece of music, and then, when the opportunity presented itself, he would write it down in its entirety. He was not, in other words, taking responsibility for composing the piece; merely for being the conduit through which the piece flowed. Likewise, the exceptional performance on the playing field is one over which athletes often claim no conscious intent or even awareness.

Long-distance runners often report this feeling of euphoria once they have passed some critical distance. While it is fairly easy to characterize these atypical psychological states, where performance is exceptional and effort minimal, it is not so easy either to explain them or to facilitate or otherwise control their appearance. One tentative explanation that may be offered is based on Solomon's (1980) opponent process theory. Here the exertion required of a sport, process A, sets in motion a counter process, B, which eventually produces a euphoric feeling. Involved in process B may be the recently discovered endorphins, morphinelike substances produced by the pituitary (Margules 1979), which act as pain killers and which may produce euphoria. "Flow" related to peak performance may be a result, either direct or otherwise, of an increase in endorphin level. This hypothesis is currently being studied by an interdisciplinary team at Temple University and the University of Pennsylvania.

One of the many implications of the notion of flow and athletic performance is that external incentives to perform well may undermine the necessary state of relaxation for this phenomenon to emerge. As Jacklin noted, if you try to concentrate you won't be able to do so. The paradoxical effect of "flow" is that it emerges without intention. Peak performance will almost inevitably result from this desirable psychological state; but one cannot be forced into it. It will emerge when the athlete is relaxed, has mastered the fundamentals of the sport, is able to concentrate on proprioceptive feedback, and is free to let his or her thoughts wander. The intention to perform well, to win, to humiliate one's opponent, to experience hatred or anger is apt to prevent the appearance of "flow," and it is just such emotional and psychological states that are so often stressed by coaches, fans, and players.[1] Were athletes encouraged to compete for the love of the game, for the sundry personal motivations that attract individuals to sports in the first place, peak performance would be more commonplace than it now appears to be, and athletes would be more satisfied both with their own and with their team's performance (Goldstein 1982).

Psychology and the Sports Fan

It is easier to study sports fans than athletes themselves, if only because they are more accessible and more numerous. Over the years, sports fans have been both vilified because of their laziness and aggressiveness, and glorified because of the economic and psychological benefits they reap upon a community. Two particularly interesting analyses of sports fans have recently been published, and we will limit our general comments to these (Sloan 1979; Zillmann, Sapolsky & Bryant 1979), followed by an examination of violence in sports and socialization and sports.

Ren Sloan (1979) reviews theories of the functions of sports for fans. These theories focus on one or more of the following: the recreational and diversionary value of sports for spectators; the provision of stimulation and vicarious risk-taking; the need either to express aggressive impulses—the familiar catharsis notion, discussed below—or to experience a momentary and not unpleasant increase in aggressiveness; and the seeking of self-enhancement, which includes the sort of basking in reflected glory (Cialdini et al. 1976) that accompanies the wearing of home-team T-shirts after a victory and referring to the victorious team as "we," instead of "they." It is this last theory that is most forcefully presented and that is stressed by Sloan as the most parsimonious for explaining fan behaviors.

Zillmann, Sapolsky, and Bryant (1979) second this notion, but also present a theory on just why a fan supports a particular team or favors a particular player. The enjoyment of watching a game is immensely enhanced if the spectator is partisan. Not only will this support for one side color the fan's interpretation of the game, for example, seeing more rule infractions by the opponent than by one's preferred side (cf. Hastorf & Cantril 1954; Mann 1974), but it will also enhance the intensity of the fan's emotional response, simultaneously reducing boredom, providing an expressive behavioral outlet, and providing the supporter of a winning team with a momentary increase in self-esteem.[2]

Aggression and Sports

Sports serve a wide variety of functions, from teaching youngsters to abide by formally prescribed rules of conduct to providing a self-contained world outside of the "serious," adult world of the workplace. When discussing aggression and sports, it is well to keep in mind the many levels of a game, only one of which may be aggressive. With respect to those sports that require bodily contact between participants of opposing sides, it is possible that for some (or even all) players, and for some spectators (but certainly not all), the aggression inherent in the game may be peripheral to other facets of the game. It is possible that for some players and, perhaps for some spectators, the violence of, say, a football game, can be transcended through involvement with the game itself and, in this way, have little effect on spectators' or players' subsequent tendencies to aggress. But for a great many players and spectators, aggression in sports does influence their subsequent hostility and aggression.

On numerous occasions, violence has erupted at athletic events. Lever (1969) has suggested that the war between El Salvador and Honduras may be traced to a soccer match between those countries. In 1964, a riot erupted at a soccer match in Lima, Peru, in which three hundred people were killed. Mann (1979) has listed instances of serious injury or death at soccer matches in South Korea, the Congo, India, Egypt, Argentina, Brazil, Mexico, and New York. Comparable violence has occurred at boxing matches throughout the world.

Do these sports tend to attract the violence-prone, or do they create violence proneness in the otherwise nonviolent? The amount of research on effects of violence upon spectators has been growing. Most of it has been limited to spectator aggression and hostility at football, soccer, wrestling, and boxing matches (e.g., Arms, Russell & Sandilands 1979; Cullen & Cullen 1975; Gaskell & Pearton 1979; Goldstein 1983; Goldstein & Arms 1971; Kelly & McCarthy 1979; Russell & Drewry 1976; Smith 1979), but an increasing amount of attention has been directed toward fan violence at what are normally thought to be noncontact sports, such as baseball and basketball (Dewar 1979; Leuck, Krahenbuhl & Odenkirk 1979).

In nearly all this research, the findings have tended to invalidate the prevailing wisdom—that viewing aggression on the playing field (or ice) serves as a healthy outlet for the spectator's own aggressiveness. In fact, in study after study, there is evidence that both players and spectators become increasingly aggressive and/or hostile during the course of a game. When pregame hostility is compared with postgame hostility at boxing, wrestling, football, and soccer matches, fans are more hostile afterward than beforehand. Such increases in aggression proneness do not occur to the same extent at benign (i.e., noncontact) sports, such as gymnastics and swimming meets. In other words, spectators tend to imitate, in emotion and even in deed, the aggressive actions they see on the playing field.

There have been a number of theoretical explanations for these effects, ranging from a social learning theory explanation (Bandura 1973; Goldstein 1975) to a social class explanation

(Taylor, 1971). (See Cromer 1979; Gaskell & Pearton 1979; Goldstein 1983; and Russell 1981 for reviews of this literature.) It appears from these analyses that distinctions must be made between various types of spectator violence, and that a time dimension should be introduced when discussing the effects of aggression in sports. When individual spectators are studied as subjects, the investigator invariably finds an increase in hostility or aggressiveness. Studies of violent outbursts among fans at athletic events tend to find that, as the game progresses, violent incidents in the stands (as well as on the playing field) increase. But there is an altogether different type of spectator violence that is not generally examined in such research, which we might call collective (as opposed to individual) violence. Perhaps the best example of this type of collective violence is what the British call "soccer hooliganism." Here, gangs of youngsters engage in what most appropriately can be referred to as mock or ritualized warfare before, occasionally during, and after soccer matches. While a great deal of aggressive display occurs, serious injuries are fairly rare. These aggressive displays may have more in common with ego identities than with any sort of imitative aggression. That is, the behavior engaged in by youth gangs is symbolic, a way of expressing and creating one's identity as an outsider (see Marsh, Rosser & Harré 1978; Taylor 1971).

We must also take note of the immediate versus long-term effects of sports violence. In the short run, as attested to by the studies reviewed above, spectators are more apt to be hostile after viewing an aggressive sport than before. But such increases in hostility, unless they are acted upon, dissipate over time—perhaps in a matter of a few hours—returning the observer to his or her pregame level of aggressiveness. But there may be long-range consequences of watching aggressive sports, and these may not be so readily dismissed as momentary increases in emotionality (Keefer, Goldstein & Kasiarz 1983). The amount of, and the tolerance for, aggression on the playing field, as presented by athletes, officials, management, and sports broadcasters/writers may influence the attitudes and behaviors of countless fans and nonfans in numerous ways, a topic which we now discuss under the heading of socialization.

Socialization and Sports

As noted by Kenyon and McPherson (1974), the study of socialization in, and through, sports may take many avenues.

Here we will examine primarily the development of attitudes and values as a function of exposure to sports, particularly as presented in the mass media.

Though the socializing effects of sports have been commented upon by a number of sociologists and psychologists (e.g., Denzin 1975; Erikson 1972; Mead 1934; Piaget 1972), almost none of the theories proposed takes into account the relatively recent growth of sports spectatorship. It has traditionally been argued that participation in sports teaches the young participant competence, role-taking skills, temporal perspective, a cooperative as well as a competitive spirit, and cognitive and motor skills, thus preparing him or her for participation in the nonplay business of daily social intercourse. But the nature of sport has changed since midcentury, and many of the assumptions about the positive effects of sports are now being questioned. Television, in particular, seems to have had at least two important effects on the nature of sports and organized play engaged in by youngsters. Increased coverage of sports by the television networks has led to an increase in the formalization and "professionalization" of sports and has reduced the intrinsic motivations of sports participants (e.g., Deci 1975; Goldstein & Bredemeier 1977).

Whereas fifteen years ago, pre-high-school youngsters could play hockey, soccer, or football only in "pickup games," today there are dozens of junior leagues, replete with uniforms, sponsors, coaches, and all other trappings of their senior counterparts, including an emphasis on outcome (winning), rather than process (play). There seems to be a conscious attempt to model amateur sports on professional sports. Here is a sampling of popular opinions about what that modeling entails (taken mainly from Michener's *Sports in America,* 1976):

> I will demand a commitment to excellence and to victory; that is what life is all about. (Vince Lombardi)

> Winning isn't everything, it's the only thing. (attributed to Lombardi)

> To play this game you must have fire in you, and there is nothing that stokes fire like hate. (Lombardi)

> Every time you win, you're reborn; when you lose, you die a little. (George Allen)

> The winner is the only individual who is truly alive. (Allen)

In this country, when you finish second, no one knows your name. (Frank McGuire)

Defeat is worse than death because you have to live with defeat. (Bill Musselman)

Nice guys finish last. (Leo Durocher)

And, from former President Gerald Ford:

> The reason I make reference to those winning seasons at Michigan is that we have been asked to swallow a lot of home-cooked psychology in recent years that winning isn't all that important any more, whether on the athletic field or in any other field, national and international [*sic*]. I don't buy that for a minute. It isn't enough just to compete. Winning is very important. Maybe more important than ever. (Quoted in Butt 1976)

If you will permit a little "home-cooked psychology," inherent in these remarks is the notion that losers are in some fundamental sense inferior to winners; that one's opponents ought to be despised; that success, strength, and emotional detachment are to be valued above all else. What, in fact, is embodied by these remarks is conservative, stereotypically masculine, middle-class ideology (Prisuta 1979; Schafer 1978).

That such values are in fact transmitted to young sports fans is evident in a study by Prisuta (1979). High school students in Michigan were given a questionnaire on the relationship between values and their exposure to televised sports. Prisuta states of the results: "The high school sports viewer is more authoritarian, more nationalistic, and generally more conservative. He is also more sportsmanlike, and more oriented toward need-determined expression. These relationships remain fairly constant, even when using partial correlations to control for other variables such as demographics, peer values, etc." (p. 97). There is further evidence, as well, that an element of racism finds its way into televised broadcasts of professional football games (Rainville & McCormick 1977).

If sports broadcasters convey essentially masculine, conservative, and sometimes racist values over the air waves, they are perhaps equally as guilty of errors of omission as of commission. Absent from their endless pronouncements is much mention of sport as process or of the potential and actual social and economic roles of sports. It is as though a theater critic failed to discuss the play he has just seen, and instead only reports that Laurence Olivier is 5'9", weighs 164 pounds, and has a quick face with expressions. What the audience wants to know is what the play is about; what happens; what does it mean; why should anyone care? There are sports fans who would like to know this, too, about sports. Sports can, of course, be appreciated on the superficial level of the outcome. But they can also be appreciated for providing the spectator with drama, with tension and its management, with aesthetic appeal, with the level of skill displayed, the level of cooperation achieved (that much under-used and somewhat old-fashioned notion of teamwork), and with important recreational value. Sports are not about athletes, but about athletics.

Attribution and the Interpretation of Sports

What I have just discussed involves the interpretation of a complex and multileveled event by a broadcaster, sports fan, or athlete. Attribution theory (Heider 1958; Kelley 1967) is concerned with the causal explanation for behavior and its outcomes. How should an event be explained? Broadcasters choose to interpret the outcome of an athletic contest largely in terms of the personal characteristics of its participants, a tendency widely shared by athletes and fans. Of course, the precise interpretation will depend upon whether the favored team won or lost, and on whether one is interested in explaining the performance of a single athlete or a team (Roberts 1978). If a team won, the victory is apt to be interpreted as the result of good coaching, ability, high levels of motivation, good teamwork, and the loyal support of the crowd. On the other hand, if one's team lost, personal referents are not as likely to be made. Here we find explanations in terms of the lucky break of the opposition, the close or unfair call by the referee, the bad weather, or a host of other extrapersonal factors, including bad coaching (Goldstein & Bredemeier 1977; Rejeski & Lowe 1980).

Another attribution theory has served as the basis for several recent studies (e.g., Rejeski & Lowe 1980; Roberts 1978). Its interpretations of outcomes can range from luck to ability, and include consideration of expectancies, past performance, motivation, task difficulty, and other information about the game (such as whether playing home or away, and so on). What is of importance here is the fact that the attributions one makes will affect both one's choice of activity and the personal consequences of that activity, such as whether it will raise or lower self-esteem, the expectations one has about future performance, and therefore one's motivation and actual performance in subsequent activities. In other words, how we interpret a game will influence how we perform in later games. None of this implies that interpretations or attributions are correct or incorrect; only that the attributions we do make influence performance. If we carry this line of reasoning to the training of athletes, it implies that such commonly-used techniques as the analysis of videotapes of prior performance may be less helpful than instilling in athletes a sense of competence and ability without, at the same time, ruling out the important role of situational and non-personal factors.

Summary and Conclusions

Sports psychology is in an early stage of development. This can be seen by the relatively simple theories employed, by the fairly primitive methodology employed in much sport research, and by the emphasis on performance, to the near exclusion of satisfaction. Likewise, there is little concern with the social, economic, or political consequences of sports. Sports are often viewed, in a selective way, as a microcosm of society, in which competition and victory are predominant values. Rather than adopting a social-Darwinist position, this essay argues that sports should be viewed both as integral to a society and as reflective of the values of that society.

Owing to the lack of precise definition and measurement instruments, as well as to the fact that personality is perhaps best viewed as a situationally variable and impermanent set of personal characteristics, research by sports psychologists on personality and performance has been inconsistent in its conclusions and implications. One must take into consideration not only attitudinal and behavioral characteristics of athletes, but also the structure of the sport at issue and a host of environmental characteristics in attempting to improve prediction of sport performance. A growing number of reports by athletes and sports psychologists on peak performance, under what are described as effortless and nonconscious conditions (termed "flow"), suggests that perhaps performance in sports may be improved by not trying to improve performance, but instead by focusing on the personal satisfactions attendent upon participation in competitive athletics. In other words, much athletic training may suffer from a misplaced emphasis on performance. Performance will improve when athletes are fully involved in their sport for the purpose of personal satisfaction.

It has become increasingly clear in the past five or ten years that aggression in sports, particularly in combative sports such as ice hockey, boxing, and football (both European and American varieties) is not a "safety valve" or indirect outlet for player and spectator hostility, but instead a stimulus to further aggression. The number of acts of violence, both among players and spectators, tends to increase during the course of a game, and, in the case of fans, to continue immediately afterwards. Not only does sports violence appear to lead to further violence among players and fans, but it may well have more enduring and pernicious consequences. In particular, there is tacit approval of such violence by players, sports broadcasters, officials, and management, implying to sports fans that violence is an appropriate response to rule infractions or personal insults and that the outcome of the game is of greater importance than either sportsmanship or abiding by the rules of the game.

Televised sports, perhaps more than other forms of spectatorship, tend to emphasize conservative economic and political values. And, of course, how an event is interpreted will determine how one approaches similar events in the future. In other words, the attributions that athletes, broadcasters, and fans make about athletic performance and outcomes will influence how sports are perceived and performed subsequently.

Notes

1. A thorough analysis of the "flow" experience is not possible in the brief space available here. It should be noted that the psychological state here referred to as "flow" is not unique to athletic performance, but also appears in self-reports of artistic and creative endeavors. I have recently come to believe that it is also similar to the behavioral and cognitive state accompanying child abuse, spouse abuse, and various other instances of escalation of aggression (Goldstein, Davis & Herman 1975; Goldstein, Davis, Kernis & Cohn 1981). One interpretation of these diverse events with perhaps a common psychological property is that when the behavior to be performed is socially desirable, as it is in athletics or art, it is wise for the actor to lose sight of the goals of one's actions; when

the act may lead to undesirable consequences, as in punishing a child, the actor should keep the goal of punishment for some specific end clearly in mind, lest what may be called an "automatic" state be entered, with serious harm to the victim.

2. It should be noted that Zillmann et al. (1979) found no support for the widely accepted social facilitation hypothesis, namely, that the more spectators there are at any moment, the greater the increase in arousal, and hence in emotionality. This was not so in the studies they reported.

References

Adler, P., and P. A. Adler. 1978. "The Role of Momentum in Sport." *Urban Life* 7(2): 153–76.

Arms, R. L., G. W. Arms, and M. L. Sandilands. 1979. "Effects on the Hostility of Spectators of Viewing Aggressive Sports." *Social Psychology Quarterly* 42: 275–79.

Atkinson, J. W. 1957. "Motivational Determinants of Risk-taking Behavior." *Psychological Review* 64: 359–72.

Balbus, I. 1979. "Politics as Sports: The Political Ascendency of the Sports Metaphor in America." In A. Yiannakis et al., eds., *Sport Sociology: Contemporary Themes,* 2d ed. Dubuque, Iowa: Kendall/ Hunt.

Bandura, A. 1973. *Aggression: A Social Learning Analysis.* Englewood Cliffs, N.J.: Prentice-Hall.

Butt, D. S. 1976. *Psychology of Sport.* New York: Van Nostrand.

Cialdini, R. B., R. J. Borden, A. Thorne, M. R. Walker, S. Freeman, and L. R. Sloan. 1976. "Basking in Reflected Glory: Three (Football) Field Studies." *Journal of Personality and Social Psychology* 34: 366–75.

Cooper, L. 1969. "Athletics, Activity and Personality: A Review of the Literature." *Research Quarterly* 40: 17–22.

Cromer, G. 1979. "Football Hooliganism in England." In S. G. Shoham and A. Grahame, eds., *Israeli Studies in Criminology,* vol. 5. Ramat Gan: Turtledove.

Csikszentmihalyi, M. 1976. *Beyond Boredom and Anxiety.* San Francisco: Jossey-Bass.

Cullen, J. B. and F. T. Cullen. 1975. "The Structural and Contextual Conditions of Group Norm Violations: Some Implications from the Game of Ice Hockey." *International Review of Sport Sociology* 10(2): 69–78.

Deci, E. L. 1975. *Intrinsic Motivation.* New York: Plenum.

Denzin, N. K. 1975. "Play, Games and Interaction: The Contexts of Childhood Socialization." *Sociological Quarterly* 16: 458–578.

Dewar, C. K. 1979. "Spectator Fights at Professional Baseball Games." *Review of Sport & Leisure* 4: 12–25.

Doust, D. 1973. "Opening the Mystical Doors of Perception in Sport." *Sunday Times of London,* 4 November, 30.

Dundes, A. 1978. "Into the Endzone for a Touchdown: A Psychoanalytic Consideration of American Football." *Western Folklore* 37:75–88.

Erikson, E. H. 1972. "Play and Actuality." In M. W. Piers, ed., *Play and Development.* New York: Norton.

Feather, N. T. 1968. "Change in Confidence Following Success or Failure as a Predictor of Subsequent Performance." *Journal of Personality and Social Psychology* 9:38–46.

Fensterheim, H. 1980. "A Behavioral Method for Improving Sport Performance." *Psychiatric Annals* 10(3).

Fisher, A. C. 1976. "Current Status and Future Direction of Personality Research Related to Motor Behavior and Sport: Three Panelists' Views. In Search of the Albatross." In A. C. Fisher, ed., *Psychology of Sport.* Palo Alto, Calif.: Mayfield.

Gaskell, G., and R. Pearton. 1979. "Aggression and Sport." In J. H. Goldstein, ed., *Sports, Games, and Play.* Hillsdale, N.J.: Erlbaum/Wiley.

Ginsberg, G. L. 1980. "Aggression and Self-mastery in Football." *Psychiatric Annals* 10(3): 13–20.

Goldstein, J. H. 1982: "Sports Violence." *National Forum* 62:9–11.

———. 1975. *Aggression and Crimes of Violence.* New York: Oxford University Press.

———. 1983. *Sports Violence.* New York: Springer-Verlag.

Goldstein J. H., and R. L. Arms. 1971. "Effects of Observing Athletic Contests on Hostility." *Sociometry* 34:83–90.

Goldstein, J. H., and B. J. Bredemeier. 1977. "Sport and Socialization: Some Basic Issues." *Journal of Communication* 1975. 27:154–59.

Goldstein, J. H., R. W. Davis, and D. Herman. 1975. "Escalation of Aggression: Experimental Studies." *Journal of Personality and Social Psychology* 31:162–70.

Goldstein, J. H., R. W. Davis, M. Kernis, and E. S. Cohn. In press. "Retarding the Escalation of Aggression." *Social Behavior and Personality.*

Hardaway, F. 1979. "Foul Play: Sports Metaphors as Public Doublespeak." In A. Yiannakis et al., eds., *Sport Sociology: Contemporary Themes,* 2d ed. Dubuque, Iowa: Kendall/Hunt.

Hastorf, A. H., and H. Cantril. 1975. "They Saw a Game: A Case Study." *Journal of Abnormal and Social Psychology* 49:129–34.

Heider, F. 1958. *The Psychology of Interpersonal Relations.* New York: Wiley.

Hofstadter, R. 1955. *Social Darwinism in America.* Boston: Beacon Press.

Jones, J. M., and S. A. Williamson. 1976. "A Model of Athletes' Attitudes Toward Sports Performance." *International Journal of Sport Psychology* 7(2): 82–106.

Keefer, R., J. H. Goldstein, and D. Kasiarz. 1983. "Olympic Games Participation and Warfare." In J. H. Goldstein (ed.) *Sports Violence.* New York: Springer-Verlag.

Kelley, H. H. 1967. "Attribution Theory in Social Psychology." In D. Levine, ed., *Nebraska Symposium on Motivation,* vol. 15. Lincoln: University of Nebraska Press.

Kelly, B. R., and J. F. McCarthy. 1979. "Personality Dimensions of Aggression: Its Relationship to Time and Place of Action in Ice Hockey." *Human Relations* 32:219–25.

Kenyon, G. S., and B. D. McPherson. 1974. "An Approach to the Study of Sport and Socialization." *International Review of Sport Sociology.* 9:127–39.

King, J. P., and P. S. K. Chi. 1979. "Social Structure, Sex-roles, and Personality: Comparisons of Male/Female Athletes/Nonathletes." In J. H. Goldstein ed., *Sports, Games, and Play.* Hillsdale, N.J.: Erlbaum/Wiley.

Kolonay, B. J. 1977. "Effects of Visual-motor Behavior Rehearsal on Athletic Performance." Master's thesis, Hunter College of the City University of New York.

Kroll, W. 1970. "Current Strategies and Problems in Personality Assessment of Athletes." In L. E. Smith, ed., *Psychology of Motor Learning.* Chicago: Athletic Institute.

Leuck, M. R., G. S. Krahenbuhl, and J. Odenkirk. 1979. "Assessment of Spectator Aggression at Intercollegiate Basketball Contests." *Review of Sport and Leisure* 4:40–52.

Lever, J. "Soccer: Opium of the Brazilian People." *Transaction* 7(2): 36–43.

Lorenz, K. 1966. *On Aggression.* New York: Harcourt, Brace.

Lowe, B. 1977. *The Beauty of Sport: A Cross-Disciplinary Inquiry.* Englewood Cliffs, N.J.: Prentice-Hall.

Lüschen, G. 1970. "Cooperation, Association, and Contest." *Journal of Conflict Resolution* 14:21–35.

Mann, L. 1974. "On Being a Sore Loser: How Fans React to Their Team's Failure." *Australian Journal of Psychology* 26:37–47.

———.1979. "Sports Crowds Viewed from the Perspective of Collective Behavior." In J. H. Goldstein, ed., *Sports, Games, and Play.* Hillsdale, N.J. Erlbaum/Wiley.

Margules, D. L. 1979. "Beta-endorphin and Endoloxone." *Neuroscience and Bio-Behavioral Reviews* 3:155–62.

Marsh, P., E. Rosser, and R. Harré. 1978. *The Rules of Disorder.* London: Routledge & Kegan Paul.

Martens, R. 1975. "The Paradigmatic Crises in American Sport Per-sonology." *Sportwissenschaft* 5:9–24.

Mead, G. H. 1934. *Mind, Self and Society.* Chicago: University of Chicago Press.

Michener, J. A. 1976. *Sports in America.* New York: Random House.

Murphy, M. 1977. "Sport as Yoga." *Journal of Humanistic Psychology* 17(4): 21–33.

Murphy, M., and R. A. White. 1978. *The Psychic Side of Sports.* Read-ing, Mass.: Addison-Wesley.

Ogilvie, B. C. 1968. "Psychological Consistencies Within the Personal-ity of High-level Competitors." *Journal of the American Medical Association* 205:156–62.

————. 1979. "The Personality of Those Women Who Have Dared to Succeed in Sport." In J. H. Goldstein, ed., *Sports, Games, and Play.* Hillsdale, N.J.: Erlbaum/Wiley.

Ostrow, A. C. 1974. "Personality Research and Sport: Methodological Considerations." *Physical Education* 31(2): 95–96.

Piaget, J. 1972. "Some Aspects of Operations." In M. W. Piers, ed., *Play and Development.* New York: Norton.

Prisuta, R. H. 1979. "Televised Sports and Political Values." *Journal of Communication* 29(1): 94–102.

Rainville, R. E., and E. McCormick. 1977. "Extent of Covert Racial Prejudice in Pro Football Announcers' Speech." *Journalism Quar-terly* 54:20–26.

Ravizza, K. 1977. "Peak Experiences in Sport." *Journal of Humanistic Psychology* 17(4):35–40.

Rejeski, W. J., and C. A. Lowe. 1980. "The Role of Ability and Effort in Attributions for Sport Achievement." *Journal of Personality* 38:233–44.

Roberts, G. C. 1978. "Children's Assignment of Responsibility for Winning and Losing." In F. Smoll and R. Smith, eds., *Psychological Perspectives in Youth Sports.* Washington D.C.: Hemisphere (Wiley).

Rushall, B. S. 1972. "Three Studies Relating Personality Variables to Football Performance." *International Journal of Sport Psychology* 3:12–24.

————. 1978. "Environment Specific Behavior Inventories: De-velopmental Procedures." *International Journal of Sport Psychol-ogy* 9:97–110.

Russell, G. W. 1981. "Aggression in Sport." In P. F. Brain and D. Ben-ton (eds.), *Multidisciplinary Approaches to Aggression Research.* Amsterdam: Elsevier.

Russell, G. W., and B. R. Drewry. 1976. "Crowd Size and Competitive Aspects of Aggression in Ice Hockey: An Archival Study." *Human Relations* 29:723–27.

Sage, G. H. 1972. "An Assessment of Personality Profiles between and within Intercollegiate Athletes from 8 Different Sports." *Sportwissenschaft* 2:409–18.

Schafer, W. E. 1978. "Sport and Male Sex-role Socialization." *Sport Sociology Bulletin.* Reprinted in W. N. Widmeyer, ed., *Physical Activity and the Social Sciences.* 2d ed. Waterloo, Ontario: University of Waterloo Press.

Sloan, L. R. 1979. "The Function and Impact of Sports for Fans: A Review of Theory and Contemporary Research." In J. H. Goldstein, ed., *Sports, Games, and Play.* Hillsdale, N.J.: Erlbaum/Wiley.

Smith, M. D. 1979. "Towards an Explanation of Hockey Violence: A Reference Other Approach." *Canadian Journal of Sociology* 4:105–24.

Snyder, E. E., and E. Spreitzer. 1979. "Structural Strains in the Coaching Role and Alignment Actions." *Review of Sport and Leisure* 4:97–109.

Solomon, R. L. 1980. "The Opponent-process Theory of Acquired Motivation: The Costs of Pleasure and the Benefits of Pain." *American Psychologist* 35:691–712.

Suinn, R. M. 1972. "Removing Emotional Obstacles to Learning and Performance by Visual-motor Behavior Rehearsal." *Behavior Therapy* 3:308–10.

———. 1976. "Body Thinking: Psychology for Olympic Champions." *Psychology Today* 10:38–44.

Taylor, I. R. 1971. "Soccer Consciousness and Soccer Hooliganism." In S. Cohen, ed., *Images of Deviance.* London: Penguin.

Whitman, R. M. 1969. "Psychoanalytic Speculations about Play: Tennis—The Duel." *Psychoanalytic Review* 56(2): 197–214.

Zillmann, D., B. S. Sapolsky, and J. Bryant. 1979. "The Enjoyment of Watching Sport Contests." In J. H. Goldstein, ed., *Sports, Games, and Play.* Hillsdale, N.J.: Erlbaum/Wiley.

PART III
The Literary-Folkloric Interpretation

Sport is both a metaphor for American life and an
escape from the banality or complexity of life. It is an
expression of values fundamentally important to the
American people, a reinforcement of those values,
and at times an illusion that certain of those values—
like equal opportunity—truly exist in the society.
Sport thus offers the writer an ideal microcosm for
analyzing and criticizing these American characteristics.

—Michael Oriard,
Dreaming of Heroes:
American Sports Fiction (1981)

The Popular Sports Hero is more a concrete illustration of [Constance] Rourke's thesis in *American
Humor* that the accretion of folk materials, legends,
and crude sketches that cohere about a cultural figure
lead to his birth in serious fiction.

—Christian K. Messenger,
Sport and the Spirit of Play
in American Fiction (1981)

Issues and Contentions

During the 1960s, American literature, especially the genre of fiction, began to explore in earnest the possibilities of contemporary sporting experience as a rich source for the serious writer to draw upon for subject matter. Due to the pervasive medium of television and expanding opportunities for leisure-time activities, it was a period when the public became increasingly sensitized to sports experience from both the participant's and the spectator's points of view. Thus, the fiction writer aware of both these special viewpoints was in a position to charge his work with levels of meaning that could readily engage an audience.

That there has been an ongoing literary tradition of sporting experience in America, with archetypal origins in our ancestors' confrontation with the challenges of the frontier, is re-examined in my introductory essay to this section—*"North Dallas Forty* and the Tradition of the American Sporting Myth."* This piece observes, in part, that as society has become more and more subjected to the dehumanizing trends of urbanization and the proliferating technology of this century, the generally positive outlook of our prototypal sport literature has taken on negative connotations, particularly in those stories and novels structured around the systematized experience of the individual participant within a team setting.

By the early 1970s, Melvin D. Palmer noted in *Quest,* a journal for physical education professionals, that the tenor of the times had contributed to the public acceptance of anti-heroic character types in popular fiction, a situation increasingly evident in those works inspired by the realm of sports. In this light, Palmer observed that contemporary sport's "extremely organizational context . . . all too often takes the natural player and changes, corrupts, or destroys him by killing the childlike and primitive spontaneity and joy that should characterize games."

A decade later, Christian K. Messenger in his *Sport and the Spirit of Play in American Fiction* (1981) expanded upon the classic play-game theories of Huizinga and Caillois, as well as those of other theorists, to come up with a "play spirit" theory that seeks to explain all our writers' intuitive dependence on sport to enhance their personal visions of the American experience, whether positive or negative. Thus, in striking a common center in our literature, Messenger allowed himself sufficient room to analyze the cultural impact of play and sporting experience on classic authors who preceded the day of organized sports, as well as on those who have appeared through the time of William Faulkner. Fittingly, this section includes Messenger's introduction to his impressive study, in which he presents an overview of the "play spirit" concept as it relates to the "three heroic models" which have given "shape to more than a century of American play, game, and sport in fiction."

William Beezley's essay on the folkloric tales and traditions surrounding the college football player ("Counterimages of the Student Athlete in Football Folklore") appears here in follow-up to Messenger's contention (which echoes folklorist Constance Rourke's findings) that the accumulation and dissemination of folk material surrounding popular culture figures precede and inspire their appearance in serious fiction. The three essays that follow, each in its own way, demonstrate the validity of this assessment.

In "Religion and Sports: Three Muscular Christians in American Fiction," Robert J. Higgs not only reveals how a writer depends on familiar folkloric elements but also extends his theory of the socially symbolic import of the athlete advanced in *Laurel and Thorn: The Athlete in American Literature* (1981). In some areas of American culture, religion and sport have come to be thought of as intimately related, and here Higgs shows how three of our novelists' special sensitivity to this interrelationship gives rise to their respective visions of modern American life, particularly as their outlooks are dramatized through the experience of a main character conditioned by sports.

In "The Failure of Games in Don DeLillo's *End Zone*," Gary Storoff presents a provocative analysis of the novel which has become one of the most highly praised sport-centered fictional works in a critical sense. In transcending fiction's usually melodramatic treatment of intercollegiate football to suggest that the larger game is the one we find ourselves involved in off the field—the struggle to communicate with our fellows—*End Zone*'s critique of the human condition may be the most penetrating and all-encompassing use of the sport-game metaphor yet, according to Storoff.

While our serious fiction may not have yet produced a black version of *End Zone* or *Rabbit, Run* or even a *North Dallas Forty,* there have been some noteworthy achievements which focus in part, if not wholly, on the literary role of the black person who has been tempered by American sports or game experience. In "The Black Literary Experience in Games and Sports," Lloyd W. Brown extends his description of the racist effects of white-oriented games and sports on blacks in America to those in the Caribbean region, asserting that the neocolonial influence of the United States in this area has brought with it the sociocultural impact of the games and sports which typify our culture.

Whether from the black point of view or from the white middle-class perspective of John Updike's Rabbit Angstrom, the sport-centered literature discussed in this section shows how in recent years it has been a revealing mirror of American social and cultural habits.

13

North Dallas Forty and the Tradition of the American Sporting Myth

WILEY LEE UMPHLETT

When *The Sporting Myth and the American Experience* first appeared in 1975, I was pleasantly surprised at the critics' warm reception to my rather scholarly but less than exhaustive treatment of a popular subject area. In particular, various sources who reviewed the book called it "a welcome book, the first of its kind," and "a valuable preliminary study of an important theme in American literature," and—even more flattering—"an important archetypal model for further investigations of the subject."[1] Most reviewers seemed to agree that the book's chief virtue was a strikingly original approach to the interpretation of a neglected area of American fiction.

In my attempt to demonstrate that a literary tradition of sporting experience had originated with writers like Washington Irving and James Fenimore Cooper, I contended that its development, beginning with the contrasting but complementary experience of these authors' athletic character types (Brom Bones and his social conflict and Natty Bumppo and his frontier involvement) and evolving through modern variations of these archetypes, has created a symbolic dramatic pattern that I call the "Sporting Myth" in American fiction.[2]

Then when James Michener drew on some of my ideas as the basis for his chapter on the contemporary athlete in *Sports in America* (Random House, 1976), I was pleased, of course, but somewhat taken aback to discover that he had attempted to fit real-life sports heroes like Don Meredith, Hal Greer, and Robin Roberts into the mold of the "Sporting Myth," finding, not surprisingly to me, that they did not fit its fictional behavior pattern.[3] In refutation of Michener's application of the Myth, my research into a large number of serious fictional works controlled and directed by American sports experience had led me to conclude that fictional characters of a sporting background, either in solitary or in team sports, do not parallel real-life models so much as they exhibit pervasive and commonly identifiable characteristics which afford the reader a larger grasp and understanding of the complexities, ambiguities, and contradictions of American experience. In a significant number of novels and stories that I came across, it was increasingly evident that when American writers create characters who are conditioned by sporting endeavor, game competition, or some kind of athletic activity, distinctive, singular behavior traits symbolic of our cultural heritage as a people establish themselves.

In particular, male literary characters conditioned by American sporting experience all seem to espouse an ingrained adulation of the primitive and a preference for the simple as opposed to the complex and sophisticated; accordingly, they assume postures and attitudes that are anti-urban, anti-establishment, antisocial, and antifeminine (mainly because woman represents socialization). They also exhibit a narcissus complex which makes them antagonistic toward anyone or anything that would undermine their self-esteem or status; and as men in motion who behave instinctively, they come across as basically innocent, childlike figures who dream of remaining forever young while fearing their ultimate adversary—death.

The fictional pattern of the sporting hero—the experience of encounter—finds its most appropriate expression today in the microcosm of competitive team sports whose literary origins can be traced to the archetypal social and frontier experiences of Brom Bones and Natty Bumppo respectively. But in the contemporary literary hero of sporting background these antithetical experiences of confrontation have become intermingled, creating within his emotional makeup an irreconcilable conflict between the natural and the societal. In other words, the psychological tension in the contemporary sporting hero seems to derive from the fact that he exists as a composite of the Brom Bones–Natty Bumppo character makeups which focus on the conflict between the complex or societal and the primitive or natural. Because sporting activity, as both a source and means of individualized expression, has become so much a part of the American way of life, a perceptive writer attuned to the humanistic implications of modern sports can correlate the resources of the Sporting Myth and the oblique fictional process to express an intensely personal vision of life.[4] To illustrate how the Myth has continued to express itself through a writer's intuitive control of its resources, I intend to focus here on Peter Gent's *North Dallas Forty* (William Morrow, 1973), perhaps the finest novel about professional football to appear thus far, but one whose 1979 film version sparked a degree of controversy concerning the supposedly self-destructive life-style of today's pro football player.[5]

The hero (or anti-hero, if you will) of this novel is a naturally talented, but socially disoriented, wide receiver named Phil Elliott who, as we shall see, comes across as a representative character in the tradition of the sporting hero in American fiction, primarily because he personifies all the Myth's characteristics which I have identified above. Whereas most fiction dealing with professional athletes seems to be controlled by a pulp-magazine kind of emphasis on melodramatic situations— for example, an ongoing feud between team players or a former star's comeback in the big game—Gent's work reflects the serious novel's approach to incorporating the organic ingredients of theme, dramatic conflict, characterization, and structure in the sweep of his canvas, thus enhancing his special talent for dramatizing the internal conflict and emotional pain of his main character. The overall dramatic effect is a highly compelling reading experience, one that transcends the level of pure narrative appeal to get at something seriously wrong with contemporary society—although many readers must have felt that Gent's prime purpose was to expose the Dallas Cowboy organization, since Gent himself had formerly played for Dallas.[6] Such a reaction merely points out what I have previously suggested; that our familiarity with an area of real-life experience may prompt us to interpret fictional experience in a directly representational manner, thus obscuring an author's underlying intent and the fact that his work could be about a great deal more than, in this case, the rather restricted area of professional football. To test my assessment, we need first to look closely at the structural makeup of *North Dallas Forty,* particularly as it defines the experience of the novel's central character.

The pattern of Phil Elliott's encounter experience is structured around eight days during the football season which graphically reveal his growing disillusionment with the overly organized system of professional football. To dramatize this
situation, Gent focuses on his hero's frustrated attempts to find
himself as an individual both off the field and within the pro
football jungle—from the playing field right up to the Dallas front
office. For Elliott, playing football has degenerated into merely
participating in a finely tuned system wherein "opponents and
teammates alike are his adversaries"—a relationship in which
there is "no team, no loyalty, no camaraderie; there is only him,
alone."[7] Like the traditional sporting hero, Elliott lives according
to the integrity of his own personal code of behavior and also
according to what he calls a religion of survival, wherein he must
rely on his own basic instincts. His is a faith, however, which is
naturally mistrustful of institutionalized religious experiences
like, for example, the shallow inspirational talks of the team's
devotional leader. Significantly, he maintains a close identity
with the blacks on the team, whose unsophisticated and natural
air of primitive well-being has contributed to Elliott's understanding that they "always seemed to have more fun" in anything they did. But whereas most of the blacks have learned to
adapt to the demands of the system to survive, Elliott, in the
literary tradition of the sporting hero, is compelled to go his way
alone.

The structural form of Elliott's odyssey to discover self is
circular, beginning with his instinctively natural, but socially
noncommital, outing with teammates on a dove hunt, then moving through a series of events on the field and off, which are
highlighted by flashbacks of his broken marriage, a variety of
sordid experiences with alcohol, drugs, and sex, and intermit-
tent clashes with the Dallas coaching-managerial establishment,
finally ending in tragedy one week later in the ironically natural
setting of the ranch house of his most recent girl friend. The
cylical development of the novel underscores Elliott's innate
affinity with nature and the outdoors—his true religion and one
of the most pervasive characteristics of the Sporting Myth. In
fact, throughout the novel, Elliott, like Natty Bumppo, his frontier ancestor, keeps referring to the suburban countryside and
what the encroachment of both the city and technology is doing
to it, thus establishing a dramatic contrast between the way the
natural environment could be and the way it really is. His par-

ticipation with three drunken teammates in the travesty of a
dove hunt at the beginning of the novel is one of Gent's most
vivid metaphors for the way in which modern man has abused
his natural right to relate meaningfully to his natural surroundings. Instead of abiding by the ritual of the hunt, the players
persist in wantonly slaughtering the helpless birds, apparently
only for the thrill of the kill. But while the others indulge themselves in the massacre, Elliott passively resigns himself to the
role of a disenchanted onlooker until, as he expresses it: "We
returned cold, tired, drunk, and empty-handed. Jo Bob had
thrown the remaining doves at passing cars" (7).

The ritual of the hunt is ironically presented here as frustrated,
sterile experience, not only to emphasize the negative role of the
sporting hero in contemporary literature but to set the tone of
the story and introduce the reader to Elliott's inner conflict,
which pervades the novel. Appropriately, when Elliott meets
Charlotte Caulder, an appealingly independent ranch woman
who represents the kind of life-style he is strongly attracted to,
he reveals to her through hunting imagery why he thinks the
quality of contemporary life has declined:

> Hunting used to be the way energy was balanced. A good hunt
> was a great combination of muscular and emotional energy.
> But now hunting just degenerates into butchery, which creates
> more energy rather than depleting it. Almost all human en-
> deavor is that way. That surplus of energy is the cause of
> crimes of passion and spectator sports. (178)

Spectator sports, Elliott feels, have been created to function as
the artificial rendering of modern man's natural heritage while
the remaining "natural energy depleter" and the "savior of human sanity" is sexual identification and satisfaction, which he
has determined from his self-oriented outlook is the last frontier
for achieving the ultimate balance between self and the natural
environment. Phil Elliott's story, we may conclude is yet
another fictional variation of the contemporary obsession for
sexual experience as a substitute for self-realization, this time as
it is expressed from the unique viewpoint of the sporting hero.

Even though heterosexual experience plays a major role in
Elliott's life-style, both in actual involvement and vicariously
through the lurid locker-room tales of sexual prowess shared in
by his teammates, his is an ambivalent attitude toward women,

as with most sporting heroes in our literature. In fact, Elliott's feelings are instinctively homosexual in nature, especially toward his best friend on the team, quarterback Seth Maxwell. It is a relationship that he himself admits to, though, and one which he attributes to the rash of game injuries both he and Maxwell have endured together over the years—a "brotherhood of mutilation," which he considers to be "a very large part of [their] strange relationship" and "maybe even a homosexual bond" (140). The fraternity of athletes bound together by their ability to stand up to pain and injuries takes on distinctive sexual overtones in this novel of grown men clinging to the vestiges of waning youth through their common identity with a game. In this sense, and in his casual relationship with women, whose sexual favors offer a way to expand ego and hopefully discover self, Elliott is a brother to John Updike's has-been athlete, Rabbit Angstrom.

Charlotte Caulder, however, is the most exceptional female he has ever encountered, whose independence and purposefulness Elliott sees as malelike, contrasting markedly with the socializing instincts of his former wife, who, like most football wives who make their "special catalyst" particularly evident at postgame parties, had fostered disharmony among the players. In Gent's satirical portrayal of football wives we observe the recurring literary evidence of the female affinity for social constraints which oppose the natural expressiveness of the male sporting-type character. Charlotte, on the other hand, functions as much more than a social force and a sexual object in Phil Elliott's life: She becomes ultimately the one person who offers him the key to finding himself. The ranch scene in which Charlotte castrates a calf while Elliott reluctantly assists her is a pointedly significant and symbolic moment in their understanding of the unique interrelationship of their roles. In this highly graphic account of what is considered by the male mind to be the most repellent and abhorrent physical debilitation, Charlotte asserts her authority naturally enough for Elliott to sense that the ultimate emasculation is not so much a physical condition as it is to be a slave to a system, whether it be marriage or professional football. Significantly, she offers him the freedom to be himself by coming to live on her ranch, an invitation that heightens the conflict within his own mind of whether to continue abiding by the system or to go his way alone.

While sex represents one avenue taken by Elliott in his intense search for self, others are drugs and alcohol. By the end of *North Dallas Forty* the major characters have indulged in a prodigious amount of pills and marijuana, as well as a torrent of alcohol. As Elliott himself puts it: "I was high on something all the time—codeine, booze, grass, speed, fear; in fact, I doubt that during a season I was ever in a normal state of mind . . ."(154). But true to the performance code of the traditional sporting hero, "doing something better than anyone else in front of millions of people" is Elliott's ultimate high, and to maintain his intensity of purpose and the "ability to endure pain" in one of the most violent of sports, Gent suggests through Elliott's experience that the professional football player is greatly dependent on drugs as both a pain deterrent and an emotional stimulant. Within this situation lies the source of much controversy surrounding the film version, but because in both the film and the novel, drugs are used off field as well as on, the oblique fictional process would probably have us believe that their use represents not only a physiological need but, in a larger, more metaphorical sense, a psychological necessity to shield the self against the harsh realities of an apparently indifferent world, as symbolized by the system of professional football. Ultimately, though, it is Elliott's possession of drugs that precipitates both his final clash with the Dallas front office and his decision to break with football by taking up Charlotte's offer to live on her ranch.

Although the coaching staff has labeled Elliott as immature and unable to take the game of football seriously because of his propensity for clowning and joking on the field and off, his attitude persists as yet another buffer to what he sees of the prevailing system around him. In Elliott's own mind his problems with coaches and the front office have been compounded by the injuries he has suffered during his career—"five major operations, plus numerous muscle tears, breaks and dislocations" (49). As a result, Elliott contends that he hasn't had the opportuity to play up to his full potential. Revering the act of quality performance as his sporting hero brothers do, Elliott shares their naturally expressive need to participate meaningfully in the sacrosanct world of the game. But because management now looks upon him as "damaged" property, he knows that he must somehow make his peace soon or the system "would be shopping for a new piece of equipment" (23).

But Elliott's increasingly antagonistic attitude toward management's coldly detached approach to problem solution has created a seemingly irreconcilable emotional conflict between his inherent love for a game and his growing detestation of a system which inhibits the individualistic and freely expressive manner of the prototypal sporting hero. As Elliott instinctively understands involvement in sports,

> There is a basic reality where it is just me and the job to be done, the game and all its skills. And the reward wasn't what other people thought or how much they paid me but how I felt at the moment I was exhibiting my special skill. How I felt about me. That's what's true. (265)

Over the long run, then, Elliott comprehends his participatory role in the special sense that there is really only "the game. Not the end, the winning or losing, but the means: the game." With the sporting hero of American literary tradition, the game or sporting act itself has always been understood in terms of the experience of pursuit and not in the achievement of a goal. Because of his emphasis on game experience as both an end in itself and a means to self-realization, Phil Elliott stands in the direct line of this tradition.

Professional football as it is represented in *North Dallas Forty,* then, exists as a metaphor for a large area of modern experience, suggesting that today there may be many people—and not just professonal football players—who find themselves in a psychological predicament or moral dilemma similar to that of Phil Elliott. At particular points throughout the novel, Elliott observes and comments on events reported in the newspaper or over his car radio—reports of scandals, violence, and murders—asides that inform the reader of serious problems that exist outside the isolated world of the football game, yet suggesting that Elliott's life could be a microcosm of what is happening at large in contemporary society. Occasionally, in the insulated comfort of his late-model car, he observes the malaise of the passing scene, as at one point:

> It was the afternoon rush hour and I was going against the grain of the traffic escaping north to the suburbs. I passed miles of glazed eyes, tight jaws, and hands tensely gripped on steering wheels, people rushing home, dazedly thankful that the world had held together for another day. (61–62)

If there is a sickness that pervades the game of professional football, Gent intimates through his hero's experience that it is perhaps only a reflection of a more widespread and malignant illness within society itself.

Consequently, as a contemporary version of the sporting hero who seeks a symbolic return to his natural heritage but who is frustrated in his quest by both an unfathomable system and frustrating societal demands which entrap rather than free, Phil Elliott is involved in a search that is apparently doomed to failure. From time to time, he can reflect from his vantage point in the city that

> the land was still out there and not that hard to reach. Sometimes I felt that knowledge was what kept me from going totally crazy in Dallas. . . . But lately that fantasy didn't seem to hold. How could I return to the land? I had never been there in the first place. (170)

It is through this denial of his natural heritage, then, that we observe Elliott's encounter experience taking shape as a conflict between trying to realize the romantic identity of his heritage or giving in to the edicts and demands of the Dallas coaching-managerial establishment. Even his best friend, Seth Maxwell, who as the team's quarterback represents the organizational philosophy of his coach, cannot offer Elliott any consolation and in the end cops out on him because in reality he functions as a lackey to management. To Maxwell's attitude that the best way to get along in a system is to join it, Elliott ironically underscores his own theory of the game as an enjoyable end in itself when he remarks, "People don't talk about football teams anymore, they talk about football systems, and the control long ago moved off the field" (263). True to the code of the sporting hero, Elliott maintains his individualistic stance through the novel's climax and even through its tragic denouement.

After the critical New York game, which Dallas loses by one point and in which Elliott ironically enjoys one of his best days, the Dallas coach calls him before a tribunal of club and league officials. It is a powerful scene, one in which intense personal confrontations are staged to spotlight Elliott's ultimate clash with management. Informed that he has been under investigative surveillance for the past week, Elliott is accused of "conduct unbecoming professional football," specifically that of indulging in illegal drugs and carrying on an illicit affair with the fiancée of the team owner's brother. The dramatically charged setting also invites the Dallas coach to make one of the most paradoxically revealing comments in the entire novel when he criticizes Elliott as being "dangerous to organization for the same reason you are desirable" (281). Although he is categorized as a superior athlete, Elliott must pay the ultimate price for trying to be an individual in a system in which the individual must be sacrificed to the good of the organization. It is a familiar theme in American literature, but here it finds unique expression through Gent's skillful application of the resources of the Sporting Myth. Banished from league play, Elliott realizes once again that the "game wasn't on the field, it never had been." The real game had been played by the Dallas coach and his staff, who looked upon the game of football as a complex brand of technology requiring a systems management control. Charlotte had been right, he reasons: "I must have a value to myself and that has to come from inside, not from achievements in the world" (287). Once again the peculiar code of the sporting hero expresses itself through Elliott's awareness that to overcome the personally restrictive forces of the system, he must find a way to be himself.

In spite of the novel's violently shattering ending, Gent manages to convey the basic posture of the sporting hero up to the very last line of his story. Returning to Charlotte's ranch where he has decided his true destiny lies, Elliott confronts the sporting hero's most feared adversary when he discovers that an estranged acquaintance of Charlotte's, having come upon her and her black ranch hand in bed together, has shot them to death in a fit of jealous rage. Elliott's first impulse is to kill the murderer, but his efforts are frustrated, as if to dramatize the literary convention of death's role as the most formidable antagonist of the sporting hero. Thus, for Elliott there can now be only one recourse—self-renewal through nature—and after the police complete their investigation, he walks out of the ranch house to confront the natural force he innately understands by looking "out over the silent rolling pasture . . . [and] listening for sounds of life in the distance" (294). Bringing his hero full circle from the grotesque dove hunt of eight days previous to this final symbolic scene at the ranch, Peter Gent has constructed from both the resources of the American Sporting Myth and the oblique writing technique of the serious novelist a remarkable first novel that transcends the mundane level of a popular sport to tell us a great deal about the identity problems of the individual in contemporary society.

Notes

1. The quotations are from *Choice, Journal of Modern Literature,* and *Library Journal* respectively.

2. In using the term *sporting* as opposed to *sports,* my intent is to suggest an attitude toward a code of behavior or a set of values derived from our frontier heritage. The term *sports,* on the other hand, connotes the system of organized games and contests as affected by societal needs. *Myth* I interpret as a symbolic pattern of action or frame of literary reference representative of and common to a culture, which a writer uses either consciously or subconsciously to give his readers a better understanding of, and a deeper insight into, themselves and their culture.

3. See Michener, *Sports in America,* 224–68. Michener's assumptions suggest that even reputable and experienced fiction writers may critically misconstrue what ought to be the connotative function of serious fiction. The fictional process, I believe, is not intended to create a *direct* representation of life as the nonfiction writer would attempt it in, say, a biographical work. If such were the case, the experience of reading fiction would be journalistic in nature, akin to looking at the world as a mirror image. Instead, the fictional process ought to be dependent on an *oblique* approach to describing experience so that the reader may perceive nuances of character and insights into human behavior which a mirror representation would overlook by its very directness. In fact, the mirror or visual representation projected by the film version of *North Dallas Forty* may be the major contributory factor to audience misinterpretation of literary intent and the resultant controversy surrounding what this film is probably trying to say.

4. Hemingway, of course, is the most obvious example of a writer who depended on sporting experience to project an attitude toward life, but one should also note other outstanding examples in the writings of William Faulkner, Nelson Algren, James Jones, Philip Roth, Irwin Shaw, John Updike, and Bernard Malamud, to mention some established writers who have relied on the Myth.

5. The fact that I ignored this novel in *The Sporting Myth* (Lewisburg: Bucknell University Press, 1975) was not because I underrated it at the time but was rather due to my feeling then that I had reviewed sufficient material to illustrate the major points of my thesis. Because professional football keeps growing in popularity, *North Dallas Forty* is a prime example for updating the Myth, I think.

6. Note, however, that for obvious reasons the "Cowboy" generic term is never mentioned in this novel.

7. Peter Gent, *North Dallas Forty* (New York: New American Library, Signet edition, 1974), 24. All subsequent quotations are from this edition, with pagination noted in the text.

14

Introduction to *Sport and the Spirit of Play in American Fiction: Hawthorne to Faulkner*

CHRISTIAN K. MESSENGER

Play, Game, Sport

Sport has been a vital part of the American experience for the last 150 years. Its patterns have celebrated and reflected the American panorama, shifting from exuberant free-form play on the frontier to encapsulation in a modern stadium. Americans have had to subdue and civilize a vast continent, confronting nature in the raw and often calling on only their own "raw" physical natures as tools or weapons in an unequal contest. From the outset American society has been close to elemental conflict with nature and expressly reliant on physical strength, endurance, and courage. At the same time, America's religious heritage has engendered a profound mistrust of play and sport. This singular American experience required Americans to bring their physical natures into conjunction with the tenets of the mind and the yearnings of the spirit. Their sport has contributed to and been shaped by that American spirit, which is often most fundamentally itself when "at play."

The sports hero in American fiction has been a special figure, a

man apart from mass man: whether Davy Crockett, Natty
Bumppo, Frank Merriwell, Jack Keefe, or Pedro Romero. Because of particular skills, he is lionized and given heroic status.
What happens to this hero is typically described in a series of
encounters between the player and his society. While the focus
is consistently on physical sport—from the hunt, eye-gouging
matches, and country frolics to championship fights, college
football, and professional baseball—the competition described
often turns ironic, abstract, and metaphorical. Here the play
spirit predominates in metaphors of control and loss, mastery
and tragic defeat. These metaphors enable authors such as Hawthorne, Fitzgerald, and Faulkner to invoke play in order to deal
with the full complexity of human relationships both in and out
of the arena and to define modes of American conduct.

Sport in American life has always been contradictory. It liber-
ates in play, but it binds its players to the most strenuous work.
Such irony leads to even greater ironies: a frontier people becomes the greatest industrial nation in the world, its free-form
roarers become heroes in urban stadiums.[1] The real descendants
of Davy Crockett and Mike Fink are Babe Ruth and Dizzy Dean.
The Edenic New World becomes a country of disciplined Alger
boys striving for success, embodied in a schoolboy hero such as
Frank Merriwell and most poignantly caught in the figure of a
Jay Gatsby, who plays his magic illusions across the face of
society. America's puritanical society with its fierce work ethic
has nurtured a deep suspicion of play, thus fostering the need to
express this play spirit in fully sanctioned activities such as frontier games and school and popular sport. Reuel Denney stated,
"In the American culture as a whole, no sharp line exists between work and play."[2] Gregory Stone best expressed these contradictions in modern America when he observed, "sports that
were once work [hunting and fishing] are never played, but these
engage the 'players'—the amateurs. Sports that were never
work [team sports] are always played, and these engage the
'workers'—the professionals."[3] Play and game, sport and work.
The terminology is most often fluid and ambiguous in the American experience.

The relations among play, game, and sport are constantly being reinterpreted, but it is important to establish categories at the
outset that will be used throughout this study. In its broad
definition, play signifies something "simulated" or "not real,"
any activity whose main end lies outside itself. Johan Huizinga

in *Homo Ludens* (1938) characterized play as having freedom, separateness, and regulation. Roger Caillois, who, after Huizinga, has most elaborately classified expressions of the play spirit, retained Huizinga's characteristics of play and added three more: uncertainty, unproductivity, and make-believe. For Huizinga, play could be both a competition for something *(agon)* or a representation of something *(mimesis)*.[4] Caillois went further, identifying four categories of play: *agon* (the contest, competition with rules); *alea* (games of chance which render decisions independent of the players): *mimicry* (acting on the part of participants and simulation by the audience): and *ilinx* (the irrational whirling state induced by hypnosis, drugs, or any emotional exaltation.[5] Caillois conceives of the "as if" or improvisatory quality of games that replaces and performs the same function in *mimicry* that rules do in *agon*. He also plots these expressions of play along an axis from *paidia* (the most spontaneous of free play) to *ludus* (the most rule-oriented and organized variant of play).

Caillois was inclined to isolate play from reality in the progression of play-profane-sacred, stating that the sacred and play resemble each other but only to the degree that they are both opposed to the practical life.[6] He was dubious about what has happened to play in the modern world, stating that the modern equivalent of a festival is war in all its destructive potential. Caillois believed that one is freer in play than in life. However, his vision of the sacred was one of rigid captivity by a unity; thus play was for Caillois a movement leading down away from the profane in freedom rather than toward a captive prostration before the sacred. Yet everything we know of the ritual motions by which we approach the sacred suggests that our actions of rule-obeyance, motions of grace, cordoning off of a ritual space, the creating of festal time, begin in play. More helpful, while still incomplete, is a progression of reality-play-sacred conceived by the linguist Emil Benveniste, who suggests that play offers an inverted and broken image of the sacred which he defines as "the consubstantial unity of myth and rite."[7]

The current prevailing play theory, best expressed by Eugen Fink and Jacques Ehrmann, is that play is not an activity which can be contrasted to other phenomena such as "reality," "culture," or "the sacred," but that "play is an essential element of man's ontological makeup" because the "decisive phenomena of human existence are intimately related to each other."[8] Play is "a basic existential phenomenon,"[9] and need not be contrasted or compared to anything except itself. Play has great range; it dictates the form of rules that we determine as expressing "work" or "seriousness," while it controls, amplifies, and derigidifies experience. Play may also move through ritual toward final things and an ultimate expression of reality in the sacred.

Ehrmann, in the strongest critique of Huizinga and Caillois to date, states that their error was to define play in opposition to reality and the sacred. He argues that reality cannot be considered an innocent starting point for defining what play is but rather must be the outcome where "it is dissolved in the manifestations analyzed,"[10] where play has produced spatial and temporal illusions that become the content of the real. Our so-called reality is played for, a product of culture, whereas our so-called sacred is approached through ritual. We play our reality, our work, our religion. We play for control, as a talisman, out of fear, for exuberance, and for creativity. Ehrmann concludes there is no *a priori* "real" or "sacred." Play is not Huizinga's ennobled mimesis or Benveniste's inverted image of the sacred. The gratuitousness of play is only apparent because it is part of a circuit which reaches beyond spatial and temporal limits; one cannot subtract or depreciate the value of play because its utility is in the relocation and redistribution "in pursuit of *immediate* [italics Ehrmann] satisfaction of needs and desires."[11] Play cannot be defined in isolation because "to define play is *at the same time* and *in the same movement* [italics Ehrmann] to define reality and to define culture."[12]

When the categories of play are applied by theorists constructing an order of games, the task is often perceived as vast. Even the master organizer Caillois writes that "the multitude and infinite variety of games at first causes one to despair of discovering a principle of classification," but he also firmly states "that to a certain degree a civilization and its content may be characterized by its games."[13] A game is a rule-oriented variant of play which does not necessarily need a physical object but which absorbs a player or players and takes place in arbitrary time frames and artificially agreed-upon arenas. The definitions of game are synthesized by John Loy, who writes that games are "any form of playful competition whose outcome is determined by physical skill, strategy, or chance."[14] These categories may encompass the role of the athlete (physical skill), the role of the games player or trickster (strategy), and the dramatic naturalistic element of fate (chance). Loy connects play to sport through game when he adds the elements of competition in games to the features named by Huizinga and Caillois: freedom, separateness, uncertainty, unproductiveness, order, and make-believe.[15]

Huizinga had established the linguistic congruences of "play" and "competition" in his search for the similar roots of play terms throughout the Indo-European language system. He traced the English "play," "to play," from the Anglo-Saxon *plega, plegan,* which derives from roots in Frisian and Old German, the oldest of which meant "to take a risk, to expose oneself to danger for someone or something." The *agon* or basis of competition is always stressed in Huizinga's concepts of play. The object for which we play and compete is first and foremost victory, but victory is associated with all the various ways in which it can be enjoyed. We play for victory as a communal triumph with mass acclaim as in modern sport spectacle; we play for the honor and esteem of society; or we play for intense self-knowledge. The root of the Greek word for "prize" yields "athlete," and Huizinga notes, "here the ideas of contest, struggle, exercise, exertion, endurance and suffering are united." He concludes that in ancient athletics "we are still moving in that sphere of serious competition" labeled "agonizing," "involving as [ancient athletics] do mental and physical hardship."[16]

In general, the competitive element defines sport as a more intense game. Sport is an organized game with a variety of rules possessing internal coherence, and it is an institutionalized game that may be an external expression of the order of society responding to or underscoring a national pattern. Sport in American society dramatically portrays the heroic striving of the individual in the contest where he pursues satisfaction in a wide range of behavior from the most splendid moments of isolated achievement to the mass adulation of the crowd.

Caillois grouped sport with other competitive games in his *agon* category. Huizinga cast a very dubious eye on all modern spectacle. Neither scholar focused on sport but suggested initial directions for further study. Caillois attempted to prove the essential distance that existed between play and the sacred, stating that play is born in human invention while the human worshiper is defenseless and prostrate before the sacred.[17] For this reason, Caillois could not adequately deal with predatory sport that highlighted man-in-nature. The isolated experience of the hunter is in a realm that approaches the sacred through ritual motions, but Caillois denied that play was born in the sacred. In reality, the hunter is a throwback to the primitive sportsman, whose sport was an expression of training for warfare skills as well as a religious ceremony.[18]

Huizinga wished to show the surviving play spirit in modern institutions, though he did not find that spirit in sport. When Huizinga commented in *Homo Ludens* on the relation of play to modern sport, he was firm in his view that, in modern life, "sport occupies a place alongside and apart from the cultural process."[19] He observed, "the great competitions in archaic cultures had always formed part of the sacred festivals," but "this ritual tie has now been completely severed; sport has become profane."[20] As of now, except for isolated ritual sport of the greatest solemnity, modern play, game, and sport are relentlessly secular, and contemporary play theory no longer countenances a separation of play from reality. This separation was particularly noticeable among pioneering play theorists as well as sociologists and historians of religion whose firm categories excluded play from sport, sport from cultural functions, and play from the sacred. Huizinga, Caillois, and Mircea Eliade, for example, were comparativists in their landmark scholarship. With a commitment to ancient, medieval, and nonwestern cultural models, they sought to identify pure embodiments of play and the sacred set against the "real" or the "profane."[21] All were uncomfortable with what they felt to be a disastrous twentieth century and its diluted expressive forms. They consistently resisted acknowledgment of the ritual qualities surviving in modern secularized mass observances in their comments on "degenerated" or "irreligious" human behavior, where the intensity of their subject, they felt, had collapsed into debasement and caricature. However, today, that subject is studied with validity as secular ritual in a large number of variations.

Modern America is a long way from Huizinga's medieval pageant of play and contest or his conception of the initially integrated nature of play and the sacred in ancient cultures. Although Huizinga and Caillois by the force of their rhetoric and the breadth of their scholarship argued against the purity of sport, the fact is that sport has swiftly become an immensely influential secular ceremony, part of the ordinary life of the society at large,[22] and a subject of intense investigation. Since the conceptual work of Huizinga and Caillois in characterizing and classifying play, sport itself has accumulated a welter of meanings, and a summary suggests a multiplicity of associations in many contexts: sport is its own system, an institutionalized game demanding physical prowess; games are dramatic models of our psychological lives; sport is popular art as well as applied art; sport regulates social interaction, ritualizing collective unity and pride; sport weds man to technological civilization while supposedly giving him relief from it; sport acts as a transitional institution between work and play; sport is studied as social imagery and is "a currency of communication on every level of American life"; sport is found to be "the success story of the twentieth century, the modern way up the ladder"; sport is the "rationalization of the Romantic" in the modern world; and, coming full circle to confront the heart of Huizinga's argument, sport is flatly labeled a natural religion.[23]

Models of Sports Heroism

The history of American fiction is, as critics such as Richard Chase, Leslie Fiedler, Daniel Hoffman, and Theodore Gross have pointed out, the history of individual, larger-than-life American heroes. The American hero from Natty Bumppo through Captain Ahab, Huckleberry Finn, Henry Fleming, and Nick Adams has had a conflict "between free will as a function of natural liberty and determinism as a result of surrender to society."[24] American Sports Heroes have had to continually make themselves up or redefine their roles in the absence of a place in a traditional culture.

Huizinga dismissed much of modern sport as "a thing *sui generis,* neither play nor earnest,"[25] stating in *America* (1918) that "if we compare the tense athlete in his competitive harness with the pioneer hunter and Indian fighter, then the loss of true, free personality is obvious."[26] In this comparison are grounds for tracing not so much the decline of the play spirit, which is *not* so "obvious," but, more accurately, the metamorphoses of the play spirit. These changes mirror and dictate changes in the fiction about sport as well. That America has always been bewildered about what constitues work and play suggests a tremendous tension in the society *between* work and play. The modern athlete on a sports team does not resolve this tension but actually embodies this paradox, as did Hester Prynne and Pearl in their free play in *The Scarlet Letter,* Rip Van Winkle in "Rip Van Winkle," Natty Bumppo in *The Pioneers,* and Thoreau in the "Higher Laws" chapter of *Walden,* as classic American literature confronted the dilemma in differing ways.

Brian Sutton-Smith states that the "primary paradigm" for play is activity taken up voluntarily, usually by a solitary player. The result of the activity is individual gain "in cognitive or creative organization."[27] This definition best describes the play of characters in classic American literature. However, the play of athletes in the organized competition related in modern fiction more closely resembles Sutton-Smith's "secondary paradigm" in which play organizes collective forms of human communication and "reflects the enculturative processes of the larger society."[28]

The modern sports hero exemplifies a paradox in American society: his drive for individual excellence and acclaim (in the primary paradigm of play) is confronted by democratic consensus, which is adoring and hostile by turns. His drive upward through the classless society celebrates idealism and individual striving that turns, as the American dream turns, toward acquisition, wealth, and power. The success myth champions accommodation to social norms, the prudence of Benjamin Franklin's maxims, and the ability to be a team player (in the secondary paradigm of play). Whatever talent he is blessed with, most often physical grace, power, and creativity masked by an inability to express himself, the sports hero confronts the established society in the largest metaphor, the team itself. Sports heroes are individually isolated in their performing skills, which set them off from mass society, but it is in the performance itself that their status as isolates is severely tested for the mass audience. Here is where the primary and secondary paradigms of play clash in discordant drama.

To deal with the proliferation of meanings that the sports hero has acquired in differing historical periods, it is necessary to draw some broad outlines of sports heroism. Three specific heroic models will be discussed at length in this study. They are the Ritual Sports Hero, the Popular Sports Hero, and the School Sports Hero. While I see the delineations quite clearly, it is inevitable that there is some overlap and direct influence among the three figures—they are not rigidly separated parallel tracks coursing through the critic's imagination. These three heroic models give shape to more than a century of American play, game, and sport in fiction.

The Ritual Sports Hero antedates both the Popular and School Heroes in his wisdom and probity as well as in his personal, isolated frame of competiton. An Adamic figure who seeks self-knowledge, he competes to learn what he is capable of against self or natural adversaries. He has origins in sacred ceremony as well as state ritual. He has specifically American origins in the accounts of wilderness heroes, in ordeal and captivity narratives. His exploits are prefigured in the accounts of the great early naturalists, explorers, and historians such as John James Audubon, Meriwether Lewis, and Francis Parkman, as well as in the journals of trappers, scouts, and hunters. He is a figure of both surpassing skill and great dignity and is only incidentally defined by a community or society with which he is most often in conflict. His sport is often formalized as ritual, and then sport becomes a way of knowing in the present and a dance toward the dramatic ordering of ultimate meaning, the sacred, for which he has played and has risked the loss of his secular, temporal selfhood.

The Popular Sports Hero has born in exuberant playfulness on the American frontier in the early nineteenth century. He was deeply democratic, raw, humorous, and unlettered. As a hunter, physical wild man, gambler, or shrewd confidence man, he expressed the strength and vitality of westward expansion and growth. He was physically prodigious and boldly manipulative in an environment that demanded such power and deception for survival. His sport grew out of his work with horse, rifle, and riverboat. Gradually, the Popular Sports Hero was refined and scaled down to fit into the modern arena of industrial society where he played for a team before huge crowds. In this volume, "popular" consistently refers to the *sport* and not to the hero. Obviously, by 1900, School Sports Heroes are just as visible in the culture as Popular Sports Heroes; so can Ritual Sports Heroes be clearly recognized under certain circumstances. "Popular" sport is here defined as that activity which evolves out of the daily life of the culture which is captivated by it. "Popular" sport first denotes the games and contests of the frontier and later the spectatorial pastimes of an industrial urban society. The determination of popular sport is as an end in itself, a thoroughly secular spectacle.

The School Sports Hero grew from the development of a militant sporting ethic in the Eastern colleges in the post–Civil War period. He was more genteel than the Popular Hero and nurtured through American education, privilege, and the assimilation of war through symbolic sports conflict. The School Sports Hero heralded a shift from transcendental speculation in the universities to preparation for the trials of a driving, materialistic American business society and world leadership. The School Sports Hero competed not only for personal victory but for a larger self-discipline and the approbation of an admiring society which then christened him as potential leader. The figure was a prominent symbol of the American aristocracy's last great involvement in national life and affairs and was the most influential American sporting hero at the beginning of the twentieth century.

The three heroic figures diverge at a number of crucial points. The Ritual Hero plays for self, for his own pride or revelation. The School Hero competes for himself only incidentally. He competes for society's praise to establish his place as leader or spokesman. The Popular Hero competes for immediate extrinsic rewards: money, fame, records. The Ritual Hero plays for the growth of spirit, the School Hero for character and recognition, and the Popular Hero for recognition and reward. For the Ritual Hero, sport is a revelation; for the School Hero, a test; and for the Popular Hero, a contest.

The Ritual Sports Hero renounces all public pressures and rewards. His sporting motions and victories are serious and private. His personal *agon* is with nature or a force representing nature. He exemplifies the individual set apart and he always deals with primary experience. To the degree that all players and sportsmen undergo personal, individual experience, we can say that they are all Ritual Heroes but that School and Popular Heroes subordinate the primary lessons of mastery and victory to externally offered prizes, subordinate intrinsic rewards that can be enlarged upon to extrinsic rewards eagerly accepted.

The School Sports Hero is at the midpoint between ritual and the spectacle of the Popular Sports Hero. The School Hero is an elite son who has the common touch, an uncommon man of ability and discipline who undergoes the tests of sport to learn not only about himself, as did the Ritual Hero, but about lessons in courage and discipline that he can apply to life and society outside the arena. The School Hero plays for externalized goals as well as personal gratification but ultimately bends his skill and heroism to society's will and tasks. He is most aware of his place in a society in which he desires a leadership role. He makes a prudent investment in society, its continuity and health. The

Popular Sports Hero is not sensitive to his conflicting roles. He dominates the *agon* as he would all his problems, while he roars out that he is the best, beats down all competition, and wins at any cost. He is a superhero of folklore who expresses our most expansive optimism, while he possesses none of the self-knowledge of the Ritual and School Heroes, and none of the School Hero's sense of duty.

For the Ritual Sports Hero, play is often work of the most creative and healing sort. The School Hero plays in preparation for life's work. The frontier Popular Hero at first found his sport growing out of work roles in the natural environment and ultimately worked at his play for spectators who were seeking playful respite from their work. Within their play, these heroes respect or grudgingly submit to certain norms. On the frontier, the hunter or woodsman as Ritual Hero exhibited his "fair play" by ackowledging the sovereignty of powerful nature and the limits of the physical body. The School Hero respected the stated rules of the game because they prepared him for "playing fair" by observing other rules in society. The Popular Hero respected the power of his competitors, dueled the authority of the team, or fought the record book containing the inhuman accomplishments of past heroes.

None of the three figures developed along the same paths. The Ritual Sports Hero cannot be reduced to a formulaic pattern. He is a mythical hero performing large, well-established motions and is timeless, creating his time out of all time. While his American setting has enormously magnified his stature as hunter and naturalilst in a pristine wilderness, he has links to primitive sacrificial sports and the sports of antiquity where rites sustained culture. Cooper and Thoreau bequeath to Hemingway and Faulkner ritual heroes who perform acts of pride and humility, perception and mastery. They all wished to show sport as a rule-limited activity with limitless reference in a world with consequences for the player. If the hunt cannot rearrange and irrevocably alter lives outside its rite, it may ontologically celebrate reality that can be lived both *with* and *in,* controlling, if briefly, nightmares of personal history, and perhaps establishing, if imperfectly, a link with the sacred.

The School Sports Hero, on the other hand, affords a classic study of how a formulaic pattern in a culture grew into an established popular literary formula: that of the boys' school sports story, and how that convention would be subsumed by the ironic

and satiric statements of authors such as Fitzgerald, Hemingway, and Faulkner. The Popular Sports Hero is more a concrete
illustration of Rourke's thesis in *American Humor* that the
accretion of folk materials, legends, and crude sketches that
cohere about a cultural figure lead to his birth in serious fiction.[29]
The Popular Hero's development is jagged, long-drawn-out, and
must be tracked through several large metamorphoses: the country's shift from frontier to urban culture, from outsized backwoods heroes to scaled-down team members, from southern to
northern emphasis, and from pre–Civil War to post–Civil War
setting. The birth of the Popular Sports Hero in fiction is expressly connected with the development of American journalism
and its interaction with traditions of American humor in reporting and narration.

Before beginning extensive examination of these three sports
heroes, it is important to reiterate that their broad outlines do
not preclude cross-fertilization. Two sporting heroes may begin
in similar fashion—Davy Crockett and Natty Bumppo, for example. But where Natty becomes a Rousseauistic philosopher-
hunter, internalizing his sporting lessons while instructing the
settlement in the correct use of sport, Crockett's fictional persona is created through carelessly sown tales of giantism. He is a
raging public patriotic symbol and a popular consensus hero.
Two hunters. Two divergent courses toward idealism and
humorous realism. Two very different breeds of sportsmen. Yet
they both begin as natural gentlemen obeying wilderness laws
and performing adeptly in sporting rites. Natty Bumppo, however, is in part the genesis of the upright college sports hero of
1900 in his living by a rigorous code. Coming full circle, Fitzgerald's Yale all-American Tom Buchanan in *The Great Gatsby*
is a School Sports Hero but is also prefigured in the blustering,
violent athletes of nineteenth-century backwoods tales which, of
course, take their outsized conceptions of roarers from Crockett
almanacs, among other sources.

Before the Civil War, the beginnings of a fully national literature presented the sports hero as an individual in contest on the
frontier with other men or with nature. There the Ritual Sports
Hero expressed the heritage of English play forms in ceremony
as well as a new world expression of survival skill and mastery.
The Ritual Sports Hero and the Popular Sports Hero survived
side-by-side in sober achievement or in comic bluster before the
Civil War. After the Civil War, the sports hero was most clearly

defined on a team to which he was subordinated—military, industrial, educational, societal. He was the uncommon man now representative of the conflict between the individual and the modern organization. He now could best be seen as the School Sports Hero, the modern gentleman sportsman with a code, and as the Popular Sports Hero, the raucous superman of modern spectacle. The modern Ritual Sports Hero is then part of a reaction against collectivized and regulated sports figures.

Thus, American fiction for more than a century and a half has reported both somberly and hilariously on a nation of players and spectators during a great shift in American sport and leisure from spontaneous work-related sport on the frontier to the sport of modern organized industrial society. Whether an aged hunter, steamboat pilot, school football star, rube pitcher, bullfighter, or boxer, the sports hero in fiction has always been the individual performer in a contest. This contest has been with nature, with a solitary adversary, or within a formalized team rivalry. Most fundamentally, however, the sports hero has most often fought the harsh battle with himself as well as in the arena, the public performance taking on a deeper perspective through the private struggle. American sport in fiction celebrates the nation's youth, innocence, and power while focusing on all the tragic contradictions implied in the obverse themes of death, experience, and impotence. Sport has become a binding myth for an intensely organized, competitive society growing from a brawling adolescence into aggressive adulthood. The text of that myth is recorded in sport's varying presentation in our fiction.

Notes

1. Christopher Lasch comments on the irony that "the appearance of an escapist conception of 'leisure' coincides with the organization of leisure as an extension of commodity production." Lasch, "The Corruption of Sports," *New York Review of Books,* 28 April 1977, 30. [Ed. note] See Chapter 2, p. 65.

2. Reuel Denney, *The Astonished Muse* (Chicago: University of Chicago Press, 1957), 118.

3. Gregory Stone, "American Sports: Play and Display," in John H. Talamini and Charles H. Page, eds., *Sport and Society: An Anthology* (Boston: Little, Brown, 1973), 74.

4. Johan Huizinga, *Homo Ludens* (Boston: Beacon Press, 1955), 13.

5. Roger Caillois, *Man, Play and Games,* trans. Meyer Barash (New York: Free Press of Glencoe, Macmillan, 1961), 8–26.

6. Ibid., 160.

7. Emil Benveniste quoted in Jacques Ehrmann, "Homo Ludens Revisited," in Ehrmann, ed., *Game, Play, Literature. Yale French Studies* 4:35–36.

8. Eugen Fink, "The Oasis of Happiness: Toward an Ontology of Play," in Ehrmann, ed., *Game, Play, Literature,* 19.

9. Ibid., 22.

10. Ehrmann, "Homo Ludens Revisited." 34.

11. Ibid., 44.

12. Ibid., 55.

13. Caillois, *Man, Play, and Games,* 11, 83.

14. John Loy, "The Nature of Sport: A Definitional Effort," in M. Marie Hart, ed., *Sport in the Socio-Cultural Process* (Dubuque, Iowa: William C. Brown, 1972), 50 (hereafter referred to as "Hart"). Loy expands on definitions initially formulated by John M. Roberts and Brian Sutton-Smith, "Child Training and Game Involvement," *Ethnology* I (1962): 166.

15. Loy, "The Nature of Sport," 55.

16. Huizinga, *Homo Ludens,* 39, 50–51.

17. Caillois, *Man and the Sacred,* trans. Barash (Glencoe, Ill.: Free Press of Glencoe, 1960), 158–61.

18. Gunther Lüschen, "The Interdependence of Sport and Culture," Hart, 33; Allen Guttmann, *From Ritual to Record* (New York: Columbia University Press, 1978), 23.

19. Huizinga, *Homo Ludens,* 197.

20. Ibid.

21. Caillois, *Man and the Sacred;* Mircea Eliade, *The Sacred and the Profane,* trans. Willard R. Trask (New York: Harcourt, Brace, 1959); René Girard, *Violence and the Sacred,* trans. Patrick Gregory (Baltimore: Johns Hopkins University Press, 1977).

22. Guttmann, *From Ritual to Record,* 23.

23. "Sport as system . . . ," Loy, "The Nature of Sport," 57; "sport as institutionalized game . . . ," Marshall McLuhan, "Games: The Extension of Man," *Understanding Media: The Extensions of Man* (1964), Hart, 147; "games as dramatic models . . . ," McLuhan, "Games: The Extension of Man," 150: "sport as popular art . . . ," Edgar Z. Friedenberg, Foreword to Howard Slusher, *Man, Sport, and Existence,*" Hart, 181; "sport as regulated social interaction . . . ," Nicholas Petryszak, "The Cultural Evolution of Barbarism in Spectator Sports: A Comparative Analysis," *Sport Sociology Bulletin* 6, no. 1 (Spring 1977): 26 (Petryszak quotes P. E. Frolich, "Sports and Community," Ph.D. diss., University of Wisconsin, 1952, 274); "sport weds man to technical civilization . . . ," Lewis Mumford, "Sport and the Bitch Goddess," *Technics and Civilization* (New York: Harcourt, Brace and World, 1934). 305: "sport acts as transitional institution . . . ," Arnold Beisser, *The Madness in Sports* (New York: Appleton-Century-Crofts. 1967), 41; "sport as social imagery . . . ," Denney, *The Astonished Muse,;* "sport as currency of communication . . . ," Robert Lipsyte, *SportsWorld* (New York: Quadrangle, *New York Times* Book Co., 1975), 51; "sport as success story . . . ," John R. Tunis, *The American Way in Sport* (New York: Duell, Sloan and Pearce, 1958), 18; "sport as rationalization of the Romantic . . . ," Guttmann, *From Ritual to Record,* 89; "sport is natural religion . . . ," Michael Novak, *The Joy of Sports* (New York: Basic Books, 1976), 19.

24. Daniel Hoffman, *Form and Fable in American Fiction* (New York: Oxford University Press, 1965), 4.

25. Huizinga, *Homo Ludens,* 197.

26. Huizinga, *America, a Dutch Historian's View from Afar and Near* (New York: Harper & Row, 1972), 115–16.

27. Brian Sutton-Smith, "Introduction," Sutton-Smith, ed., *Play and Learning* (New York: Gardner Press, 1979), 1.

28. Ibid.

29. Constance Rourke, *American Humor* (New York: Harcourt Brace Jovanovich, 1931), 159, 279–80, 283–84, 287.

15

Counterimages of the Student Athlete in Football Folklore

WILLIAM H. BEEZLEY

"Any player who gets straight A's is letting his teammates down."[1] Alex Karras's pointed summary of the conventional attitude of football players toward academia expresses as well the folkloric view of football players held by other students and many faculty members. In keeping with this former University of Iowa all-American's assessment, I intend to concentrate here on the college football player (the most representative student-athlete) in campus folklore.

Ever since students from Princeton and Rutgers played the first intercollegiate football contest in 1869, three major folk types have cavorted on the college gridiron, and variations of these types have continued to appear in fiction, drama, and film. Chronologically these are the "tramp athlete," first showing up in the 1880s and flourishing until about World War I; the "Dumb Jock," who appeared in the 1920s, and to some extent still survives today; but who was superseded in the 1950s by the "jock"—known in the more formal parlance of athletic directors and the press releases of the NCAA as the "student-athlete." By the 1960s, the jock even came to represent athletes of both sexes. The different guises of these athletic types have generated legends, tales, jokes, riddles, aphorisms, and general student lore which reveal that a substantial body of folklore has built up around them over the years.

In the folk tales about varsity athletes, the tramp athletes were football players of extraordinary skill, recruited by team members or team captains to play for their university. They acquired the nickname "tramp" from students because they bummed around from one campus to another, offering their services to the highest bidder. The best known real-life story about these early recruiting practices concerns one James Hogan, who was attracted to New Haven to play for the old Blues, beginning his career as a college athlete at the ripe old age of twenty-seven. As an inducement to come to Yale, he received a ten-day holiday in Cuba, then moved into the most luxurious dorm on campus, took his meals at the University Club, and received a $100 scholarship, free tuition, and a monopoly on the sale of game programs. He was also appointed an agent of the American Tobacco Company, receiving a commission on every package of the company's cigarettes sold in New Haven. Facts of Hogan's "scholarship" can be documented, but the facts needn't interest us here.[2] What's important is that stories (with all kinds of imaginative embellishments) soon circulated about Hogan's recruitment, and the details of Hogan's deal at Yale soon inspired other tramp athletes on other campuses and set a market price for star players. These stories gained credence because of the extremely loose eligibility rules that permitted even graduate students and younger faculty to join the varsity. Although immediate efforts were made to prevent all but undergraduates from joining the team, nonstudent tramp athletes occasionally appeared on campus well into the twentieth century. Consequently the lore about them flourished—particularly that which concerned their outlandish recruiting tactics—until the dumb-jock type emerges in the 1920s.

The characteristics of the dumb jock reveal several differences from the tramp athlete. As a regularly enrolled full-time student of the university, he was expected not only to attend classes but to pass his courses. If he fell behind or came down with a failing average, he was immediately ineligible for sports. By this time, the eligibility and participation rules had become more systematized, and the faculty saw to it that these regulations were enforced. Finally, the tales and the portraits of the dumb jocks as they first appeared in literature and in the movies demonstrate that these athletes were fully integrated into the student life of the university; unlike the tramps, the dumb jocks did not form a group apart. A typical early tale concerns the player who has failed a French test and consequently cannot play in the big game unless he passes his teacher's makeup test: "I'm going to read you five questions in English," she says. "They will be *yes* or *no* questions, but you must answer them in French to show me that you have gained something from this course."

The French teacher begins: "Is the new coach tougher than the old one?"

"Oui."

"Did you start in last week's game?"

"Oui."

"Will you start in the next game?"

"Oui."

"Will the home team win?"

"Oui."

"Will you place a $5 bet for me?"

"Oui."

The teacher then concludes, "Your French was good in each answer, and you made no mistakes, so I will give you a passing grade."[3]

The context of dumb-jock stories prior to World War II has several features: (1) The athlete is enrolled in genuine classes leading to a degree. (The classes that cause him trouble are the same ones that often cause trouble for other students as well: usually chemistry, foreign languages, and math.) (2) The pressure on the professor to retest the athlete comes from the students and, as in numerous cases, the alumni. (The coach and his assistant are not yet involved in seeking a second chance for the player.) (3) Finally, we learn in these stories that the teller believes that the player is indeed a dumb jock who could not pass the normal exam. The teller also understands that the player must pass some kind of test or he will not play in the next game. As the next story reveals, the player who fails may be not only ineligible in an upcoming game, he may also flunk out of the university completely.

The story: Three pro football players were talking about why they had left college. "I was a senior at Cornell," said the first, "but I wasn't grounded in calculus, so I didn't have the slightest idea what the professor was talking about."

The second said, "Trigonometry did me in. Ran me right out of Kansas State in my junior year."

The third player, late of Alabama, stared moodily into space.

Suddenly he spoke, "Say, did you guys ever run into a thing called long division?"[4]

After World War II and the tremendous expansion of university enrollments as a result of the opportunities provided through the G.I. Bill, there was a concomitant expansion of college athletic programs. As a result, the dumb-jock stories took new twists. The coach now became prominent in the stories, usually trying to pressure faculty to assist his prize athlete, and often revealing that he was only slightly less ignorant than his player. Also after World War II, recruiting stories begin to focus on the coaches' problems in getting athletes admitted to their college in the first place. Here is a variant of the tale we have already discussed.

When Wally Butts coached the Georgia Bulldogs, he had a fullback who just couldn't pass history. Came the week of the big game and the player was declared scholastically ineligible. Butts went to the professor and asked if the boy could take a second examination. The professor said he was giving some others, who were nonathletes, a second exam, so he saw no reason why he shouldn't allow the same for the football player.

So Butts "boned up" the fullback for several nights. The results were pretty discouraging, but the fullback went to the classroom to take the exam anyway. In about an hour, he came rushing out, his face beaming. "Coach, I made 90," he said. Butts was amazed. But before they could leave the building the professor came rushing out of the room. "Wait," he said, "I can't pass that boy. He had the same answers as the student who sat next to him." "Well," said Butts hopefully, "they were the same questions, why not the same answers?" "That's what I thought," replied the instructor, "until I came to the tenth question. The other student had written, 'I do not know the answer.' Your boy wrote, 'I don't know the answer EITHER.'"[5]

This postwar story and other versions of it show several new elements: the prevalence of the coach in arranging the makeup test, prepping his player, and taking him to the exam. The fact that this is not an easy special test means that the player must resort to cheating but still fails because of his basic stupidity. The changed campus environment and the changed substitution rules provoked Yale coach Herman Hickman to comment that he would like to see three-platoon football, "one to play on offense, one to play on defense, and one to go to class."[6]

Another dumb-jock story of this time concerns college admission examinations: The coach was trying to coax a gigantic but peanut-brained fullback through a special oral entrance exam. But the prospect responded to each question with nothing but a shrug of the shoulders. Finally one professor asked, "How much is three plus three, young man?"

When the prospect answered, "Eight," the coach jumped in to try and save the situation. "Wait a minute," he said to the professors. "Please don't be tough with the poor guy. Can't you see he's nervous? After all he only missed the right answer by one."[7]

The situation of a coach unwittingly demonstrating his own ignorance may be the result of all the inexperienced men who became coaches after the Second World War, a great many of whose own college experience had been limited to little more than playing football. Also we note a shift in this tale from trying to keep the player in school to trying to get him admitted to school in the first place, a type of story that becomes more and more apparent in these years. Another variant is often told about Herman Hickman:

Some of Hickman's Tennessee friends came by his office at Yale and brought a big tackle with them. "I could see immediately that he was going to have trouble getting into Yale," said Herman. "So partly to show off to my friends, I said, 'How is his Greek?' and they shot back, 'He *is* Greek, it's his English that we're worried about.' "[8]

Other tales of the dumb jock explain how coaches separated the players into positions. Knute Rockne took his players out to a wooded field and told them to run from one side to the other. Those players who dodged the trees became backs; those who ran straight ahead into the trees became linemen. Dana X. Bible, who coached Nebraska before going on to establish a national reputation at Texas A & M, said he used the following method: "If a player was big and dumb, he played the line." "What about the backfield?" someone asked. Bible responded, "they don't have to be big."[9]

By the 1950s, the dumb jock was overshadowed by the student-athlete, as this type is now officially known to athletic administrators, booster clubs, and the NCAA hierarchy. The shift in emphasis during this time results from three factors: unlimited substitution that resulted in a doubling, then a tripling, and even a quadrupling of the number of players on football teams; the development of professional football so that players aspired to play on a pro team for a living rather than obtaining some other career training in college; and finally, the superior football skills of almost all the players. College athletes had become specialists in football—or basketball, or baseball—with diminishing numbers of regular students, who, as walk-ons, could make the varsity team, let alone become stars on the squad. After World War II, the student-athlete became a physically talented, socially mobile celebrity whose career aims had little to do with a college education. Naturally the folk tales about him changed as well.

The most common tales of the student-athlete are those about recruiting immigrant or farm boys to the college campus to play football and maybe pick up an education along the way. The recruiting experience gives many prospects their first inkling of a way to escape the drudgery of the mines, farms, or ghettos. A joke that made the rounds some years ago pokes fun at two immigrant factory hands and their limited vision of football, education, and mobility. In this version, the two are talking:

"Hey Stosh, my oldest boy is going to college. I guess they can't call us stupid Polacks anymore."
"That's great, Chester. What college is he going to?"
"Marquette!"
"Oh, Great! What Marquette is that? The A & P Marquette over on Main Street or the National Marquette on Grove Street?"[10]

This ethnic joke, however short its view of social mobility, reveals something about workingmen who know that college can make life better. The knowledge that football offered a way to fill the cupboard attracted players to college, while college recruiters used this lure to pull them up from the mines and in from the prairies. Many sons of immigrants have played the game, and many sons of the poor have strapped on shoulder pads. Both possess a drive that comes from having known poverty, and since World War II there have been very few rich kids who have made it big in sports. Dick Butkus had a simple enough explanation for football: " . . . football's too rough if you don't really want it. Maybe those rich kids have a different sort of competitive mechanism. They don't need material success."[11] Immigrants, country boys, and ghetto kids recognized that playing football has shorter hours than farms and fewer injuries than steel mills and hardrock mines. In short, football offered a way to a better life.

The fans of college football covered their insecurities about the arrival of these new groups in large numbers after World War II by telling ethnic and racial jokes. Several immigrant groups and blacks had already arrived on campus (except in the South) before 1945 but never in the overwhelming numbers that now appeared to engulf the traditional student body of well-to-do, white young men. Stories such as the following about a football game played between the Poles and the Italians served to allay anxiety over loss of status: "The Poles and the Italians played to a scoreless tie through the middle of the fourth quarter, when a factory whistle blew, and the Poles and the referee thought it was the end of the game and ran off the field. So the Italians finally scored . . . ten plays later." This same story is told about a game between the University of Texas and Texas A & M. After the Longhorns and the referee leave the field, the Aggies manage a touchdown after only five plays, perhaps suggesting that an education at College Station does have some reward.[12]

Another example of the ethnic jokes that appeared at this time concerns the recruitment of a Czech player by an Ohio State coach who brought him to campus for his physical examination. The Czech kid "was asked if he could read the bottom line of the eye chart. 'Read it?,' he said, 'I played with *him*.' "[13] Despite ethnic jokes such as these, most stories focus on college recruiting, rather than on the college recruits themselves.

The most common recruiting tale describes the technique used by coaches who drive the back roads looking for prospects. Knute Rockne claimed that when he recruited in the Pennsylvania coal region he would "ask the farm boys how far it is to the next town. If he points with his finger I drive on. If he picks up the plough with one hand and points it, I sign him up." This story has been told many times, perhaps most often about Bronko Nagurski. Bronko's coach, Don Spears, told it this way: "I was driving past a farm, up in the woods along the Rainy River which separates Minnesota from Canada, when I noticed this big, strong farm boy, plowing a field . . . without a horse, just pushing the plow. I stopped to ask directions. The boy pointed . . . with the plow." Of course, Spears then recruited him. James Michener claims the same tale for Pennsylvania, saying fans swear that Chuck Bednarik had "picked up a plough in each hand to give directions."[14]

From the turn-of-the-century tramp athletes to the modern-day student-athletes, the recruitment of football players has remained a major concern of the university administration. And it has spawned many stories about what star players are offered or what they might receive for their services. The National Collegiate Athletic Association attempts to prevent the abuses or punish the colleges it cannot stop, making the recruiting scandal, as Michael Roberts says, "as trite a tradition as the pep-rally bonfire on campus."[15]

In fact, stories of payoffs and gifts swirl around all the great players. Take Hugh McElhenny, a southern California prep sensation. Unable to decide on a four-year school, Hugh enrolled in Compton Junior College where he had a remarkable freshman season. Just before the Compton Relays in which he was expected to star as a sprinter, he left school, married his high school sweetheart and headed for his honeymoon and big-time college football. Newspapermen speculated on his destination. Some said California, some Washington, Michigan, or Indiana. One refused to guess the final destination but said that "the trail, wherever it was going, had been well marked with strategically-placed $20 bills" so Hugh would not lose his way. Gossips whispered about fantastic deals once he arrived in Seattle and began playing with the University of Washington Huskies. McElhenny admitted every rumor. "Ah, yes," he would confess, "they gave me four cars and put $40,000 in my bank account. Four companies promised me lifetime jobs and several gas stations. I found $20 under my pillow everytime I scored."[16]

After World War II, coaches not only had to recruit star players, they also had to bring to campus whole squads to play two-platoon football. Coaches themselves have contributed much to this folklore of recruiting. Nebraska's Tom Osborne said he had heard about one player who had been offered $10,000 in cash. UCLA's Terry Donahue remarked: "I've heard a story of a prospect who reputedly got a total package worth about $30,000 that included land, farm equipment, tractors and livestock. I absolutely refuse to accept the truth of that, but I know an assistant coach who'll stand up and swear that it happened."[17]

These stories about big payoffs either trail off into snickers about the NCAA's ineffectual reaction or end abruptly with quips about the college "pro" who turns professional. The NCAA has an investigative committee and elaborate procedures to suspend teams that violate the recruiting rules. Both provoke sneers. The committee is understaffed, its procedure awkward, and the rules legalistic and impossible to enforce. The NCAA puts schools on probation, usually for the few nit-picking items that the committee has managed to document. Coaches, players, and fans laugh at the high seriousness of the NCAA and its fastidious enforcement of the letter, not the spirit, of the rules. A perfect example comes from Tim Salem, a freshman quarterback at Minnesota, where his father was the coach. "The other day I ran out of money," the younger Salem reported, "so I asked Coach for $5. He told me I'm a player now and the rules don't permit a coach to give a player money."[18] No one should think the coach was kidding.

Most often a session of recruiting stories ends as the teller quips that when the highly recruited star left the campus he became "the only college player in history who had to take a cut in pay to turn pro." Quarterback Frankie Albert supposedly introduced McElhenny to the 49ers with these words. Others have repeated them about everyone from Red Grange to O. J. Simpson.

Recruiting occupies so much of the coach's time that he dreams of the perfect player—talented, intelligent, hardworking, and financially self-sufficient—who recruits himself. Once Herman Hickman thought he received a letter from this perfect recruit:

Dear Coach:
 I have admired you for a long time as a player, coach, and television star, so I would like to come to your wonderful University and play football under your expert tutelage. I scored 6 touchdowns last year from my left halfback position and passed for 10 more. I also intercepted 15 passes while playing safety man on defense. I did all the punting, fieldgoal kicking, and kicking off. My punts averaged 46 yards, but I did miss one extra point (which was partially blocked by a defensive tackle).
 I weigh 200 pounds and run the 100-yard dash in 9.8 seconds on the track team. Of course, I probably can do no better than 10 flat in full football equipment. I played left field on the baseball team and batted .418.
 I rank second in a class of 179 and have an I.Q. of 145. I have taken 4 years of Latin, 4 years of math, and 4 years of science.
 I would like to visit your campus and, of course, pay my own expenses. My father who owns several coal mines in this section would like to send four linemen along to block for me.

Their average weight is 220 pounds, and they are all "A" students. Father said he would take care of all their college expenses.

I know you are a busy man, Coach Hickman, but if you are interested please write me.

Hickman's dream ended when he learned that the letter had been written by a rival coach, Wake Forest University's Peahead Walker.

In another version of the same folktale: a college freshman football player was interviewed by a big university coach. "Yes," said the student, "I can run 100 yards in less than 10 seconds, with full uniform. I block so well that last season four of our opponents had broken legs. As for passing, I can pass about 60 yards on the average—into the wind. As for my grades, I have always been on the dean's list." The coach was impressed. "But son," he said, "every one of us has some weakness or deficiency. What is yours?" "Well," said the candidate, "I am inclined to LIE a little."[19]

Recruiting remains the crucial job of the college coach. He must find talented players, if he expects to win games regularly. Using trick plays and lots of luck, a coach can sometimes spring surprises and grab a few games that his team wasn't supposed to win. But he can't do it consistently. Coaches remind each other about this, not by talking turkey, but by remarking on chicken salad.

A few years ago when Maryland defeated the highly favored Clemson squad using a tricky kickoff-return double-handoff, the Tigers coach, Frank Howard, went into the Terrapins' locker room to offer congratulations. He cautioned the new coach that the next game would not even be close. Repeating some coaching wisdom, he drawled, "It's mighty tough to make chicken salad out of chicken shit two times in a row." Duffy Daugherty made the same connection between finding excellent players and winning. "Everyone knows that recruiting is the name of the game," explained Duffy, "and that you can't make chicken salad out of chicken droppings just as you cannot compete successfully in bigtime football without the blue chip athletes."[20]

Another anecdote that demonstrates the coach's dependence on successful recruiting recalls the time a college president decided to help his coach find some players who could be enticed into transferring to his school. The executive made a national tour. When he returned to his own campus, he called in his coach, and gave him a report:

"How did you make out?" asked the coach.

"Well, I saw one team that went through a 14-game schedule unbeaten, untied and unscored on. The amusing thing about it is that their line averaged 145 pounds, their backfield 135, and they had not a passer or kicker," reported the president.

"Well," said the coach. "I don't suppose you wasted any scholarships on them?"

"No," replied the president, "but I hired their coach as your successor."[21]

The players, when they talk about recruiting, repeat different themes. For many the campus visit is their first trip away from home and the adventure means a great deal to them. They describe the plane trip, the accommodations, and the meals in the exacting detail of a summer traveler showing home movies. They comment extensively on campus social life; the parties they attended, the beers they drank, and the coeds they did or did not seduce.

Several Indiana University players told stories that Pat Nutz has collected and analyzed in "Recruiting Practices of College Football Teams." All of them told stories about the meals, with comments restricted to quantity ("big dinner," "big meal," "ran up a bill of $138 at dinner"), lodging (had to sleep in "a motel," "the athletic dorm," or worse, "the campus dorm"), and opportunities for a good time on campus, especially the drinking ("first thing we did was get some beer," "got drunk with the players every night," "got drunk and at midnight went skiing") and the girls.

"Clowns" and coeds appear in nearly every story. Football humor generally runs to pranks, destruction of property, and fighting. One prospect, for example, described what he considered a great party: "A player took an axe, knocked out the windows, then hit cars and things and got away before the cops came." "Looney Terry," showing a recruit around Tulane and New Orleans, "got into arguments and fights everywhere." The varsity bully, including his adventures in bars and frat houses, often serves as the comic figure in recruiting stories.

Coed flirts appear even more frequently in recruiting tales. These girls use a promising smile to lure recruits to campus. Sometimes they do more than smile, according to the narrator.

One offensive guard told about a visit to an Ohio college campus where he and three other recruits were met by four coeds in a Winnebago camper. The girls entertained them until 4:00 the next morning, promising more Winnebago trips it they decided to play football there.[22]

The most famous coed recruiting tale concerns Joe Namath's visit to Notre Dame. Namath flew to South Bend, visited the coach, and wandered around campus to see the facilities. After his tour, he asked where all the women were. "I nearly had a heart attack," Joe says in his version, "when I found out they didn't have women. They said, 'There's a girls' school just across the lake.' I said, Man, I don't *swim* after my women. I want them, like so they can come up to *my* place. I don't want to talk to them on no pay telephone."[23]

Stories about coeds who promise a roll in the back seat or in bed circulate in every discussion of recruitment and have a permanent place in novels about football. This use of sex to attract football players has been described graphically in Jay Cronley's *Fall Guy,* and confirmed in such exposés as *Meat on the Hoof.* Gary Shaw, the author of the latter volume, recalled his recruiting visit at Rice University. His two player-hosts spent the afternoon discussing where to get him a woman for the night (Shaw gasped at the possibility). At the University of Texas, the recruits were entertained by beautiful coeds, including the University Sweetheart. "Every prospect had three coeds surrounding him," Shaw said of his Austin visit, "and like me, stood goggle-eyed and speechless as they told us how much they wanted us to come to Texas. If you are seventeen and there are three or four beautiful twenty-one-year-old women standing around, telling you to do something, you are apt to do it."[24] These tales about women and recruiting lead to another cycle of stories about the college jocks and sex on campus. One round of these tall stories concerns the "promiscuous cheerleader." Later, when the players join the professional players, they encounter similar stories about "Detroit Shirley" and other camp followers.[25]

The lore of the student-athlete also concerns his trouble with academic work. But now the stories focus on special jock classes, gut or crib courses, ranging from underwater basket-weaving to the study of the unintelligible. Many stories about these special jock courses are repeated over and over on campuses. And recently, reflecting the many abuses that have been uncovered, these remarks have even been extended to stories about falsified records and fixed transcripts so that athletes don't take classes at all. An example of this shows up in the "light bulb cycle."

"How many jocks does it take to change a light bulb at Arizona State?"
"I dunno."
"Only one, *but* eleven get one course credit for it!"[26]

Of course, there are many other features of this kind of folklore. The players have an image of themselves and their game, a special vocabulary, superstitions, slogans, legends, and heroes. The fans and boosters also make up part of the folklore, but these are topics that will be treated more appropriately in another place.[27]

Notes

1. Quoted in Dave Klein, *The Pro Football Mystique* (New York: New American Library, 1978), 200.

2. John Richard Betts, *America's Sporting Heritage, 1850–1950* (Reading, Mass.: Addison-Wesley, 1974), 126–27; John A. Lucas and Ronald A. Smith, *Saga of American Sport* (Philadelphia: Lea and Febiger, 1978), 210–14.

3. Reed Harris, *King Football: The Vulgarization of the American College* (New York: Vanguard Press, 1932), 113–14.

4. Mac Davis, *Great American Sports Humor* (New York: Pocket Books, 1950), 81–82.

5. Harold V. Ratliff, *"I Shook the Hand . . ."* (San Antonio, Tex.: Naylor Co., 1948), 193.

6. Herman Hickman, *The Herman Hickman Reader* (New York: Simon & Schuster, 1953), 39.

7. Scott Anderson, *The Funniest Football Stories of the Century* (Los Angeles: Price, Stern, Sloan, 1979), 13.

8. Hickman, *Reader,* 20–21.

9. Representative examples of these tales can be found in Michael Bonifer and L. G. Weaver, *Out of Bounds: An Anecdotal History of Notre Dame's Football* (Blue Earth, Minn.: Piper Publishing, 1978), 60; Gene Ward and Dick Hyman, *Football Wit & Humor* (New York: Grosset & Dunlap, Tempo Books, 1979), 98; George Ratterman and Robert Deindorfer, *Confessions of a Gypsy Quarterback* (New York: Coward-McCann, 1962), 32.

10. Wells Twombley, *Blanda: Alive and Kicking* (Los Angeles: Nash Publishing, 1971), 274.

11. Dick Butkus and Robert W. Billings, *Stop-Action* (New York: E. P. Dutton & Co., 1972), 92.

12. Mac E. Barricks, "Racial Riddles and the Polack Joke," *Keystone Folklore Quar-*

terly 15, no. 1 (Spring 1970): 11; Jack Keels, "U T Jokes," #47, University of Texas Folklore Archives, Department of Folklore, Austin, Texas.

13. Anderson, *Funniest Football Stories,* 18.

14. John Wiebush, "Bronko Nagurski: The Living Legend," in *More Than a Game,* ed. John Wiebush (Englewood Cliffs, N.J.: Prentice-Hall, 1974), 81–82; Arthur Daley, *Pro Football's Hall of Fame* (New York: Grosset & Dunlap, 1963), 83; James Michener's introduction to Jack McCallum with Chuck Bednarik, *Bednarik: Last of the Sixty-Minute Men* (Englewood Cliffs, N.J.: Prentice-Hall, 1977), ix.

15. Michael Roberts, *Fans! How We Go Crazy over Sports* (Washington, D.C.: New Republic Book Co. 1976), 39.

16. Jim Scott, "Hugh McElhenny: He Always Ran Scared," *Quarterback* 1, no. 10 (July 1970): 52–53.

17. *Raleigh* (N.C.) *Times,* 27 Feb. 1979, 3-C.

18. "They Said It," *Sports Illustrated,* 22 Sept. 1980, 22.

19. Hickman, *Reader,* 10–11; Duffy Daugherty with Dave Diles, *An Autobiography of Duffy Daugherty* (Garden City, N.Y.: Doubleday, 1974), 64–68; Anderson, *Funniest Football,* 3.

20. Klein, *Football Mystique,* 180; Daugherty, *Duffy,* 71.

21. Anderson, *Funniest Football Stories,* 29.

22. Pat Nutz, "Recruiting Practices of College Football Teams," Indiana University Folklore Archive, 77, 129.

23. Martin Ralbovsky, *The Namath Effect* (Englewood Cliffs, N.J.: Prentice-Hall, 1976), 193.

24. *Fall Guy* (New York: New American Library, 1978), 55; *Meat on the Hoof* (New York: St. Martin's Press, 1972), 25, 27–28.

25. Gary Alan Fine and Bruce Nel Johnson, "The Promiscuous Cheerleader: An Adolescent Male Belief Legend," *Western Folklore Quarterly* 39, no. 2 (April 1980): 121–22; Neil Offen discusses "Detroit Shirley" in *God Save the Players!* (Chicago: Playboy Press, 1976).

26. Story told me by Whitaker Alan Powell, Winston-Salem, N.C., 2 Dec. 1980.

27. A forthcoming study of football's lore is my *Locker Rumors: Folklore and Football* (Chicago: Nelson-Hall). Other collections in the University of Texas Folklore Archive suggest possible approaches to this field. These include John Edward Escobedo, "Football Proverbs"; Kathleen L. Stone, "Traditions of Football Games and Their Functions;" Amy Pulver, "Cheerleading Performance as Folklore"; Charles Ballard, "Small Town (Paris, Texas) High School Football as Native Folklore"; Andrew L. Chesson, "21 Athletic Legends"; and Becky Wagstaff, "Superstitions of a Football Coach."

16

Religion and Sports:
Three Muscular Christians in American Literature

ROBERT J. HIGGS

In a 1971 newspaper article, Lester Kinsolving relates the following incident:

> "Your Son is our quarterback and You are our coach,"
> prayed Miami's Catholic Archbishop Coleman F. Carroll,
> while delivering the invocation for the Miami Dolphins–
> Atlanta Falcons football game.
> "We sometimes get blitzed by heavy sorrows or red-dogged
> by Satan," continued the Archbishop. "Teach us to run the
> right patterns in our life so that we will truly make a touch-
> down one day through the heavenly gates, as the angels and
> saints cheer us on from the sidelines."

In reporting this notable invocation, the well-known Catholic reporter sarcastically added: "And when that final gun goes off dear Lord, lead us out of the parking lot of life through the interchange of Purgatory, on the freeway into Heaven, with our fenders undented, our spirits undaunted and our metaphors untangled. Amen."[1]

Increasingly the American public is beseeched to believe that sport, especially football, and religion go hand in hand. In fact, the phenomenon has become so widespread that *Sports Illustrated* recently devoted a three-part series to the subject, and the author, Frank Deford, coined the telling term "sportianity," a "jocks-for-Jesus" movement spearheaded by the FCA (the Fellowship of Christian Athletes) and AIA (Athletes in Action).[2] Sportianity is a Christian myth and largely American, but a look at the arms races around the world indicates that all religions and nations have their athletically muscular adherents. This in fact is the thesis of Thorstein Veblen's theory of the leisure class, according to which sport and religion are two of the four "employments" of a predatory culture, the other two being, not surprisingly, government and warfare.[3]

It is appropriate to refer to Veblen on sports and religion, for no other social philosopher has given more attention to the subject than he. It is not my intention, however, to affirm or refute Veblen's sometimes seemingly simplistic views on this complex and controversial matter. My purpose instead is to contribute to a deeper understanding of the kinship of sports and religion in our society by an examination of three distinct types of muscular Christians in three popular American novels—*The Rector of Justin* (1964) by Louis Auchincloss, *Elmer Gantry* (1928) by Sinclair Lewis, and *Joiner* (1968) by James Whitehead.

The muscular Christian has been a familiar figure in modern literature since the publication of Charles Kingsley's novels in Victorian England, while the theme of the combination of physical strength and moral rectitude dates back to Juvenal's *mens sana in corpore sano* (sound mind in a sound body) and the epic ideal of *sapientia et fortitudo* (strength and wisdom). By the seventh century A.D., the latter had degenerated into a rhetorical commonplace,[4] and later a similar fate befell *mens sana*.[5] Today these ideals remain in the limbo of platitude, *sapientia et fortitudo* surviving only in the comic-book rendering of Captain Marvel's acronymic SHAZAM (*S* for the wisdom of Solomon, *H* for the strength of Hercules, etc.); and *mens sana in corpore sano* existing as practically the sole possession of the Boy Scouts and the national service academies. We know, however, that the synthesis of mind, body, and soul is not a subject to be taken lightly. Arnold Toynbee attributes the breakdown of Greek civilization to the isolation of the intellectual from the social body,[6] and Robert Frost reminds us that the greatest attempt that ever failed was that which tried to express matter in terms of spirit; and spirit, in terms of matter.[7] An attempt at synthesis, then, is, it seems, inevitable, if Robert Frost said so as a poet and Bear Bryant as a coach.

This union of opposites was the informing ideal of Greek education, as it was of English education in the Victorian period and to some degree of American education as well. In his 1869 inaugural address at Harvard College, President Charles William Eliot, almost as if he had Teddy Roosevelt in mind, called for the education of "the aristocracy which excels in manly sports, carries off the honors and prizes of the learned professions, and bears itself with distinction in all fields of intellectual labor and combat; the aristocracy which in peace stands for the public honor and renown, and in war rides first into the murderous thicket."[8]

Frank Prescott, the Rector of Justin in Auchincloss's novel, aptly symbolizes the athletic aristocracy espoused by Harvard's Eliot. A staunch advocate of martial valor, Frank "passionately believed that an age of heroes had died with his father in the red clay of Virginia and that a generation of jackals now gorged itself on the bloated carcass of valor."[9] The young Frank, "the athlete and social leader," is also a Christian, and he uncompromisingly evaluates the character-shaping institutions he attends against the severe standard which the Hellenic-Christian synthesis suggests. At St. Andrews, religion has been shaped by the neglect of the body, so that Frank finds it everything that a school should not be. The headmaster cares only for the souls of his boys and reviles the human body as "an unlovely thing." (54) At Balliol, religion has suffered through neglect of faith, at least as seen in Frank's famous master, Dr. Jowett, in whose plump, soft figure Frank also sees evidence of neglect of the body. Dr. Jowett is "full of alternatives" and believes that "Christianity has been better stated by Plato than by Christ." To Frank, on the other hand, Christ is the supreme position in the Trinity. A knowledge of Plato and the Greeks may be important for the minister and educator-to-be, but Christ would definitely be the keystone of education at Justin Martyr school.

It is necessary to keep in mind that the eponym of the school Frank has made famous had tried to reconcile "the thinking of the Greek philosophers with the doctrines of Christ" (127). Frank, in turn, carries this reconciliation to every aspect of life at Justin, for everything, he feels, is interrelated: "the clean collar, the shined shoe, the hard-played game, the deeply felt prayer" (220).

As doctrinaire as Frank may appear, he should not be taken as a platitudinarian, for he is a complex and convincing character. Because the role of physical strength is decisive in his life, his world view, like that of many of his stripe, cannot be imagined without the playing fields of Justin. Hence clichés lurk just beneath the surface of his ministry, and one student refers to the school as "a red pile of red brick, shrouded in the fog of its headmaster's platitudes" (148). Frank is well aware of the ironic kinship of clichés and ideals, but what he is uncertain about is not idealism, but reality. He would have eagerly rushed first into combat along with his father in the Civil War or with Charley Strong, the Golden Boy of Justin, in World War I had he had the chance. He has, in fact, longed for battle to determine if he were a man, or "real," as he confesses to Charley. He dies, as he predicted, in his sleep, his strength untested by combat, and his recriminations for hating acknowledged. His consolation, if any, comes from the realization that he has helped "a few boys," among them Charley, whom he sought to rescue from the effects of war and the designs of his own daughter Cordelia.

A muscular Christian of another stripe is Elmer Gantry, the archetypal evangelical bounder. Elmer is converted to the cause in college by Judson Roberts, the praying fullback from the University of Chicago, and in the same strong-armed manner of Old Jud, Elmer uses his fists to knock out sinners and sprinkles his sermons with metaphors from the gridiron. He exhorts his listeners to get on "our team," make two yards for the Savior, while he leads them in the "Hallelujah Yell," which he himself wrote:

> Hallelujah, praise God, hal, hal, hal!
> Hallelujah, praise God, hal, hal, hal!
> All together, I feel better,
> Hal, hal, hal,
> For salvation of the nation—
> Aaaaaaaaaaa—men![10]

As Elmer rises in the world, he abandons sport metaphors for more cultivated ones, mainly because he realizes that "if you're to reach the greatest number and not merely satisfy their spiritual needs . . ., you gotta explain great literature to 'em." On one occasion, however, during his visit to London, he resorts again to primitive methods. At this time Elmer considers himself as both a Lancelot and an up-to-date John Wesley, but realizes at the last moment that the English would more than likely prefer another type:

> He was going to say that it was the strong man, the knight in armor, who was most willing to humble himself before God; and to say also that love was the bow on life's dark cloud, and the morning and evening star, both. But in a second of genius he cast it away, and reflected, "No! What they want is a good, pioneering, roughneck American!" And that he was, splendidly. (406)

As late as *Gideon Planish* (1943), Elmer is still going strong, is still a "handsome buck," and still a "fine upstanding type of manly leader."[11] Listed in *Who's Who,* Elmer is thought to be a graduate of Harvard and to come from one of the oldest Massachusetts families. Characteristically, among the many organizations which he either heads or is prominent in are MEB (Modernistic Educational Bureau) and DDD (Dynamos of Democratic Direction). If he lives until 1954 he will, there is no doubt, become active in the Fellowship of Christian Athletes.

While a major influence upon Frank Prescott is St. Justin, Elmer's spiritual ancestors are, in his view anyway, Sir Lancelot and John Wesley. But Elmer shows clearly a much later influence, the Christ of Bruce Barton's *The Man Nobody Knows* (1925), which, says Lewis satirically in *Gideon Planish,* "like *Das Kapital* or Shakespeare or the Koran, [has] inspired a generation and enriched an age." According to Lewis, Barton proved that "Christ Jesus was not a peasant, but a society gent, a real sport, a press agent and the founder of modern business" (179). Barton did nothing less than to make Christ all things to all people, and Elmer Gantry is—whether intended or not—a savage parody of Barton's Jesus. "Athaletics" Jesus would have been in favor of, for Barton in effect says so. Jesus, Barton shows, was a fighter, and so is Elmer. Christ was a businessman, an executive, and so is Elmer, who gets things done and who reassures his fellow bromides that were Christ living he "would be a Rotarian." I am not saying that Barton would have approved of Elmer (who would?), but I do assert that Lewis shows how easy it is for a bounder inspired by the winning philosophy of team sports to be all-round in the same way which, according to Barton, Jesus was. It is no wonder that Lewis called the book an "Epistle to the Babbitts."

A third type of Muscular Christian is Sonny Joiner, titular hero of James Whitehead's remarkable novel with a Southern setting. To Joiner, a six-foot, seven-inch, multi-pound NFL tackle from Mississippi, who is also a strange composite of murderer, grade school teacher, and avid student of history and art, the trouble with ideals is that they are often too harsh and uncompromising, especially when not moderated by sensualism; and "the devil in all the myths" of a better world, he thinks, is Plato. If Plato had had his way, Joiner believes, the world would never have had to put up with Southerners (both Negroes and Whites), Jews, or Mongolians.[12] He also discredits the Greeks because of the way they treated women. Yet when asked to speak before civic clubs, he talks more about classical ideals than about Christ, mainly because if there is anything on earth Joiner abhors it is the public Christian, an attitude which helps explain his demolishment of a pulpit at a Billy Graham crusade in Jackson, Mississippi. Among the many objections Joiner has to proselytizing Christianity is the simplistic alternatives held up to potential converts. In the biggest football stadium in the state Billy Graham, according to Joiner, is telling "the people, nobody in the whole freaking place will be alive in a hundred years, and where *will* you be in a hundred years? In Heaven, Brother? In Hell, Brother, Sister?—waving the floppy red Bible and driving off the rain with his left hand . . ." (196).

Joiner believes in hell, resurrection, and Christ, but not in any conventional or shallow sense. What kind of Christian is he, then? He is, I think, a *secret* Christian, which he obviously could not claim to be but which he says one must be. Unlike Elmer Gantry, Joiner is not a hypocrite, and unlike Frank Prescott he does not have an overriding sense of duty. He acts decisively only in what seems to him extreme situations: when Foots Magee, punched-out ex–Detroit Lion and hopeless segregationist, feels "obleeged" to shoot Negroes, and when Stream, a former teammate and fastidious abstractionist, who gives him such "squirrelly stuff" to read as D. H. Lawrence and Wallace Stevens, chides him about his conduct. Joiner kills Foots, and after he tries to kill Stream remains, it seems, the only character in this novel of the 1960s Southern civil-rights movement who has compassion without any compelling moral obligations, unless it is Sheriff Davis, the only good Southern sheriff perhaps in all of literature.

Where does Sonny Joiner derive his views of the secret Christian? Not in the virtual library of impressive books on history and art that he discusses, but ultimately perhaps from a book not even mentioned. I refer to Dietrich Bonhoeffer's *Letters and Papers from Prison*. I base this argument not only on the use of "secret Christian" in *Joiner* but also on the term *metanoia,* both of which are crucial to Bonhoeffer's last view of the world. Admittedly Joiner mentions *metanoia* in his discussion of Luther, but its thematic importance in the novel cannot be fully appreciated unless looked at in connection with the idea of the *secret* Christian in the manner of Bonhoeffer. He prophesied a day "when men will be called again to utter the word of God with such power as will change the world. . . . Until then the Christian cause will be a silent and hidden affair, but there will be those who pray and do right and wait for God's own time."[13] To be a Christian does not mean to be religious in a particular way, to cultivate some particular form of asceticism . . . but to be a man. It is not some religious act which makes a Christian what he is, but participation of the suffering of God in the life of the world. This is *metanoia*" (22–23).

Nevertheless, Bonhoeffer argued, one must love life and participate fully in it even in the apocalypse, and this Sonny Joiner does, quite unlike the legions of self-pitying absurd heroes in American literature who flee the world rather than involve themselves in it. To many people of Bryan, Mississippi, Sonny Joiner is so involved in the world as to be public nuisance number one, but to the careful reader he will emerge as the opposite—a secret Christian.

Joiner, thus, is a repudiation of public muscular Christianity whether practiced in the manner of a Gantry or a Frank Prescott. Different in intention and aims as these latter two are, the one self-serving, the other God-serving, they nevertheless think of themselves as Christian soldiers in the army of the Lord. Not so with Sonny Joiner. Though a violent individual on the field and at times off, he belongs to a less militant tradition and hence a much more silent one. It is the kind of silent tradition articulated by Walt Whitman in "To Him That Was Crucified," which opens as follows:

> My spirit to yours dear brother,
>> Do not mind because many wounding your name
>> do not understand you,
> I do not sound your name but I understand you. . . .

Sonny Joiner would appreciate this poem, but not Frank Prescott or Elmer Gantry.

In his biography of Martin Luther, Richard Marius writes, "Jesus has become a name we apply to any current ideal of man. In our own century Jesus has been depicted as a soldier sighting down the barrel of a rifle in a World War I poster. He has been a great scoutmaster for the Boy Scouts, and he has been a kindly Rotarian in the minds of business classes. He has been a rather vacuous-looking shepherd in thousands of picture books for city children who have never seen sheep, and he has been a rock singer in several stage productions that have attempted to translate the New Testament into the language of beats and hippies. . . . But all this is to say that we take him no more seriously than we take a billboard along the highway."[14] To the list of the Jesuses Marius mentions I would add these portraits of the three Muscular Christians described herein. While we do not take them seriously either, we are inclined to take seriously the rituals of the playing field in honor of God, country, and physical prowess that have made these three individuals what they are.

Notes

1. Lester Kinsolving, "Exploiting Athletes in Religion Questioned," Johnson City (Tenn.) *Press Chronicle,* 12 January 1971, 10.

2. See the series "Religion in Sport," *Sports Illustrated,* 19, 26 April and 3 May, 1976.

3. See *The Theory of the Leisure Class* (New York: Macmillan Co., 1912), especially p. 21.

4. For a discussion of the ideal of *sapientia et fortitudo,* see Robert E. Kaske, "*Sapientia et Fortitudo* as the Controlling Theme in Beowulf," *Studies in Philology* 55 (July 1958): 423–57: reprinted in *An Anthology of Beowulf Criticism,* ed. Lewis B. Nicholson (South Bend, Ind.,: University of Notre Dame, 1963).

5. Bruce Haley, "The Cult of Manliness in English Literature: A Victorian Controversy, 1857–1880," Ph.D. diss., University of Illinois, 1963, 235. For the controversy over "muscular Christianity" in England, also see Haley, pp. 46–49, 63–86.

6. *A Study of History* (New York: Oxford University Press, 1939), 4:238–39.

7. "Education by Poetry," *Selected Prose* (New York: Collier Books, 1956), 41.

8. Nathan N. Pusey, Introduction, *A Turning Point in Higher Education* (Cambridge, Mass.,: Harvard University Press, 1969), 17. [Ed. note] Respecting participation in athletics during Theodore Roosevelt's day, a personal code of conduct—a badge of

honor, as it were—had begun to express and assert itself among that select group of prep school and college students known as varsity athletes. Because not everyone was skilled enough to participate in varsity athletics, those who did were looked up to as exemplars of the dedicated play and honest, disciplined life-style that others might emulate through observation. With its brand of muscular Christianity, the code of the American athlete was peculiar to school-college athletics, and since its inception, our changing social values may have altered it considerably, but since the 1890s it was always most popularly and influentially expressed in the vast outpouring of boys' sport fiction. Notwithstanding the radical changes in behavior patterns and social values of adolescent boys since that time, this genre continued to adapt to the times that produced it, while expressing the constant ideal of quality performance derived from the Hellenic-Christian synthesis, which, it was thought, contributed to character development through sports involvement.

9. Louis Auchincloss, *The Rector of Justin* (Boston: Houghton Mifflin, 1964), 57. Subsequent references are to this edition.

10. *Elmer Gantry* (New York: Harcourt, Brace, 1927), 197. Subsequent references are to this edition.

11. *Gideon Planish* (New York: Harcourt, Brace, 1943), 374. Subsequent references are to this edition.

12. *Joiner* (New York: Alfred A. Knopf, 1973), 114–15. Subsequent references are to this edition.

13. Dietrich Bonhoeffer, *Letters and Papers From Prison* (New York: Macmillan Co., 1953), 188. Subsequent references are to this edition.

14. Richard Marius, *Luther* (Philadelphia: Lippincott, 1974), 46–47.

17

The Failure of Games in Don DeLillo's *End Zone*

GARY STOROFF

Gary Harkness, the protagonist of Don DeLillo's brilliant but enigmatic novel *End Zone,* desperately searches for a game that will provide his life with significance. Having failed at three other schools, he is given his last chance to succeed at Logos College. Here, Harkness tests alternative games designed to organize his life coherently and finds in each instance that the game fails because he perceives too clearly the contrast between man's contrived portrayal of experience in games and the world as it actually is—irrational, disorderly, and ambiguous. In the novel, games assume a much greater significance than the football contests Gary enjoys. A game becomes for Harkness a device for ordering his life, and he discovers that all men use games for the same purpose: to define and order existence. In the end, the game becomes coextensive with civilization itself.[1]

His first experience with game playing is through his father's idea of success, for his father is a salesman who sees personal worth in terms of sales volume. A former football player himself, Harkness's father envisions his job as an athletic contest, with sports language defining his effort to succeed: "Suck in that gut and go harder."[2] He is a successful and ambitious man who cannot understand his son's perpetual failure, but beyond his father's safely circumscribed business-game world, Gary senses

235

only a spiritual vacancy. In Gary's words, "Beyond these honest latitudes lay nothing but chaos" (14).

Like his father, the people Harkness encounters at Logos College all employ game techniques to order their lives. Another father-figure, Coach Emmett Creed—whose name underscores his religious sense of games—is convinced that only through football can one acquire a clear sense of self and a healthy inner life. He also believes that self-transcendence can be achieved by total commitment to the game; self-sacrifice, pain, and hard work result in victory on the field and off. His motto, "It's only a game, but it's the only game" (12), emphasizes his concentrated vision, a vision he imparts to his team through complicated football plays and the private language describing them. Much like God as he stands in his tower watching the patterns he has created, Creed is worshiped by his team because he has become "famous for creating order out of chaos" (8). Indeed, he even extends his influence well beyond the gridiron, for his rules include such social concerns as being courteous, writing home, dressing neatly, and so forth. Although he demands "the maximal effort" (84), he makes the choices for the team, thus lessening for them the burden of choice.

Because Creed reduces the complexity of experience for Harkness ("When the Coach says hit, we hit. It's so simple." [28]), football does offer a reprieve from chaos and uncertainty. As Harkness points out, "the football player travels in the straightest of all lines . . . , his actions uncomplicated by history, enigma, holocaust or dream" (3). Gary feels "reduced in complexity" (24) because as a halfback he enjoys a clear sense of role, a clearly defined function assigned by Creed, and a private language of plays known only to him and his team—a knowledge that brings a pervasive sense of harmony and order. Because Creed is a source of order, *all* the athletes deeply appreciate his effort to provide a structure for their lives, and thereby forgo the responsibility of choice. One player worries that his beard may disrupt Creed's regulated world, while the team's inept quarterback slavishly depends upon Creed's assurance that he has selected the "correct" play. As the team is losing their most important game, a player assures Harkness that they will "come back," that Creed will win for them in the end. Even losing does not shake their almost religious faith in him.

Yet inevitably, Harkness must step outside the realm of game and enter the "end zone," literally the field beyond the playing area but symbolically the full realization of an imponderable reality. When he makes this step, he realizes that the sense of order and rationality assumed by Creed is illusory; that Creed, like his father, has betrayed him with a game and a language that encloses experience more complex and mysterious than a game will allow. In a lengthy report of a game between Logos and West Centrex Tech, their chief rivals, Logos is defeated in a violent, brutal contest that discloses the irrationality masked by the game's rational and orderly rules. Indeed, Centrex's number 62 actually uses the rules to inflict unnecessary pain, thereby suggesting a return to primordial chaos and disorder. At the end of the game, one of the Logos players, Jessup, gives up all pretense of civilized game-playing when he fights with 62. The game with Centrex is doubly ironic because it is so crucial: Although the Logos team has done extremely well that season, the Centrex victory makes their previous triumphs meaningless.

Through DeLillo's description of the game, the two football teams acquire symbolic significance. While Logos College is a liberal arts school, its opponent is named "West Centrex Biotechnical Institute," and the victory of the technical college over Logos suggests the ascendency of technology over liberal humanist faith in our contemporary culture. Pitted against technology, human limitations seem discouragingly immediate. The players of Centrex Tech are even comparable to machines due to their metallic, silver-and-red uniforms and their well-executed plays. After several Logos players are severely injured during the game, the Centrex team seems more inhumanly invincible. Onan Moley notes that Centrex is "the kind of team that gets stronger and stronger. . . . They'll just keep coming" (100), and the Logos team is utterly exhausted by half-time. The Centrex players are identified only by numbers, except for the quarterback Telcon, whose name implies his computerlike function. Even though Logos plays uninspired and disappointing football, their mistakes and injuries remind us of their essential humanity as opposed to Centrex's mechanical perfection. Also, the Logos colors emphasize the connection of the team with natural life itself. As Bing says, "Our uniforms are green and white. . . . The field itself is green and white—grass and chalk markings. We melt into our environment. We are doubled in the primitive mirror" (112).

This "melting" Bing refers to is repeated with ironic implications in a second football game played later, one clearly intended to parody the Centrex-Logos humiliation. The Logos team spontaneously begins playing in a snow storm and finally becomes almost lost in the snow. As the teams play, they add more and more rules, making the game more predictable and less specialized while denying life's irregular and conditional nature. For these players, even conventional football regulations and rules make life too chaotic. When the game finally ends, their rigid rules permit only one tactic—running the ball. Ironically, however, they have become a static group indistinguishable from one another in the storm. Associated with the snow, the players exemplify the unifying force of death through their deification of order, regularity, and predictability at the expense of life's unpredictable and impulsive nature.

Harkness seeks refuge in football, then, but ultimately discovers that the game cannot prevent the encroachment of the irrational reality he flees. As Bing points out, football paradoxically "harks back" to the primeval. Despite football's intricate player structure and complex rules and plays, its violence recalls an uncivilized era when no games were played. Although Gary says, "My life meant nothing without football" (18), ultimately he must confront the futility of evading the absurd through games. Indeed, the very shape of a football—unlike the round tennis ball, baseball, or basketball—maximizes chance, for a player cannot possibly anticipate the direction of the bounce. DeLillo concludes that "sport is a benign illusion, the illusion that order is possible" (89), but he has created an ironic novel in which his protagonist penetrates that illusion to the void beneath.

Harkness also tries to find stability from another father-figure, Major Staley, an Air Force ROTC instructor who celebrates modern technology by transforming nuclear war into an elaborate game. "We'll get together with [the enemy] beforehand," Staley assures Harkness, "and there'll be an agreement that if the issue can't be settled . . . we keep our war as relatively humane as possible" (63). In making football analogous to nuclear war, DeLillo is not merely making the facile, popular observation that violent sports are our surrogates for modern war. As "Zap" Zapalac, the professor, says, "I reject the notion of football as warfare. Warfare is warfare. We don't need substitutes because we've got the real thing" (135). Instead, DeLillo communicates a much more profound insight: The nature of civilization demands—even in something so chaotic as war—the regularity, uniformity, and stability that a "game" (however loosely defined) provides. Faced with the utterly unthinkable prospect of nuclear war, our world can do little else than codify and systematize it; transform it into manageable and contained patterns which won't threaten us so much. Finally, we are all runners in the arms race. In the book, Major Staley represents this impulse, and although he is an amusing caricature of the devotee of military technology, he is a frighteningly real element of our modern world.

As such, Harkness is attracted to him, for Staley's game, like Creed's, organizes life with a new language that describes and reduces life's complexity. Like football, war is played according to rules ("we'll use only clean bombs"), complete with game plays using the language of weapons technology ("maximum attack posture," "collateral damage," "x-ray pulse intensity," "interval recognition bombing"). While Creed resembles a god on the football field, Staley believes that "the bombs are a kind of god" (62). Harkness is urged by Staley to join the Air Force "team," "the most self-actualizing branch of the military" (128). In the Air Force as on the gridiron, Harkness would have a specific role and a definite function, and Staley emphasizes that his recruit would also have a unique advantage because of his athletic prowess. Since Harkness would not call his own "plays," choices would be eliminated and guilt would disappear.

But like Creed, Staley ultimately fails to offer a viable game for Harkness. In a lengthy war game Staley plays at the end of the book, the entire world is devastated through "rational and orderly" use of weaponry. The fallacy of Staley's conception of an impersonal and predictable technocratic world order is shattered by a simple instrument of technology: the ringing telephone, which reminds him of his wife and children who would perish in a "rational" war. And in a parody of the technocracy Staley idealizes, Gary's friend Bloomberg imagines the role of "an anguished physicist" who invents "the super-megaroach aerosol bomb" (176). The consequence of Staley's impersonal game theory is revealed by Bloomberg's tongue-in-cheek nihilism: "I came to the realization that one terminal bomb more or less makes small difference in this ever-expanding universe of ours" (177). Once again, Harkness is compelled to step from an illusory ordered world into an "end zone" of fragmentation and chaos.

The "language game," the third pervasive game in the novel, is

much more subtle than Creed's or Staley's games, but is nevertheless crucial because all the characters are unconscious players. The notion of DeLillo's "language game" derives from Ludwig Wittgenstein, to whom DeLillo alludes late in the novel. The
allusion is embedded in Gary's last visit to Taft, the "mystical"
football player:

> Poster of Wittgenstein, I thought. Maybe that's what he'd had
> up there, or almost had. Dollar ninety-eight poster of
> philosopher surrounded by Vienna Circle. Two parts to that
> man's work. What is written. What is not written. The man
> himself seemed to favor second part. Perhaps Taft was a stu-
> dent of that part. (192)

DeLillo's allusion is adopted without quotation marks from a
letter Wittgenstein wrote to his publisher Ludwig von Ficker in
1919 in which he comments on his intentions in his book *Tractatus Logico-Philosophicus:*

> The book's point is an ethical one. I once meant to include in
> the preface a sentence which is not in fact there now but which
> I will write out for you here, because it will perhaps be a key
> to the work for you. What I meant to write, then, was this: My
> work consists of two parts: the one presented here plus all that
> I have *not* written. And it is precisely this second part that is
> the important one. My book draws limits to the sphere of the
> ethical from the inside as it were, and I am convinced that this
> is the ONLY *rigorous* way of drawing those limits. In short, I
> believe that where *many* others today are just *gassing,* I have
> managed in my book to put everything firmly into place by
> being silent about it.[3] (Emphasis Wittgenstein's)

Wittgenstein emphasizes in the *Tractatus* the limits of language
and its inability to communicate the nature of the ethical, mystical, and transcendental realm of meanings. In his letter to Ficker, he scorns those metaphysicians who are just "gassing"
about transcendental reality, which to him *does* exist but is inef-
fable and "unthinkable."[4] He therefore cannot write about the
mysical sphere but acknowledges its reality by his silence. Indeed, the last sentence of the *Tractatus*—"What we cannot speak
about we must pass over in silence"[5]—insists upon the existence
of the mystical realm that Taft meditates upon in *End Zone.*
Also, Billy Mast's course in "the untellable" is yet another hid-

den allusion to Wittgenstein's philosophy; both Taft and Mast are trying to find meaning in their lives by embracing Wittgenstein's concept of a unified—but unthinkable and unsayable—Ideal.

Wittgenstein himself abandons this quest for unity in his *Philosophical Investigations,* the book in which he develops his famous theory of "language games."[6] In attempting to explain language's purpose, he argues that language is not a *picture* of reality, nor does it *depict* the world. Instead, there are diverse types or families of language "games"—some describing the world, but others which assert or report or command. There are countless "language games," then, each having its own set of "rules." The conviction that a word actually communicates accurately or completely the "reality" it designates is a delusion. Thus Wittgenstein argues that the meaning of a word depends entirely upon its function and its context (its "game"); it is like a tool with countless uses.[7]

DeLillo ingeniously incorporates Wittgenstein's doctrines into his narrative by having his characters constantly speak at cross-purposes, never noticing that they are indeed speakers in different contexts, players in different language games. For instance, Dennis Smee wonders about the proper role, the "function" of captains on a football team. Billy Mast immediately supplies a precise mathematical definition of the word *function:* "A rule of correspondence between two sets related in value and nature to the extent that there is a unique element in one set assigned to each element in the corresponding set, given the respective value difference" (122). Clearly, neither concept of "function" is the complete or total one. This divergent use of a word occurs many times throughout the novel, as in the football game when Jessup and Gary differ in their use of the word *black:*

> "Fee-uck, man. This game is still on. I get that sixty-two yet. I get his ass and whip it into shape. Damnright. I get that shitpiss sixty-two and beat his black ass into the ground."
> He's white," I said.
> "I know he's white. They're all white. Everybody's white. Those black fucks" (112).

Jessup's racist use of the word *black* differs completely from Gary's racial identification. Jessup's meaning is intimately connected to his actions, particularly his aggressive nature, and to

the racist and profane hazing typical in collegiate and professional sports. DeLillo demonstrates artistically Wittgenstein's
thesis: that the "meaning" of a word is not constant and unyield-
ing but is entirely relative to its purpose in a particular context,
to the multifarious forms of human activity in the world.

The implications of the language game are enormous for Harkness, who wants to abandon appearances in favor of an essential
and basic reality. But he recognizes that since any word can
convey only a *partial* "reality" rather than a totality of experience, man's inadequacy must be as basic as his language: he can
never know "truth." Knowledge must necessarily be fragmen-
tary and incomplete because of the inevitable "failure" of language games themselves. In a deceptively humorous incident,
Gary attempts to "know" a pile of manure he sees in the desert,
but realizes the inability of language to express the object's ontological reality:

> It was overwhelming, a terminal act, nullity in the very word,
> shit, as of dogs squatting near partly eaten bodies, rot repeat-
> ing itself; defecation as of old women in nursing homes fouling
> their beds; feces, as of specimen, sample, analysis, diagnosis,
> bleak assessments of disease in the bowels; dung, as of dry
> straw erupting with microscopic eggs; excrement, as of final
> matter voided, the chemical stink of self discontinued; offal,
> as of butchered animals' intestines slick with shit and blood;
> shit everywhere. . . . (70)

In some contexts, or games, the object is "shit"; in others,
"feces," "dung," "excrement," or "offal"—and each word leads
Gary to the inevitability of death. Even this seemingly simply
defined object becomes enigmatic and unknowable—Harkness
ponders "shit's infinite treachery," "this whisper of inexist-
ence"—for it cannot escape the chaos of the verbal context.
"Perhaps it was easier to die than admit that words could lose
their meaning," Gary says (42); but even at *Logos* College no
one has discovered words adequate to picture a shifting and
impalpable world.

Harkness's dilemma is mirrored by the other characters in the
novel, all of whom formulate games of varying complexity to rid
themselves of a sense of the absurd. Wally Pippich, for example,
uses "a little word-play" (124) to construct a public relations
game which totally falsifies reality. The enthusiastic teacher

"Zap" Zapalac uses "ploys and counterploys" (173) against his students, who are themselves playing games with him when they create an imaginary student named "Robert Reynolds." Myna, Gary's girl friend, wears bizarre costumes and gains weight to avoid "the responsibility of beauty"; presumably, "beauty" would force her to play yet another game not to her liking. Esther and Vera Chalk play a game in which certain words are forbidden. Many of the characters also play games in order to hide from the horror of a sudden, meaningless death. Norgene, for instance, is given his strange first name to ward off bad luck, but we see the futility of his game when he is killed in a tragic car accident. Bloomberg devises a history game—"Who was the greater man?"—to escape history, but is continually reminded of his own horrible past: his mother's murder by a lunatic. Finally, Coach Tom Cook Clark plays the part of a sophisticated, suave, eloquent man who seems to have everything in control—until he kills himself early one morning. Cook's funeral becomes an elaborate game in which the team evades the true meaning of Cook's suicide: The players comment on "how good the embalmed corpse looked" and Creed praises him as "a fine inter-denominational example of all those fortunate enough to have been associated with him" (55). Throughout the book, then, we are made to see the futility of people's games in the face of the absurd.

Indeed, DeLillo's novel itself could be seen as a perverse "antigame," an artistic refutation of the popular, nonserious college football novel.[8] Unlike the teams usually celebrated in this genre, Gary's team not only loses the "big game," it plays sloppy football. No all-American, Gary smokes pot and evades the draft. The mythical football hero on college campuses always dates the Homecoming Queen, but Gary self-consciously selects the heaviest, worst-dressed girl on campus. Football players supposedly take the simplest courses to graduate, but DeLillo's players quote Wittgenstein, argue theology, enroll in bizarre "exobiology" courses, and study "the untellable." DeLillo satirizes all the black athletes named after U.S. presidents (e.g., Roosevelt Grier) through sleek and fast "Taft" Robinson—named, presumably, after America's only three-hundred pound president. DeLillo, then, consistently reverses the "rules" of one of the most familiar novelistic forms of popular culture, sport fiction. In so doing, he artistically acknowledges the idea of failed rules that his novel so emphatically inculcates.

But the character who finally convinces Harkness of the futility of games is Taft Robinson, the extraordinary fullback who renounces football. Renowned for his speed, Taft opts for "stasis" and silence as he retreats to a solipsistic world of the "smoky languid dream" (192). Although Taft has been enticed to enroll at Logos College because Creed told him that football would lead to self-transcendence, to passing limits of "mind and body" (195), Taft chooses a mystic existence where the only reality is his own thoughts and perceptions. Inexplicably, he escapes from all game playing and merely sits alone in his room meditating, silent and still. Unable to accept such a solution for himself, Gary desperately tells Taft, "There must be something we can do" (199). But he finally accepts that there is no game, no rules, which will impose absolute order and confer unambiguous meaning. With this realization, he stops playing games too. But more than this—he stops eating and drinking. For in the "end zone," to refuse to play the game is to welcome death.

Despite its comic tone, DeLillo's novel veers perilously close to a tragic vision, a sense that even if essential "truth" were accessible, it would be too painful to bear. *End Zone* does not allow us our comfortable conception of a game as frivolous play, inconsequential and profitless, set against a background of the stable, coherent, and meaningful though mundane "reality" of our everyday world. Instead, DeLillo makes us see that the fundamental character of civilization is the game: that we are continually caught up in playing with appearances of our own making—appearances designed to conceal our own metaphysical barrenness. In the "end zone" which we all inhabit, DeLillo makes us see that our games are at best evasions, unconscious methods of escaping the void, but that for the truly thoughtful person these strategies must inevitably fail.

Notes

1. This essay was influenced by the concept of games discussed in Johan Huizinga's ground-breaking book *Homo Ludens: A Study of the Play Element in Culture* (London: Temple Smith, 1970). However, Huizinga's definition of "game" limits it to an activity "standing quite consciously outside of 'ordinary' life" proceeding "within its own proper boundaries of time and space according to fixed rules . . ." (32). As I argue in my paper, DeLillo makes no such qualifications. Also, I am greatly indebted to Jacques Ehrmann's essay "*Homo Ludens* Revisited," *Yale French Studies* 41 (1968): 31–57; cf. " . . . play in the fullest sense is coextensive with culture" (44).

2. Don DeLillo, *End Zone* (New York: Simon & Schuster, 1973), 13. All quotations are from this edition, with pagination noted in the text.

3. *Letters from Ludwig Wittgenstein, With a Memoir,* Paul Engelmann, ed. (New York: Horizon Press, 1968), 143.

4. *Tractatus Logico-Philosophicus,* trans. D. F. Pears and B. F. McGuinness (New York: Humanities Press, 1961), 53.

5. Ibid., 151.

6. Perhaps *End Zone* itself was inspired by Wittgenstein's injunction in *Philosophical Investigations,* trans. G. E. M. Anscombe (New York: Macmillan Co., 1953):

> Consider for example the proceedings that we call "games." I mean board-games, card-games, ball-games, Olympic games, and so on. What is common to them all?— Don't say: "There *must* be something common, or they would not be called 'games' "—but *look and see* whether there is anything common to all.—For if you look at them you will not see something that is common to *all,* but similarities, relation- ships, and a whole series of them at that. To repeat: don't think, but look! (No. 66, p. 31e, emphasis Wittgenstein's)

7. Ibid., no. 11, p. 6e.

8. DeLillo published part of this novel in *Sports Illustrated,* a fact that demonstrates his wry sense of humor.

18

The Black Literary Experience in Games and Sports

LLOYD W. BROWN

Quite apart from the usual run of black "jock" autobiographies, there is a significant body of literature by blacks on the importance of games in the black experience. These writers envisage sports as a metaphor of the black experience in the West, especially in the United States and the Caribbean; that is, the games that black people play, either as improvised play activities or as organized professional sports, are allegories of black-white conflicts and symptoms of the impact of such conflicts on black cultures.

In this regard both Langston Hughes and Richard Wright are interested in the improvised play of young blacks attempting to define their relationship with a world that is simultaneously exclusive and culturally influential. In the poem, "Children's Rhymes," Hughes's children base their games on play-songs which they have improvised out of their experience in direct response to an early disillusionment with American society,

> By what sends
> the white kids
> I ain't sent:
> I know I can't
> be President. . . .
> What's written down

> for white folks
> ain't for us a-tall:
> "Liberty And Justice—
> Huh—For All.
> Oop-pop-a-da!
> Skee! Daddle-de-do!
> Be-bop!'

The children's play-song is not only in itself a kind of game which allows them to satirize racism. It is also the parody of another game—the elaborate pretenses of "written down" idealism, an idealism which is tainted by the double standards that make a mockery of the American dream of liberty, justice, and equal opportunities for all. On another level the conflict between the games of black protest and the games of white hypocrisy takes on a self-consciously artistic dimension. The children's play-song and the oral mode on which it is based are linked in the poem with the bebop revolution of jazz in the 1940s. The literary games of black protest are rooted in the rhythms and sounds of oral modes (black music and the distinctive patterns of black play-songs) which are pitted against the literate ("written down") language of the white world. And this contrast between the oral and the literate is integrated with the other contrast—the conflict between the abstract idealism of the (white) literate tradition and the (nonwhite) reality of social injustice.

In Wright's *Native Son,* Bigger Thomas and his friends act out their deep-seated ambivalence toward white society in their favorite pastime—"playing white," a game of "play-acting in which he and his friends imitate the ways and manners of white folks."² Their game is actually a lampooning of three pillars of American society—the military, big business, and politics, with the players acting out the roles of generals, business tycoons, and the president of the United States. In one sense the game is the acting out of frustrations that have been fostered by a pervasive sense of powerlessness. Ridiculing these symbols of American power temporarily relieves the players' sense of impotence. At the same time this tactic underscores, by way of caricature and calculated stereotype, the heartlessness of an oppressive and exclusive social system. Moreover, both as collective therapy and as satiric comment, games of this kind provide Bigger Thomas with the temporary means of expressing those resentments upon which he does not wish to elaborate consciously—at least not in the first stages of the narrative. Significantly, when the game of "playing white" comes to an end these resentments explode into view for a brief moment when Bigger exclaims angrily on the injustice of being barred, as a black, from outstanding achievements in the white world.

But in another sense the game allows the players to experience white power, albeit vicariously and momentarily. And in this regard it reflects a yearning to be fully accepted members of the culture which excludes them—the kind of yearning which they express just before the game itself when Bigger and Gus envy white men for being able to do anything, including the flying of airplanes. In turn that combination of fascination and hatred with which Bigger views white America is duplicated in the game which the white majority culture plays at his expense. This is a far deadlier game, in which Bigger is arrested for murder and which transforms the judicial process into an elaborate form of play-acting, designed to culminate in a predetermined result. But in this game, too, the players are both repelled (in this instance by Bigger's racial identity) and fascinated (in this case by the sexual presence of another black stud accused of raping and murdering another white woman).

Sonia Sanchez's poem "On Watching a World Series Game" is quite explicit in linking white racism, as an elaborate and destructive game, with organized professional sports. The poem is apparently based on the 1967 World Series featuring the duel between St. Louis's black pitcher Bob Gibson and Boston's white superstar Carl Yastrzemski. It is also written from the viewpoint of the white spectator who bemoans the passing of baseball as a white man's game and yearns for a Great White Hope—in the form of a batter. Yastrzemski strikes out, as we may judge from the anti-Polish refrain that accompanies his appearance:

> Carl YASTRZEMSKI
> yastruski, YASTROOSKI.
> ya-fuck-it.

Sanchez's point is enforced by the poem's rhetorical structure: that is, the parallels between the racist's rhetoric and the rhythms of pitcher versus hitter offer an enlarged picture of racism as a game that is so pervasive and ingrained that it intrudes upon all aspects of society, manifesting itself not only as antiblack prejudice but also in ethnic slurs among whites themselves. Or, as Sanchez observes in summing up this complex of racial attitudes:

>   it's america's
>   most famous past time
>   and the name
>   of the game
>   ain't baseball.[3]

Baseball, then, is a dramatization of America's cultural myths (the myth of white superiority, for example). And it is an integral part of the society's flawed idealism; hence the poem, like the baseball game itself, opens with the refrains of the national anthem. Accordingly these myths and perverted ideals are drawn together in Sanchez's poem so that they are all a kind of collective ritual, which includes the black player as both participant (striving to make the ideal his reality) and victim (marked, inevitably, for derision and rejection even if he is athletically successful). But of all the major professional sports it is boxing that has dominated the imaginations of most black writers who are at all interested in organized sports as ethnic allegories. The "Battle Royal" episode of Ralph Ellison's *Invisible Man* is typical of a classic racial phenomenon; the violence of racism is internalized by its victims, who brutalize each other out of impotent rage at the white world and out of the need to prove themselves to that world.

The boxing contest between the protagonist and his schoolmates is therefore not simply a game rigged for the benefit of middle-aged white men who derive their peculiar, ethno-sexual pleasures from the spectacle of young blacks battering each other. It is also an example of the manner in which the violence of the whites' racial game is transformed by blacks into a destructively competitive violence among themselves—because of their fear of whites and their self-hating need for white approval.

In the Gordon Parks novel *The Learning Tree,* the young hero, Newt, recognizes these implications in the middle of a boxing match with a fellow black, Marcus, because it is clear that this is all for the benefit of the parasitic white racists—"dirty, white, vicious, grinning animals" about to bet on two "nigger boys" who would try to beat each other's brains out.[4] What Newt recognizes here is something that Ellison's protagonist is a long while in learning; the need to be an achiever in white American terms—that is, the need to realize the socioeconomic promises of the American Dream—victimizes blacks, and in turn they brutalize each other in attempting to realize that dream. The ethos of competitiveness which is so aptly summarized by the brutality of boxing is always an inherently damaging factor in society at large, in so far as it inhibits or damages a fully idealistic sense of community and human brotherhood. It is the more damaging when it involves nonwhites whose racial identity is a given handicap in this broader competition. In this regard the *idea* of the American Dream is not simply a hollow myth. It is also a game of pervasive social implications.

Thus the narrative of *Invisible Man* as a whole is really an extension of the "Battle Royal" episode. The protagonist's experience as the nigger boy who must be kept running is pertinent here. The running metaphor, the boxing match, his grandfather's lifelong tactic of subversively agreeing with the white world's stereotype of blacks—all of these are the games of white dominance and black survival tactics. Similarly, the political battles of the hero's Harlem experiences are further extensions of the Battle Royal; for the machinations of the white political group, the Brotherhood, and the confrontations between the black nationalist Ras and other blacks are all intrinsic to a process in which whites manipulate blacks, who in turn seek to destroy each other.

Clay Goss's play *On Being Hit* weaves these themes into a pathetic study of the promise and failure of the American Dream in the lives of black Americans. Holly, a former title contender, is now an underpaid janitor who is dying of a kidney ailment that began with too many "punches to the midsection." But notwithstanding the memories and the palpable evidence of the sport's violence, Holly still clings to the dream of "making it"—or more precisely, he persists in the assumption that he could have made it had he been given a fair chance at the championship. In Holly's personality, and in the personality of his half-envious, half-incredulous friend, Duncan, the American Dream of justice, equality, and the reward of merit is reduced to the level of mere fantasy. And boxing itself becomes a physical symbol of the psychic violence endured by those who are victimized, simply because of their race, in their pursuit of the American Dream.

Nicolás Guillen, the Cuban poet, extends the ramifications of the American Dream as hoax to the Western Hemisphere at large, especially in light of the United States's historical role in the hemisphere. His "Small Ode to a Black Cuban Boxer" therefore envisages the Cuban boxer as a participant in the American Dream as hoax in so far as he is drawn to the north by the promise of socioeconomic success. But the boxer needs to be reminded, in the metaphors of his trade, that

> . . . the North is hard and cruel.
> The very Broadway
> that like a vein bleeds out
> to scream beside the ring.

And in hemispheric terms, the exploitation of the black Cuban in a brutal sport is not only a metaphor of the black experience, it is also an allegory of America's exploitation of Caribbean resources in general:

> the very Broadway
> that oils its melon-mouth with fear
> before your fists of dynamite
> and stylish patent leather shoes . . .
> is the same Broadway
> that stretches out its snout, its moist enormous tongue,
> to lick and glut upon
> our canefields' vital blood![5]

Edward Brathwaite of Barbados is comparable with Guillen in that he too sees the games and sports of the Caribbean as extensions and internalized forms of the outsider's exploitative interests. Hence in Brathwaite's *Islands,* the poem "Rites" explores the game of cricket both as the West Indian's colonial heritage and as symptom of the West Indian's response to that heritage. The account of a match between a visiting British team and the home side hints at implications that go beyond the game of cricket itself:

> Boy dis is *cricket* . . .
> all de flies that was buzzin' out there
> round de bread carts, could'a hear
> if de empire fart.[6]

More precisely, the dramatic vignette underscores those sociopolitical considerations that are always inherent in the game of cricket. For in a colonial context cricket is never simply a pastime. From the colonizer's point of view it has always been a tool of the colonial process itself, instilling a sense of cultural loyalties among the empire's alien, nonwhite subjects. In this regard it has performed a role that is quite similar to that of the English language itself, the British educational system, or British parliamentary traditions. And from the viewpoint of the colonial, even of the normally quiescent colonial, cricket offers the nonwhite subject an exquisitely pleasant opportunity to beat the white master at his own game. To triumph over the British cricket team is an important racial and anticolonial gesture, even in preindependence times when racial pride and anticolonialism were not the most obtrusive issues in popular West Indian consciousness.

Students of anticolonial literature, especially from the Caribbean, will find these issues familiar. They are similar to the kind of irony which several writers have developed by defining their roles in terms of Shakespeare's Caliban—the "brutish" colonial who turns the language of the colonial master, Prospero, into an effective tool of condemnation and subversion. It is significant in light of this parallel with the Caliban tradition that Brathwaite chooses the folk idiom rather than standard English as his narrative vehicle in this poem. The language of the folk is an adaptation of the colonizer's language while remaining quite distinct by virtue of African survivals and historical Anglo-Caribbean usages. In this poem the idiom vibrates with an assertiveness that implies a kind of subversion of the game itself. Hence the declarative statement, "dis is cricket," suggests an assertive redefinition that wrenches the word "cricket" itself from the colonizer's air of polished gentility to the candid, even boisterous, partisanship of the colonial. And the ebullient mockery of empire ("could'a hear/ if de empire fart") implies a contemptuous, even rebellious, perspective.

While Guillen and Brathwaite describe the interaction between the Caribbean and the outsider, Michael Anthony of Trinidad concentrates on telltale contradictions within Caribbean society itself. Hence his novel *The Games Were Coming* treat popular games as symbols of Trinidad society. The immediate reference in his title is to a series of games which are to be staged after the annual Trinidad carnival, and which include the bicycle races for which the hero Leon is preparing with fanatical devotion. In one sense what Anthony calls the "chaos" of carnival is a celebration of life itself; but in another, concurrent sense it represents a certain uneasiness on Anthony's part with a lack of discipline in the society as a whole, the kind of discipline that young Leon exemplifies.

However, as an exuberant celebration of life, carnival is the antithesis of that disciplined competitiveness which is the essence of the athletic games and which, however desirable for an orderly, creative society, can become inhuman and mechanical (as it does in Leon's personality) when it is too far removed from the needs and the passionate humanity that are represented by the carnival spirit. And by extension, this is the kind of ambiguity that surrounds the games themselves. They are, ideally, a kind of celebration while exemplifying a desirable sense of order. In this context Anthony's perception of the games is intricately bound up with his responses to West Indian society as a whole. The society's vibrancy reflects a stubborn reluctance to be destroyed by all those factors that link West Indian history with black history in general—slavery, colonialism, racism, and poverty. But at the same time, these historical ills have taken their toll, fostering a perpetual sense of disorganization, a certain disorderliness that is at once beguilingly vital and depressingly self-destructive. And the self-destructiveness of the West Indian character is emphasized in the novel by one of the more negative aspects of carnival itself; in one sense carnival is really an elaborate game of sorts, played for the benefit of commercial interests that profit from the carnival—at the expense of its unheeding participants.

At this point the idea of games in Anthony's work is both uniquely regional, in Trinidad terms, and broadly cultural in its significance. And in the latter sense the idea of games or sport provides a broad symbolic background for the exploration of black history in the West as a whole.

Notes

1. Langston Hughes, *Selected Poems of Langston Hughes* (New York: Knopf, 1971), 223–24.

2. Richard Wright, *Native Son,* Perennial Classic ed. (New York: Harper & Row, 1966), 21.

3. Sonia Sanchez, *We a BaddDDD People* (Detroit, Mich.: Broadside Press, 1970), 36.

4. Gordon Parks, *The Learning Tree,* Fawcett Crest ed. (New York: Fawcett, 1963), 131–32.

5. Nicolás Guillen, *Man-Making Words: Selected Poems of Nicolás Guillen,* trans. Robert Márquez and David Arthur McMurray (Amherst: University of Massachusetts Press, 1972), 53–54.

6. Edward Brathwaite, *Islands* (London: Oxford University Press, 1969), 45.

PART IV
The Academic Analysis

What all of these writers [about sport] and their sponsors . . . have failed to perceive is that some departments of human endeavor cannot be studied empirically or otherwise examined academically.

—George Core,
"The Lower Mythology and
the Higher Clichés" (1979)

If the Twenties were the Golden Age of Sports, then perhaps the Seventies will come to be known as the golden age of sports studies. Clearly, the serious examination of sports has become academically legitimate.

—David L. Vanderwerken,
"The Joy of Sports Books:
A Tout Sheet" (1979)

Issues and Contentions

Actually, each section in this collection has drawn outstanding examples of academic analysis from the burgeoning field of sport studies, as, for example, the selections by Jeffrey H. Goldstein and Christian K. Messenger, which relate respectively to sport's individualized experience and its literary interpretation. More representatively, Gregory S. Sojka's introductory piece to this section ("Sport Culture Studies: The State of the Discipline") presents a comprehensive overview of the high level of academic achievement in recent years. This essay particularly reacts to what Sojka refers to as the "sophomoric treatment athletics have received for too many years" by educators. He goes on to cite the wide diversity of academic studies (as well as works of a more popular stripe) which have "shifted from predominantly physiological studies penned by health educators" to in-depth analyses of a psychological, sociological, philosophical, historical, and literary bent.

Nonetheless, the scoffers persist who, for various reasons, contend that sports and scholarship do not mix. In "The Lower Mythologies and the Higher Clichés," reprinted here, George Core observes that the academic mind is given to strange contortions of language and farfetched interpretations when it attempts to venture into a field that he disdainfully concludes would be better off left to those who invented it—the sports writers themselves. In a sense, Core appears to be echoing the sentiments of Paul Hoch *(Rip Off the Big Game),* which assert that academicians, especially those in the disciplines of physical education and sociology, have erred in interpreting sports wholly in terms of their own areas of specialization, contributing unwittingly to what Hoch calls "the stilted irrelevancies of the academic approach."

257

Yet, while Core's purist outlook disparages the efforts of the trained scholar who would attempt to supplant the role of the sports journalist and produce books in the "pop" culture vein, David L. Vanderwerken's rebuttal ("The Joy of Sports Books: A Tout Sheet") waxes enthusiastic over these selfsame efforts to explore and comprehend the complexities of sport, whether from a sociological, literary, historical, or even philosophical point of view, concluding that we are the richer for what has been accomplished in this growing field. Despite the points in Core's argument we might agree with, the fact remains that in recent years, as Vanderwerken contends, academic people who have turned to the field of sport studies have produced a remarkable array of influential and stimulating works dealing with the nature of American sports.

To exemplify the efforts of academicians in the classroom in recent times, Kendall Blanchard's exposition of how the anthropological study of sport has come of age, along with his objectives for researching and teaching it ("Sport Studies and the Anthropological Curriculum"), is highlighted here. Surely, some of the most seminal and influential studies about the nature of play, games, and sport have been produced by anthropologists; and while the psychological, sociological, and literary study of sport may have become increasingly legitimate, these fields admit a great debt to the theories and findings advanced by anthropology. In tracing the slow acceptance of the study of sport by his fellow academicians, Blanchard singles out the prejudices and scholarly taboos which have had to be overcome not only by the teacher of anthropology but by those in other fields as well. Thus, his conclusion that the anthropological study of sport has "great practical, theoretical, and instructional potential" is equally applicable to other disciplinary approaches as the plethora of college courses which have been springing up across the nation attest.

The future of researching and teaching sport-oriented subject matter is indeed bright, and the interdisciplinary dialogue generated by such gatherings as the Conference on Sport and Society held annually at Clemson University is further evidence of a growing awareness of the humanistic implications of sport as they are being perceived by both the education and the athletic establishments. It is the provocative interaction of these two factions which is at the very heart of this unique conference series, promising ever new and challenging insights into the humanistic approach to sport through academic study.

19

Sport Culture Studies: The State of the Discipline

GREGORY S. SOJKA

According to a recent Humanities Commission report, humanists "tell us about ourselves, stretch our imagination, and enrich our experience." They provide a "record" of how people "have tried to make moral, spiritual, and intellectual sense of a world in which irrationality, despair, loneliness, and death are as conspicuous as birth, friendship, hope, and reason."[1] No contemporary academic area of investigation provides a greater opportunity for scholars to reveal a "mirror" or "reflection" of America, it would seem, than sport culture studies in which researchers from various disciplines have begun to demonstrate just how the "SportsWorld" encompasses a microcosm of values, attitudes, and beliefs.[2]

Scholars seemingly circumscribed by a lack of training in sport studies per se or a scholarly specialization in a compatible arena should not be hesitant to embark on innovative research in this area. If academics had forever been shackled by narrow disciplinary constraints, such fields as economics, sociology, political science, and anthropology, to name a few, surely would not exist today. Similarly, they should ignore outcries from traditionalists, who—like their academic predecessors of the Middle Ages who were convinced the earth was the center of the universe—see unorthodox inquiry as heresy. Skilled and thorough researchers must clear the hurdles of academic orthodoxy to articulate crucial issues which otherwise would be pondered primarily by talk-show hosts, television commentators, and armchair or barstool quarterbacks.

The career of the University of Maryland English professor and Washington sports columnist Neil Isaacs provides an example for all future sport scholars willing to follow the path from traditional academic studies to innovative sport scholarship.[3] Unless dedicated scholars pursue sport study, we may have to read the same sophomoric treatment athletics have received for too many years. In fact, serious, detailed research by committed scholars will be necessary to stanch the inevitable "trivialization" of this area by dilettantes and dabblers in statistical sports minutiae and other shallow "cultureless" pursuits.

Until about fifteen years ago, most academic treatments were physiological and health-related research reports conducted by physical educators. Biographies and autobiographies were written (or ghostwritten) by sports journalists. The interest in physical fitness and hygiene, greatly stimulated by twentieth-century sociopolitical developments, ultimately resulted in mandatory physical education classes within the public education curriculum.[4] Most sports biographies, on the other hand, reflected a belief in the character-building values of athletic participation. Athletes, invariably depicted through exemplary lives, served as "moral" leaders from whom youngsters could learn traditional values of hard work, sportsmanship, and being rewarded for a job well done.[5]

The turbulent decade of the 1960s, however, with its anti-establishment emotional and intellectual thrust, greatly changed the manner in which Americans perceived their heroes, whether attired in three-piece suits or shoulder pads and helmet. Hitherto praised by writers, athletic role models were suddenly transformed into individuals victimized by a materialistic system hardly different from that of the business world. *Sports Illustrated,* in a 1968 series of articles dealing with exploited black athletes within the American athletic establishment, termed them "paid gladiators" and offered substantial evidence that greed and racism polluted intercollegiate athletics.[6] A number of behind-the-scenes autobiographies by athletes followed: Dave Meggyesy's *Out of Their League* (1970), Curt Flood's *The Way It Is* (1970), Bernie Parrish's *They Call It a Game* (1971), Chip Oliver's *High for the Game* (1971), Johnny Sample's *Confessions of a Dirty Ballplayer* (1970), Gary Shaw's *Meat on the Hoof* (1973), Lance Rentzel's *When All the Laughter Died in*

Sorrow (1972), and Jim Bouton's *Ball Four* (1971), which confessed that athletes were not paragons of virtue, but in fact persons susceptible to the same maladies—drug addiction, marital problems, moral turpitude, gullibility, latent homosexuality, and a plethora of vocation-related problems—that plague the general public.[7] Sports journalists likewise authored more candid volumes from their insider-perspective of the locker-room. Leonard Shecter's *The Jocks* (1969), David Wolf's *Foul!* (1972), and Jack Scott's *The Athletic Revolution* (1971) portrayed the extremes—both the athletes' greed and their exploitation by equally grasping owners and agents.[8]

Similarly, scholarly emphasis shifted from predominantly physiological studies penned by health educators to sociological, historical, and psychological inquiries by academicians motivated, perhaps, to learn more about the relationship of sport and society due, in large part, to the dominant role of televised sports. A steady flow of books, review-essays, journal articles, special journal issues, conference presentations, and even conferences devoted specifically to sport culture resulted. Paul Hoch's *Rip Off the Big Game* (1972), describes athletes falling victim to monopolistic capitalism.[9] Harry Edwards's *The Revolt of the Black Athlete* (1969) and *The Sociology of Sport* (1973) detailed the threatened black boycott of the 1968 Mexico City Olympics and its effect on his theory of sport in the first extended analyses of minority group behavior in athletic competition.[10] Seminal volumes in traditional academic areas such as philosophy, in Paul Weiss's *Sport: A Philosophical Inquiry* (1969); psychology, in Arnold Beisser's *The Madness in Sports* (1967); history, in Foster Rhea Dulles's *A History of Recreation* (1965); sociology, in George Sage's *Sport and American Society* (1970); and even geography, in John F. Rooney's *A Geography of American Sports* (1974), have also appeared.[11]

The American Historical Association, the American Sociological Association, the American Studies Association, the Modern Language Association, and the Popular and American Culture Associations encouraged thematic presentations as well as entire sport sessions. Since 1981, Clemson University has sponsored annual "Sports and Society" conferences.[12] Other institutions of higher learning such as Pennsylvania State University decided on "Sports in American Culture" as the topic for its 1983 Social Philosophy colloquium.[13] Influential journals such as *National Forum* (Winter 1982), *Journal of Popular Culture* (Fall

1974), *The Annals of the American Academy of Political and Social Science* (September 1979), *Journal of the West* (July 1978), *Journal of Communication* (Summer 1977), and *The Maryland Historian* (Fall 1973) each devoted an entire volume to the sport phenomenon. Individual articles appear regularly in the *Journal of Social History, Journal of Contemporary History, Social Sciences Quarterly, Labor History, Journal of Ethnic History,* and many others.[14] Publications regularly focusing upon sport include: *Journal of the Philosophy of Sport, Journal of Sport Psychology, ARENA, Journal of Sport and Social Issues,* and *Journal of Sport History.* The newest publication in this vein is *Arete: The Journal of Sport Literature.*[15]

The North American Societies for Sport History and Psychology of Sport and Physical Activity, the Philosophic Society for the Study of Sport, the Association for the Anthropological Study of Play, and other professional organizations also provide outlets—conferences, journals, and newsletters—for scholarly symposia and publications.[16] A few research centers such as Herbert T. Juliano's International Sports and Games Research Collection at the University of Notre Dame purposely gather materials to stimulate further investigation by serious scholars.[17] A growing number of courses offered by American universities, particularly in English, history, sociology, psychology, philosophy, and American studies departments, attracts students through eye-catching "sports" titles as well as through relevant, intellectual content. An entire academic graduate program at the University of Massachusetts at Amherst offers both masters and doctoral degrees in "Sport Management and Theory."[18]

As academicians became aware of the slighted area of sport, they began to explore the unique relationship between higher education and intercollegiate athletics, as in J. Robert Evans's *Blowing the Whistle on Intercollegiate Sports* (1974), Edwin H. Cady's *The Big Game* (1978), and John F. Rooney's *The Recruiting Game* (1980), the most controversial but thorough volume on the subject yet to appear.[19] Jay Coakley's *Sport in Society* (1982) is among the most readable of the many sociological sport studies volumes. Unfortunately, the majority of sports sociology books are conceived as texts for departmental majors, and extensive use of academic jargon renders them incomprehensible for more general audiences, who may learn more from a book like James Michener's *Sports in America.* These works nevertheless provide quantitative data and statistical analysis that can be readily utilized by humanists.[20] William Baker and John Carroll have edited a volume of original essays, *Sports in Modern America* (1981), on post–Civil War sports in our society.[21] Three 1981 volumes examining the role of athletics in American literature—Michael Oriard's *Dreaming of Heroes,* Christian K. Messenger's *Sport and the Spirit of Play in American Fiction,* and Robert J. Higgs's *Laurel and Thorn: The Athlete in American Literature*—supplement the ever-increasing number of literary-oriented sport anthologies and readers available for general classroom use.[22]

Works in progress include Charles S. Prebish's juxtaposition of sports and religion and Joan Chandler's analysis of the sport-television symbiosis.[23] The quality of recent publications signals the maturity of sports as a legitimate research area. Allen Guttmann's *From Ritual to Record* (1978), Richard Lipsky's *How We Play the Game* (1981), Steven A. Riess's *Touching Base* (1980), Kendall A. Blanchard's *Mississippi Choctaws at Play* (1982), John Dizikes's *Sportsmen and Gamesmen* (1981), Richard C. Crepeau's *Baseball: America's Diamond Mind* (1981), Benjamin G. Rader's *American Sports* (1983), and Donald J. Mrozek's *Sport and American Mentality* (1983) withstand the most assiduous scholarly tests.[24]

The recent decision by the University of San Francisco to abolish its men's intercollegiate basketball program should prompt original research into the relationship between institutions of higher education and the athletic programs they continue to support.[25] The definitive history of intercollegiate athletics remains to be written. A similar study of the NCAA certainly is a topic worthy of a doctoral dissertation by a serious student of sociocultural history, and would offer weighty counterbalance to the views of university administrators and their athletic directors, who have a real and vested interest in the success and continuance of programs.[26] The current impact of the "moral majority" as a powerful political force should stimulate research into the parallel growth of the Fellowship of Christian Athletes. The association between athletics and religion harkens back to the mainstream of "Muscular Christianity," one of the earliest rationales for mass athletic participation in American history.

Popular culture studies examine the many aspects of society

which, for better or for worse, underpin mass values and attitudes and suggest additional arenas for work. Cartoon strips (*Doonesbury* and *Tank McNamara*), successful films (*Rocky, Raging Bull, Semi-Tough,* and others), along with popular music, clothing styles, and fads could reveal both the economic and entertainment impact which sports have for such a mass-consuming society as the United States. While the relationship of sport and film remains largely virgin territory, Wiley Lee Umphlett devotes a significant amount of space to how Hollywood has treated intercollegiate athletics in *The Movies Go to College* (1984). In a forthcoming book, William Beezley will examine the cultural implications of football folklore. Biographies and autobiographies of athletes continue to flow freely from the pens of sports journalists. Serious comparison of these volumes with the many "rags-to-riches" success stories of popular entertainers, performers, politicians, and other celebrities might reveal much about the nature of hero worship and celebrity status in America. In addition, the *Wall Street Journal* has become a regular source of information concerning the "business" of sports.

Possibly the most inviting, basically unexplored topic ripe for future study remains the relationship between sports and the media, especially, although not exclusively, television. The rapid growth of professional football accompanied by a parallel evolution of television comprises a major cultural event of the twentieth century. Yet, William O. Johnson's *Super Spectator and the Electric Lilliputians* (1971), now over ten years old and dated, remains the sole book-length treatment.[27] Obviously, spectator sports, whether before live or television audiences, have not received the scholarly attention they deserve.

When French physicist J. A. C. Charles launched a hydrogen balloon before fifty thousand Parisians on August 24, 1783, he realized what earlier generations could only fantasize about in the Icarus legend and in Leonardo da Vinci sketches: air flight. "Interesting, but what use is it?" exclaimed one spectator of Charles's launch. "What use is a newborn baby?" replied Benjamin Franklin, who could foresee the practical potential of such a successful experiment.[28] Although in its infancy, sport culture studies promise, with proper nurturing, direction, and encouragement, to mature into a robust, healthy discipline which should make its creators one day proud to reflect positively upon their pioneering efforts.

Notes

1. Committee on the Humanities, *The Humanities in American Life* (Berkeley: University of California Press, 1980), 1.

2. I borrow the term "SportsWorld" from Robert Lipsyte's *SportsWorld: An American Dreamland* (New York: Quadrangle, 1975), 2, where he identifies the negative aspects of sports in our society as "a dangerous and grotesque web of ethics and attitudes." Lipsyte and I are using the paradigm of cultural anthropologists such as Clifford Geertz, who believe that a culture's components, including athletic contests, reflect the society's fundamental characteristics.

3. The following bibliography illustrates Isaacs's progression: *Approaches to the Short Story*, ed. with Louis Leiter (San Francisco: Chandler, 1963); *Tolkien and the Critics*, ed. with Rose A. Zimbardo (South Bend, Ind.: University of Notre Dame Press, 1968); *Structural Principles in Old English Poetry* (Knoxville: University of Tennessee Press, 1968); *Eudora Welty* (Austin, Tex: Steck-Vaughn, 1969); *Fiction into Film: A Walk in the Spring Rain,* with Rachel Maddux and Stirling Silliphant (Knoxville: University of Tennessee Press, 1970); *All The Moves: A History of College Basketball* (Philadelphia: Lippincott, 1975); *Jock Culture, USA* (New York: Norton, 1978); *Sports Illustrated's Basketball,* with Dick Motta (New York: Harper & Row, 1981); *Tolkien Now: Critical Perspectives,* ed. with Rose A. Zimbardo (Lexington: University Press of Kentucky, 1981).

4. This phenomenon is recounted in John A. Lucas and Ronald A. Smith's *Saga of American Sport* (Philadelphia: Lea & Febiger, 1978) and in other social histories of sports such as John R. Betts's *America's Sporting Heritage 1850–1950* (Reading, Pa.: Addison-Wesley, 1974). See also Benjamin G. Rader's *American Sports* (Lincoln: University of Nebraska Press, 1983).

5. See Rudolf K. Hearle, Jr., "The Athlete as 'Moral' Leader: Heroes, Success Themes and Basic Cultural Values in Selected Baseball Autobiographies, 1900–1970," *Journal of Popular Culture* 8 (Fall 1974): 393–401, for an analysis of several of these volumes which act as "cultural stimuli" to the public at large.

6. Jack Olsen, "The Black Athlete: A Shameful Story," *Sports Illustrated* 29 (1 July 1968, 15–27; 8 July 1968, 18–31; 15 July 1968, 28–43; 22 July 1968, 28–41; 29 July 1968, 20–35). The serialized issues were later collected in a separate volume published with the same title by Time-Life Books in 1968.

7. Dave Meggyesy, *Out of Their League* (Berkeley, Calif.: Ramparts, 1970); Curt Flood, *The Way It Is* (New York: Pocket Books, 1972); Bernie Parrish, *They Call It a Game* (New York: New American Library, 1972); Chip Oliver, *High for the Game* (New York: Morrow, 1971); Johnny Sample, *Confessions of a Dirty Ballplayer* (New York: Dial, 1970); Gary Shaw, *Meat on the Hoof* (New York: St. Martin's, 1973); Lance Rentzel, *When All the Laughter Died in Sorrow* (New York: Saturday Review Press, 1972); and Jim Bouton, *Ball Four* (New York: World, 1970.)

8. Leonard Shecter, *The Jocks* (Indianapolis, Ind.: Bobbs-Merrill, 1969); David Wolf, *Foul!* (New York: Holt, Rinehart & Winston, 1972) and Jack Scott, *The Athletic Revolution* (New York: Free Press, 1971).

9. Paul Hoch, *Rip Off the Big Game* (New York: Doubleday, 1972).

10. Harry Edwards, *The Revolt of the Black Athlete* (New York: Free Press, 1969) and *The Sociology of Sport* (Homewood, Ill.: Dorsey Press, 1973).

11. Paul Weiss, *Sport: A Philosophical Inquiry* (Carbondale: Southern Illinois University Press, 1969); Arnold Beisser, *The Madness in Sports* (New York: Appleton-Century-

Crofts, 1967); Foster Rhea Dulles, *A History of Recreation: America Learns to Play* (NY: Appleton-Century-Crofts, 1965); George Sage, *Sport and American Society* (Reading, Mass.: Addison-Wesley, 1970).

12. Contact Professor Joseph Arbena, History Department, Clemson University, Clemson, SC 29631, for information concerning this conference, which is usually held in the spring.

13. Contact Professor Daniel Doran, Health, Physical Education and Recreation Department, Pennsylvania State University, Delaware County Campus, Media, PA 19063.

14. *National Forum* 52 (Winter 1982); *Journal of Popular Culture* 8 (Fall 1974); *Annals of the American Academy of Political and Social Science* 445 (September 1979); *Journal of the West* 17 (July 1978); *Journal of Communication* 27 (Summer 1977) and *Maryland Historian* 4 (Fall 1973). Steven Riess, "Sport and the American Dream: A Review Essay," *Journal of Social History* 14 (Winter 1980): 295–303 is my source for the variety of articles and their diverse locations.

15. *Journal of the Philosophy of Sport,* Human Kinetics Publishers, Box 5076, Champaign, Illinois 61820; *Journal of Sport Psychology,* Human Kinetics Publishers, Box 5076, Champaign, Illinois 61820; *ARENA,* Richard Lapchick, Editor, P.O. Box 518, New York, NY 10025; *Journal of Sport and Social Issues,* James H. Frey, Editor, University of Nevada, Las Vegas, 4505 Parkway, Las Vegas, Nevada 89154; *Journal of Sport History,* Jack W. Berryman, Editor, Hutchinson Hall, DX-10, University of Washington, Seattle, WA 98195; *Arete: The Journal of Sport Literature,* Lyle Olsen, Editor, Department of Physical Education, San Diego State University, San Diego, Calif. 92182.

16. North American Society for Sport History, Betty Spears, President, Department of Sport Studies, Curry Hicks Building, University of Massachusetts, Amherst, MA 01003; North American Society for the Psychology of Sport and Physical Activity, Richard A. Magill, Sec./Treas., Dept. of HPRE, Louisiana State University, Baton Rouge, LA 70803; Philosophic Society for the Study of Sport, Robert Trevas, Sec./Treas., Philosophy Department, Ohio University, Athens, OH 45701; The Association for the Anthropological Study of Play, Brian Sutton-Smith, President-Elect, Graduate School of Education, University of Pennsylvania, Philadelphia, PA 19104.

17. Herbert T. Juliano, Director, INSPORT (International Sports and Games Research Collection), University Libraries, University of Notre Dame, IN 46556.

18. The program, directed by Betty Spears (see note 16 for her address), offers both M.S. and Ph.D. degrees with courses required in both theoretical areas such as history, social psychology, philosophy, and sociology of sports as well as management courses in leadership, economics, law, marketing, public relations, finance, and public policy.

19. J. Robert Evans, *Blowing the Whistle on Intercollegiate Sports* (Chicago: Nelson-Hall, 1974); Edwin H. Cady, *The Big Game: College Sports and American Life* (Knoxville: University of Tennessee Press, 1978); John F. Rooney, *The Recruiting Game: Toward A New System of Intercollegiate Sports* (Lincoln: University of Nebraska Press, 1980).

20. Jay J. Coakley, *Sport in Society: Issues and Controversies,* 2d ed. (St. Louis, Mo.: C. V. Mosby, 1982); James Michener, *Sports in America* (New York: Random House, 1976).

21. William J. Baker and John M. Carroll, eds., *Sports in Modern America* (St. Louis, Mo.: River City, 1981).

22. Michael Oriard, *Dreaming of Heroes: American Sports Fiction 1868–1980* (Chicago: Nelson-Hall, 1981); Christian K. Messenger, *Sport and the Spirit of Play in American Fiction; Hawthorne to Faulkner* (New York: Columbia University Press, 1981); Robert J. Higgs, *Laurel and Thorn: The Athlete in American Literature* (Lexing-

ton: University Press of Kentucky, 1981). These works follow the paths of two pioneering studies of American sport fiction: Leverett T. Smith's *The American Dream and the National Game* (Bowling Green, Ohio: Popular Press, 1975) and Wiley Lee Umphlett's *The Sporting Myth and the American Experience: Studies in Contemporary Fiction* (Lewisburg, Pa.: Bucknell University Press, 1975). Several anthologies of sport literature have been published recently, including Robert J. Higgs and Neil D. Isaacs's *The Sporting Spirit: Athletes in Literature* (New York: Harcourt Brace Jovanovich, 1977) and Tom Dodge's *A Literature of Sports* (Lexington, Ky.: D.C. Heath, 1980). Higgs has also edited *Sports: A Reference Guide* (Westport, Conn.: Greenwood, 1982). David L. Vanderwerken and Spencer K. Wertz have edited an anthology designed primarily for teaching purposes: *Sport: A Literary and Conceptual Approach* (Fort Worth: Texas Christian University Press, 1984).

23. Charles S. Prebish is working on a book based on his course at Penn State entitled "Religion and Sport: the Meeting of the Sacred and the Profane". Joan Chandler has published "T.V. and Sports: Wedded with a Golden Hoop," *Psychology Today,* April 1977, 64–68.

24. Allen Guttmann, *From Ritual to Record: The Nature of Modern Sports* (New York; Columbia University Press, 1978); Richard Lipsky, *How We Play the Game: Why Sports Dominate American Life* (Boston: Beacon, 1981); Steven A. Riess, *Touching Base: Professional Baseball and American Culture in the Progressive Era* (Westport, Conn.: Greenwood Press, 1980); Kendall A. Blanchard, *Mississippi Choctaws at Play: The Serious Side of Leisure* (Champaign: University of Illinois Press, 1982); John Dizikes, *Sportsmen and Gamesmen* (New York: Houghton Mifflin, 1982); Richard C. Crepeau, *Baseball: America's Diamond Mind 1919–1941* (Gainesville: University Presses of Florida, 1981); Benjamin G. Rader, *American Sports: From the Age of Folk Games to the Age of Spectators* (Englewood Cliffs, N.J.: Prentice-Hall, 1983); and Donald J. Mrozek, *Sport and American Mentality 1880–1910* (Knoxville: University of Tennessee Press, 1983).

25. An article in the *Chronicle of Higher Education* 24 (11 August 1982): 1, 11, summarizes the San Francisco situation. Beginning with its 8 September issue, the *Chronicle* will devote an entire section to "Athletics": another indication of its significant role in higher education.

26. A perfect example of such a "vested interest" is the recently NCAA-formed "independent" panel to find practical solutions to sports problems. Two athletic directors, seven chancellors and presidents, two head coaches, two faculty representatives, and the current chairman of the board of governors of the Red Cross provide its membership. The only other faculty member, Charles Alan Wright, of the University of Texas at Austin, currently chairs the NCAA's committee on infractions.

27. William O. Johnson, *Super Spectator and the Electric Lilliputians* (Boston: Little, Brown, 1971). See also his more recent "You Ain't Seen Nuthin' Yet," *Sports Illustrated,* 10 August 1981, 48–54, and "High on Cable," *Sports Illustrated,* 17 August 1981, 26–32.

28. Cited in *The American Heritage History of Flight,* ed. Alvin Josephy (New York: American Heritage Publishing Co., 1962), 41.

20

The Lower Mythology and the Higher Clichés

GEORGE CORE

The Big Game: College Sports and American Life. By Edwin H.
  Cady. University of Tennessee Press. $14.50.
From Ritual to Record: The Nature of Modern Sports. By Allen
  Guttmann. Columbia University Press. $12.95.
Jock Culture, U.S.A. By Neil D. Isaacs. Norton. $9.95.
*The Joy of Sports: End Zones, Bases, Baskets, Balls, and the
  Consecration of the American Spirit.* By Michael Novak.
  Basic Books. $12.50. Paper, $4.95.

In the United States, for at least a decade, discontent has
persistently irrupted, not only among undergraduate and
graduate students but among their teachers. Today much of the
discontent within academic walls lies in the realm of the
humanities. Tillers of these stony fields (especially literature)
have often looked enviously toward other pastures and nearly as
often have bolted. They have seen the greening of America and
of their own careers in terms of popular culture—film, comic
strips and books, soap opera, and sports—or, more grandiosely,
within the frames of ethnic studies and interdisciplinary studies.
The professor who has rushed into the world of the silver screen

Reprinted from *The American Scholar,* Volume 48, Number 2 (Spring 1979). Copyright
© 1979 by the United Chapters of Phi Beta Kappa. By permission of the publishers.

or other precincts of popular culture has often so behaved because he, in some way, has been unsuccessful in the academic marketplace—the classroom or the publishing forum or both—and because he is secretly contemptuous of his chosen discipline. He gladly exchanges the rags of his professionalism for the trappings of a subject in which he is an amateur, but he transfers the knowledge and methods of his titular discipline to the new field. The results are usually pathetic and ludicrous, and nothing is more laughable than the effort to invest a course in, say, the funny papers with the seriousness and interest appropriate to classics or history. Soon now one expects to see hermeneutics applied to *Doonesbury,* anthropology to *The Phantom,* bibliography to strips which have ended (such as *Pogo* and *Li'l Abner*), urban studies to *Apartment 3G,* and so on.

The books considered here—Edwin Cady's *The Big Game,* Allen Guttmann's *From Ritual to Record,* Neil Isaacs's *Jock Culture,* and Michael Novak's *The Joy of Sports*—are in some ways indicative of the trend that I have churlishly adumbrated; but it should be stressed that each writer has achieved success as an academician (in that he has published widely in his chosen discipline) and that each is infected by a genuine—sometimes lunatic—attraction for sports. Only Guttmann remains stiffly at academic attention. Each author is more interested in sports as such than in popular culture or interdisciplinary studies; nevertheless both fads have profoundly marked all these books.

Seldom in this country has there been much first-rate writing on sports. Guttmann momentarily waxes eloquent about London, Lardner, Hemingway, and Malamud, but he devotes more space to English and European writers. If one thinks back over the American fiction that one has read which concerns football, baseball, and boxing, it is usually not of a high order unless the sport is dealt with only in passing, as in *The Great Gatsby,* which is incidentally about football. The level of sportswriting by journalists in the United States is abysmally low. Michael Novak's belief that sportswriting is superior to the writing of any other department of the typical American newspaper results from his characteristic enthusiasm and zeal about sports. He draws this conclusion partly because most people read the sports section before going on to the remainder of the paper. What of the funnies? My distinct impression is that the typical sportswriter is less literate than the typical sportscaster is grammatical and articulate, and that the sportswriter does more violence to the language. Much of the best writing on sports has been done for *The New Yorker,* but some of it has appeared in *Harper's,* the *Atlantic,* and *Esquire.* One does not expect to find first-rate prose in *Sports Illustrated,* but it occasionally appears when a contributor like William Zinsser is enlisted. From time to time one encounters a good product of editorial whimsy—for example, the special supplement of the *New Republic* for 23 July 1977, "Rule of the Games"—a brilliant collection of essays by academics.

Given this paucity of good writing about a subject on which more words are spent than any other in this country, one can be hospitable to the efforts of the academic breed to bring the presumed elegance and erudition of the Ivory Tower to the Big Game. The fact is that if the general level of the prose in these four studies were not long since entrenched in the academy, it would set back the clock of the written language for many years. The diction and syntax of these books furnish overwhelming proof—as does the spoken commentary of a Howard Cosell or a Hank Stram—of the validity of Jacques Barzun's dictum: "The predominant fault of the bad English encountered today is not the crude vulgarism of the untaught but the blithe irresponsibility of the taught." In this case the teachers are in the dock.

Each of the four authors tries in his own way to be a sportswriter. In so doing, he transfers the worst tendencies of academic writing—tortured syntax, cant diction, passive voice, grammatical conjunctivitis (beginning every other sentence and every third paragraph with a conjunction), hedging, indirection, obfuscation—to the loose and baggy writing of the sports page. The average sportswriter habitually repairs to a bedraggled stock of clichés, shuffling and reassembling them as the occasion seems to demand. His procedure resembles that of the politician whom Orwell has described in "Politics and the English Language" and whom we have all confronted on television and in the *Congressional Record.* "Modern writing at its worst," Orwell observes, "consists in gumming together long strips of words which have already been set in order by someone else, and making the results presentable by sheer humbug." The amount of humbug in the books at hand might have made Dr. Goebbels envious. The humbuggery smacks of sociology more strongly than it does of literary history or criticism.

Sports may be approached in a multitude of ways. One way has been thoroughly mined—though with little style and purpose—by the working newspaperman. His bag of tricks is limited. Of late it runs toward gossip and the "human interest" story—toward the life of the athlete off the playing field. That approach is usually numbingly dull, whether the athlete is addicted to drugs, or is fixated on his own ego, or is inclined to express himself with his fists. Out of uniform, the athlete is almost invariably a mundane chap of little interest. Present-day sportswriters, in their efforts to avoid Grantland Rice's "nice guy" approach (sharply delineated by Novak), generally end in being half-baked rather than hard-boiled. The academic sportswriter is equally transparent and fumbling. His style is riddled with cant words (*rethink, climax,* and *structure* as verb forms); dubious coinages *(ghettoize, dichotomization);* un-hyphenated and impenetrable phrases *(organized living center groups, mass proxy color war, college athletics situation);* inelegant variation *(trance-struck);* inflated language *(ludic, cultic, intrapsychic);* and corn-pone locutions *(telling it like it is, show biz, trashing).*

Neil Isaacs, who writes for the *Washington Post* and whose latest book measures the intricacies of betting on sports, presents himself in a style that is close to being garden-variety journalism. "Big Daddy Lipscomb was something of an anomaly for pro football's PR long before he ODed." Only the word *anomaly* marks the professor who is slumming in the popular press—or is it the newspaperman slumming in academia? Occasionally Isaacs salts his text with a four-letter word to show that he has penetrated that inner sanctum of sports—the locker room. Isaacs's book, along with Novak's, is the most readable of the lot; but it has the loosest structure, and the chapters, which are often interlarded with interviews, students' comments (excerpted from papers and journals written for Isaacs's popular course, Jock Lit), and newspaper articles by the author, have the casual rambling quality of lectures, not the sharpness and symmetry of good essays.

The book that is the most ambitious and far-ranging—what members of the academic establishment now deem "insightful"—is markedly the hardest going for the reader. The substance of Edwin Cady's *The Big Game* has been mired in the viscosity of its prose. One marvels in perceiving that a man whose name appears as author or editor of twenty-five books has not mastered parallel structure. "The black student athlete must be treated by and relate to the academic and athletic communities exactly the same as the nonblack, certainly not disadvantageously." Mr. Cady has labored under the disadvantage of using a typewriter that has no hyphen on the keyboard. Nevertheless his style rises toward eloquence on more than one occasion, particularly in the conclusion: "It is, after all, the business of the Big Game to be symbolic and exemplary." One applauds the sentiment and then blanches at the unintended connotation of the word *business.*

Michael Novak and Allen Guttmann have written books that could easily be viewed as burlesque—if the academic book on sports were an established genre. In reading *The Joy of Sports,* one repeatedly confronts hyperbolic philosophical statements which it is difficult to take as anything but lighthearted and droll: "The basic reality of all human life is play, games, sport; these are the realities from which the basic metaphors for all that is important in the rest of life are drawn. Work, politics, and history are the illusory, misleading, false world. . . . Barbarians play in order to work; the civilized work in order to play." One may grant this basic statement of theme and Novak's complementary idea (which appears, *mutatis mutandis,* in the other books under review)—that sports constitute natural religions—without deciding how seriously Novak wishes to be taken when he says: "Sports are far more serious than the dramatic arts, much closer to primal symbols, metaphors, and acts"; "Sports are our chief civilizing agent. Sports are our most universal art form"; "Sports constitute the primary lived world of the vast majority of Americans"; "Play is reality. Work is diversion and escape"; "Sports are the real thing. Work is the opiate." *Amusing in its perversity, engaging in its willfulness and zest, irritating in its self-indulgence*—these and other phrases come to mind as one is beguiled and entertained by the playful Mr. Novak, a philosopher whose metaphysic is sports, an epicurean who is engulfed by his lust for games.

If the parodic element in *The Joy of Sports* (for which the very title is symptomatic) lies in Michael Novak's orchestration of his themes, in *From Ritual to Record* the same dimension appears in Allen Guttmann's solemn tone and flat-footed sociological prose as he charts—quite literally by means of seventeen tables—such profundities as "Sports Featured on the Cover of *Sports Illustrated*" during the period 1955–74. Mr. Guttmann conceals his zest for sports as artfully as Messieurs Novak and Isaacs expose their frenzied love of athletic contests. Guttmann employs Karl

Marx and Max Weber to explain the mystery of sports; he also repairs to Johan Huizinga, whose *Homo Ludens* is a canonical text for Cady, as is Clifford Geertz's "Deep Play: Notes on the Balinese Cockfight."

Everyone who now writes on sports is driven to confess his own experience on the playing fields of Eton or Hell's Kitchen or Lumberton, North Carolina (the home of Tom Wicker). My indelible experience in this department occurred in the Marine Corps, whose complement of officers is made up largely of varsity athletes and physical education majors hailing from state normal and agricultural colleges. That I ran across (at Camp Lejeune) a college dropout with whom I had played sandlot baseball and football as a child made the importance of sports seem all the more bizarre, authentic, and final. Being a marine is deadly serious play, and one of the Marine Corps's failings stems from the fact that many of its officers never go beyond the stage of being aggressive athletes and well-conditioned players, boys perpetually at physical, but not mental, attention. The military metaphor—football as a campaign—that Guttmann and Cady consider at some length strikes me as too clever by half. It is another instance of what Joseph Epstein has observed in his essay "Obsessed by Sports": "Literary men in general are notoriously to be distrusted on the subject. They dig around everywhere, and can be depended upon to find much treasure where none is buried."

The books considered here are drenched in such mythic analogues and cultural parallels. Aristotle, Roland Barthes, Norbert Elias, Sigmund Freud, James G. Frazer, Northrop Frye, Daniel Boorstin, Alexis de Tocqueville, Frederick Jackson Turner, George Steiner, Thorstein Veblen, and other cultural critics are invoked. The history of sports is also investigated: Guttmann describes Aztec and Mayan rituals in addition to Greek and Roman games, and all four writers consider the background of American sports, especially college and professional football, basketball, and baseball. Patriarchs and makers of the game, such as James Naismith and Amos Alonzo Stagg, appear in the wings. What makes *The Joy of Sports* and *Jock Culture* considerably more engaging than the two other books is that even if Novak and Isaacs don't teach American fiction (as Cady and Guttmann do), they understand the significance of character in the making of narrative. (Neither Novak nor Isaacs can create a

scene with more than one character.) The appearance of such
figures as George Blanda, Bob Cousy, Roy Jefferson, Sandy
Koufax, John Lucas, Joe Namath, and Pat Summerall enhances
each book by giving it concreteness and life. *The Big Game* and
From Ritual to Record are abstract and bloodless by comparison. Novak keenly realizes the truth of John McPhee's observation that "now factual characters can live as much on the page as
any fictional character." Factual characters constitute the bone
and marrow of Novak's interchapters, which he calls
sportsreels. Isaacs's analogous technique—the insertion of interviews and commentaries—is not nearly so effective themati-
cally or dramatically.

Neil Isaacs does deserve high marks for courageously attacking the athletic establishment of his own university, Maryland:
the director, the sports-information secretary, and the head
coaches of the football and basketball teams. Jerry D. Claiborne
and Lefty Driesell closely resemble the coaches who vied
against one another as well as their colleagues in Lexington,
Kentucky, during the late 1940s and early 1950s: Bear Bryant
and Adolph Rupp. Rupp, who was apotheosized upon his death,
was an unscrupulous man who had only two talents—winning
basketball games and amassing the material goods of this world.
He was almost as graceless in victory as in defeat. He was a
bully who represented plebeian taste at its worst (once he refused Arthur Rubinstein the "privilege," as Isaacs gleefully reports, of practicing in Rupp's coliseum). Rupp's quaint notion of
what he grandiosely called character-building led directly and
inevitably to the point-shaving scandals that ruined the careers
of Alex Groza and Ralph Beard and, later, of Bill Spivey. (These
and other athletes at the University of Kentucky were put on the
payrolls of tobacco warehouses, distilleries, and other businesses in central Kentucky, but they never did any work for the
checks they collected.) Isaacs quite properly criticizes Woody
Hayes and Jerry Claiborne severely; he could have just as well
raked Bryant with grapeshot and canister. The brutal incident
which Isaacs recounts about Claiborne—his being party to the
injuring in practice of a "walk-on" punter—is emblematic of the
callousness, indifference, selfishness, and inhumanity which frequently surface in the sports establishment—far more often, in
all likelihood, in colleges than in the professional ranks. That
this kind of coach—the relentless dictator and ruthless over-
seer—usually survives to become a greatly respected character

and cracker-barrel philosopher stands as one of the most deplorable aspects of "organized" sports.

Isaacs is joined by Novak and Cady in calling for reform in the sports establishment, but, as all these gentlemen know, the corruption in sports reflects the more profound corruption in the body politic. Isaacs argues for legalized gambling; Novak wants quasi-federal regulation and oversight for such matters as the salaries of coaches and players, broadcasting, the number of teams, and the conduct of leagues. Isaacs, Novak, and Cady would like to see college athletes treated less like chattels and more nearly like human beings and actual students. Novak speaks for all four writers in saying that "it is a corruption, not only of sports, but also of the human spirit, to treat them as escape, entertainment, business, or a means of making money."

Whether or not one views sports, especially big-time football, basketball, and baseball, as secular religions, most readers will decide that Messieurs Cady, Guttmann, Isaacs, and Novak are more persuasive on practical and moral issues than on the mythic dimensions of competitive games. None of them seems to have read Philip Rahv's "The Myth and the Powerhouse" (1953). In that essay Rahv complains that mythomania is a form of nebulous religiosity (which Novak boldly announces and gladly embraces), pointing out that myth "is a certain kind of objective fantasy" whose presence does not authenticate art or religion or culture. He argues that the mythic imagination seeks to escape from the wounds of time and from the pain of historical experience, and that it worships primitivism and nostalgia. If one applies Rahv's strictures to this context, one sees that the academic writers being considered here would have done well to free sports from the bonds of myth, both classic and homemade in origin, and bring them into the clear light of day and the bracing climate of common sense. That is what the best sportswriters of our time—Roger Angell, John McPhee, A. J. Liebling—have done. One doesn't read Liebling to discover the mythic aspect of boxing, but Liebling does create a humorously ingenious myth in describing Archie Moore as Ahab and Rocky Marciano as Nemesis in the last chapter of *The Sweet Science*. And he throws in Pierce Egan and Albert Camus as well as Melville for style and leavening. When Moore was counted out, Liebling tells us, "It was a crushing defeat for the higher faculties and a lesson in intellectual humility, but he had made a hell of a fight."

Not one of these principals has made a hell of a fight, but all have been intellectual Ahabs tirelessly voyaging on strange seas of thought. What all of these writers and their sponsors (which include the Guggenheim Foundation, the National Endowment for the Humanities, Duke University, and the Aspen Institute) have failed to perceive is that some departments of human endeavor cannot be studied empirically or otherwise examined academically. James Thurber once argued that there is no place in the modern world for the streamlined mind. The evidence that one adduces from these books indicates that there is little place in sportswriting for the academic mind.

21
The Joy of Sports Books: A Tout Sheet

DAVID L. VANDERWERKEN

From Ritual to Record: The Nature of Modern Sports. By Allen
Guttmann. New York: Columbia University Press, 1978. viii,
198 pp. $12.95.
The Big Game: College Sports and American Life. By Edwin H.
Cady. Knoxville: University of Tennessee Press, 1978. xi,
254 pp. $14.50.
Fielder's Choice: An Anthology of Baseball Fiction. Edited by
Jerome Holtzman. New York: Harcourt Brace Jovanovich,
1979. 395 pp. $12.95.
AND OTHER TITLES

If the Twenties were the Golden Age of Sports, then perhaps the
Seventies will come to be known as the golden age of sports
studies. Clearly, the serious examination of sports has become
academically legitimate. Courses on sports in several disciplines
continue to proliferate. Specialized journals devoted to the philosophy and the history of sports now exist, and it's likely that
the idea for a critical quarterly on sports-centered creative literature is germinating in someone's imagination right now.
Amherst, for one, houses an institute for sports studies. And
hardbacks multiply like NHL franchises: philosophical inquiries
into the nature and aesthetics of sports, collections of sociolog-

ical and psychological essays on sports, even literary criticism of sports-centered work. Besides these professional and technical books, a host of provocative ruminations on sports by enthusiastic amateurs adds to the lineup. All this constitutes, if not a genre, a formidable and diverse body of material. Indeed the volume of jock studies is getting as intimidating as that of Faulkner scholarship. One could almost name an All-University-Press team from the titles of the last ten years or so. Two recent competitors for berths on this imaginary squad are Allen Guttmann's *From Ritual to Record: The Nature of Modern Sports* and Edwin Cady's *The Big Game: College Sports and American Life.*

Guttmann's book is the more comprehensive of the two, examining sports both in and beyond America, both individual and team, both amateur and professional, both spontaneous and organized, while Cady focuses solely on big-time college football and basketball (a narrower scope that allows him perhaps to penetrate his subject more deeply than Guttmann). Of the two authors, Guttmann is the more consciously and elaborately systematic, attempting to "define the relationships that obtain among play, games, contests, and sports; to demonstrate what differentiates modern from primitive, ancient, and medieval sports; to interpret the social conditions that led to the rise of modern sports; to comment upon the distinctively American games of baseball and football, and, finally, to look into the American preference for team rather than for individual sports." Very clear, very logical, very ambitious. Guttmann's tight organization and his use of charts, graphs, diagrams, lists, and statistics—together with his exhaustive documentation (23 pages of endnotes)—create an illusion of scientific objectivity. Guttmann incorporates many "European scholars, especially the Germans" because they have been "much more extensively involved in the serious study of sport as a social phenomenon" than Americans. The result is a very disciplined and Germanic monograph that almost goosesteps.

On the other hand, Cady's book is relaxed, reflective, Emersonianly digressive, yet much the harder to grasp since the ideas, analogies, and images subtly modify and shift, dipping and darting within an extremely ruminative prose style, Emerson redivivus. Guttmann's book is an Earl Campbell to be compared with Cady's pure Tony Dorsett. Cady's preface, unlike Guttmann's, does not specify the book's intentions; rather, Cady shares his "personal sense of wonderment" about sports, establishes a mood for exploration and discovery, adopts the persona of the "man in the middle, the American Innocent, the seer of multiple views and variant perspectives"—a moral philosopher open to all possibilities who seeks to "puzzle out the meaning of what you see and hear in the stands and around the edges of the game." *The Big Game* is personal, experiential, with a quality of openness that may seem wise to some, waffling to others. Actually, the table of contents reveals two books: the first composed of meditations on what the Big Game is, how it came to be, what it means to American culture; and the second a series of suggestions, advice, recommendations (lectures, if you will) on the practical problems of college sports addressed to a hypothetical new university president. Cady's long involvement in intercollegiate athletics and his successful creation of a wise and experienced persona in Book 1 lend a certain moral authority to his voice in Book 2. And it is a voice worth listening to.

Despite the radically divergent approaches in these two studies, readers will find much confluence. Both books acknowledge their debts to the grand old man of this whole endeavor, Johan Huizinga, whose *Homo Ludens: A Study of the Play Element in Culture* (1938) remains *the* text to affirm, refute, or amend for every written voice in the sports colloquy. Both Guttmann and Cady believe that sports satisfy a deep need for "folly" (Cady) in life, that sports offer "moral holidays" (Cady) and "institutional time-outs" (Guttmann) from everydayness. For both, sports are life-enhancing and rehumanizing activities; they reject the notion that sports reflect some atavistic savagery in human nature. In sports, as Cady nicely puts it, we see "aggression redeemed." Guttmann and Cady wax anthropological to account for the sporting and gambling impulses in humankind. For Guttmann, sports "have their roots in the dark soil of our instinctive lives," while Cady claims that the Big Game is "in the genes."

Although Guttmann and Cady are convinced that a proclivity for sports is inherent in people, they exercise great caution on the question of whether sports are in some way a religion. Unlike Michael Novak, whose blatantly celebratory and delightfully self-indulgent *The Joy of Sports* (1976) draws running analogies between sports and religion, Guttmann and Cady are loath to claim that Yankee Stadium rivals St. Patrick's Cathedral as a house of worship. Guttmann establishes that one of the

seven characteristics of modern sports is secularism; the attachment of sport to the "realm of the transcendent has been
severed." Despite the prevalence of all the Jocks-for-Jesus
groups, Guttmann argues that the contemporary athlete knows
that the "contest is a secular event. The Sermon on the Mount
does not interfere with hard blocking and determined tackling.
Religion remains on the sidelines." Still, if the Super Bowl cannot be reconciled with Christian orthodoxy, are sports a "secular
religion" in the Novakian sense? Cady—tentatively, carefully—
says no: "I think I do not believe in the real existence of what is
sometimes called 'the secular religion.' The Big Game is not in
fact sacramental. It only feels that way at some of its highest
moments." Although Texas-Oklahoma weekend may not be sacramental, it can be a "sort of sacred, sometimes ritual."

Yet if sports are not liturgies, they do reveal national mythology and satisfy deep cultural needs. Cady emphatically declares
that the compelling secret of the Big Game lies in its ritual representation of the American Dream:

> Team against team, individual with team, person against per-
> son, person with person, team against individual: unity in di-
> versity, diversity in unity, agonism and fraternity. The new
> start, the chance for the "hungry"; democracy by compe-
> tency; self-realization and respect in cooperation, in victory
> but yet in loss; risk and fierce competition and catharsis, yet
> decorum—and all surrounded and buoyed up by the atmo-
> sphere and communal joy of the great party: this is the Big
> Game's gift of a ritual text to participants near and far.

And the Big Game's chief gift, according to Cady, is continual
cultural renewal. In contrast, Guttmann denies this notion of
"American exceptionalism," suggesting that "American sports
are less unique than they seem," yet—like Cady—Guttmann acknowledges that America's preference for team sports reflects
our self-image of cooperative individualism, in short, *e pluribus
unum.*

Although both books concentrate on the spectator's perspective (the "games we play in the seats" as Cady phrases it), Cady
and Guttmann also try to grasp what may be the extraordinary
experiences of the athlete—mystical, magical, perhaps inef-
fable. For Cady, the "real thing, the heart of light at the inmost
core of the athlete's experience, is an ecstasy." Guttmann opens

his study by quoting Roger Bannister's attempt to capture an epiphany in language. And Guttmann concludes by taking a stab at it himself: "I rush across the tennis court and return the ball with what seems to me in my enthusiasm the perfect stroke, the right stroke, the stroke dictated by the imperatives of tennis. I have surrendered myself to the rules of the game and I am, paradoxically, flushed with an ecstatic sense of amplitude and freedom."

For further insight into "athletic rapture" and all other issues regarding the experience and the meaning of sports, no better resource exists than our creative artists. Virtually every major American talent in this century has some sport-centered work in his canon. A special feature of Guttmann's book is his commentary on such works as Mark Harris's *Bang the Drum Slowly,* Bernard Malamud's *The Natural,* Robert Coover's *The Universal Baseball Association,* Don DeLillo's *End Zone.* That Guttmann focuses on baseball-oriented fiction reflects the fact that the great majority of sports-centered work is about baseball, although other sports have made some inroads, especially in the last five years. Yet baseball, unquestionably, has stimulated the greatest range of quality writing, as the recent *Fielder's Choice: An Anthology of Baseball Fiction* attests. Jerome Holtzman, the editor, has compiled twenty-seven impressive pieces by such as Lardner, Thurber, Richler, and Shaw, as well as excerpts from novels by Potok, Roth, and Brashler. No easy outs appear in Holtzman's lineup.

Lately, every month brings forth a serious piece of sports-centered fiction, if Jonathan Yardley's "Booktalk" column in *Sports Illustrated* is any indication. Moreover, several general sports literature anthologies are available, the best of which are Henry B. Chapin's collection *Sports in Literature* (David McKay Company, 1976), and *The Sporting Spirit: Athletes in Literature and Life* (Harcourt Brace Jovanovich, 1977) edited by Robert J. Higgs and Neil D. Isaacs. The selections in both are impressively catholic and provocative, although Higgs and Isaacs offer a broader scope in their collection. D. C. Heath and Company has published *A Literature of Sports* (1980), edited by Tom Dodge, and surely other such anthologies are on deck or in the hole somewhere. That many of our better talents use sports in ways similar to an earlier generation's use of Biblical myth has not totally escaped critical attention. Wiley Lee Umphlett's brave and useful study, *The Sporting Myth and American Expe-*

rience: Studies in Contemporary Fiction (Bucknell University Press, 1975), tries to account for the phenomenon and likely heralds further critical analyses of sports-centered literature.

While literary criticism of sports-related work is nearly virginal, philosophical speculation on sports has been going on for some time. Although a vast and bewildering literature exists, a consensus has established itself that the works of Paul Weiss and Harold J. Vanderzwaag merit special attention. Weiss's *Sport: A Philosophic Inquiry* (1969) kicked off the movement to treat sports with philosophic rigor, yet being first has made Weiss the victim of many late hits. Weiss's admission that he is himself no athlete, his highly speculative and abstract methodology, his conclusion that sports are not one of the highest human achievements—all have been gang-tackled since the book's appearance. The most measured and considered response is Vanderzwaag's *Toward a Philosophy of Sport* (1972), a book more firmly grounded in the concrete and less dogmatic in its conclusions than Weiss's. Vanderzwaag's strength is the preciseness and clarity of the distinctions he makes regarding play, games, sports, and athletics. Another thinker worthy of attention is James W. Keating, whose *Competition and Playful Activities* (University Press of America, 1978) is a collection of his own journal articles on such topics as sportsmanship, competition, athletic excellence, and winning. I have found Keating's work to be amazingly lucid and insightful.

What continues to interest me, however, are not the works of professional philosophers of sports, but those of the skilled amateurs, lovers (like Cady, Guttmann, Novak, Isaacs, et al.) who have felt moved to speculate publicly and lengthily on sports, those who aim at a broader potential audience than the strictly academic. Yet who are these books for? Certainly not Joe Fan, certainly not most athletes. As usual, those who might benefit most won't, or can't, read them. Perhaps sports administrators are likely candidates, although I have trouble picturing most coaches, athletic directors, front office personnel, or league officials confronting these texts. Perhaps sports journalists and broadcasters will tackle them. But, again, who in particular? Red Smith, Yes. Cosell, I suppose. But Pat Summerall or, God help us, Tony Kubek? Alas, the readership for Guttmann and Cady will primarily be people holding doctorates. And judging from the reviewing reception of these books, one can sense a kind of backlash setting in, even from fellow Ph.D.'s.

Of course, many regard the entire outpouring of sports studies with alarm, hostility, woe, and sometimes mirth. Here come the professors, the sentiment seems to run, making a field out of *the field*, note cards in hand, interrogating, speculating, analyzing, turning the joyful into the solemn. Is anything so unfunny as an academic conference on humor? So with sports, same lament. Certainly the prose of far too many sports books, as most reviewers have noted, often seems like an academic equivalent of Stengelese. Commenting on Guttmann and Cady in *Sports Illustrated,* Jonathan Yardley lefthandedly compliments the authors for being "fans at heart. Like the rest of us, they are up in the stands cheering. The big difference is that you often can't understand what they are cheering about."

Writing on a different plane for a different audience *(The American Scholar),* George Core, while sharing Yardley's scorn for such Irwin Coreyish prose, chastises such books for their mongrelized methodologies and semischolarly approaches. Core finds the attempt by literary scholars (Guttmann, Cady, Isaacs) and theologians (Novak) to transfer and apply their specialized expertise to sports "pathetic and ludicrous." The marvelously derisive title of Core's review-essay, "The Lower Mythology and the Higher Clichés," indicates his stance; his premise—one that sacks these authors like quarterbacks—is that "sports cannot be studied empirically or otherwise examined academically." This is a curiously anti-intellectual assertion from the editor of *The Sewanee Review,* the notion that sports "should not mean/ But be." Cady himself acknowledges that "play plumbs too deep for the reach of mere language," yet he, like Guttmann, strives valiantly to reach what language can reach about sports. Guttmann and Cady assume that the struggle to understand enhances, rather than spoils, enjoyment, whether of Stevens's poetry, Hitchcock's films, or the National Football League.

As for their absence of "credentials," Guttmann and Cady are sons of that rank amateur Emerson, each portraying "man thinking," refusing to cede intellectual independence to specialists. We are the richer, I believe, for the insights Guttmann and Cady provide and must accord both secure spots on the All-University-Press roster.

22
Sport Studies and the Anthropology Curriculum

KENDALL BLANCHARD

The serious study of sport is gradually working its way into the anthropology curriculum of American colleges and universities. This trend is reflected in the growing number of courses dealing with sport or some aspect of that phenomenon. Correspondingly, the volume of sport anthropology literature and the amount of research have also increased. Some anthropology textbooks now devote space to a discussion of sport (e.g., Cohen & Eames 1982, 282–90), and anthropology readers occasionally contain articles about sport (e.g., Spradley & McCurdy 1980, 316; Cole 1982, 394). Perhaps of even greater significance is the fact that anthropologists now get invited to regional meetings and national conferences to talk about sport. Clearly, the anthropological study of sport is coming of age. This essay is both a descriptive analysis of that "coming of age" and a defense of sport anthropology's importance and use in the classroom.

Sport (and Games) in the History of Anthropology

For my purposes here, I am defining sport as a gamelike activity having rules and a competitive element and requiring some form of physical exertion. It can have playlike dimensions, but has no necessary relationship to play. On the other hand, sport

284

activities have generally been included under the broader rubric *games* in the anthropological literature (e.g., "physical games" in Roberts, Arth & Bush 1959, 597). For this reason, it is difficult to treat the history of sport studies in anthropology apart from the discipline's attention to games in general.

Anthropologists have rarely been enthusiastic about the study of sport, and then only recently. During the early years of the discipline, the mid to late 1800s, anthropology literature was dominated by the classical evolutionists who devoted little time to sport and games. Limited by their dependence on secondhand field data and an adherence to an evolutionary model of culture that treated the industrialized West as the apex of human accomplishment, the early fathers were generally preoccupied with issues such as the origin of religion, cultural evolution, and the diffusion of cultural ideas between continents.

One exception to this trend was Sir Edward Burnett Tylor, often called the father of anthropology. Tylor was one of the first social scientists to recognize the importance of games as subjects of scholarly investigation. In particular, he realized that activities such as sports might provide the anthropologist with important clues about the nature of prehistoric culture contact between geographically distant groups of people. In a classic article entitled "The History of Games" (1879, 63), he argued that while some simple and natural games (e.g., tossing a ball or wrestling) had "sprung up of themselves," there were others that were "distinctly artificial," with "some peculiar trick or combination not so likely to have been hit upon twice," which could be traced from a common geographical center. In other words, certain games could be used as evidence of diffusion and contact between cultural centers in different parts of the world.

In another article, "On American Lot-Games as Evidence of Asiatic Intercourse Before the Time of Columbus" (1896, 93), Tylor discussed the similarities between the ancient Hindustani game of pachisi and the Mexican game of patolli, arguing that the parallels between the two provided solid evidence of pre-Columbian contact between the New and Old Worlds, specifically, "communications across the Pacific from Eastern Asia."

Typical of the anthropologists of his era, however, Tylor tended to treat the sport phenomenon as a vehicle for the analysis of broader cultural processes. While his periodic study of games represents a valuable contribution to our present-day

understanding of sport, it did not generate a productive theoretical framework for future sport studies.

Other nineteenth-century anthropologists occasionally mentioned sport activities in ethnographies or in the context of general introductions to culture (e.g., A. C. Haddon, *Study of Man*,
1898, 174ff.). But these issues remained secondary, with few
exceptions.

One such exception was an article written by anthropologist
James Mooney of the Bureau of American Ethnology. It was a
detailed description of the Cherokee racquet game that he published in *American Anthropologist* in 1890, providing not only a
thorough understanding of the game itself but also of Cherokee
life in general. Another exception to the tendency for anthropologists to treat sport and games as incidental was the work of
Stewart Culin. Culin, who has been called the "major game
scholar of the past 100 years . . . in the field of anthropology"
(Avedon & Sutton-Smith 1971, 55), published many important
works on the subject. Perhaps his greatest contribution was
Games of the North American Indians, an 846-page volume in
which the author systematically classifies and describes the
games and sport activities of 225 different native North American tribes (Culin 1907).

During the first five decades of the twentieth century, anthropologists, with the exception of Culin, generally ignored the role
of sport in human society. However, there were a few analyses
of sport behavior that occasionally surfaced in the anthropology
literature of the period.

In Germany, Karl von Weule published a lengthy article, "Ethnologie des Sportes," that appeared in a large volume on the
history of sport in 1925. Weule approached the subject from the
culture-history perspective, arguing that the primary focus of an
ethnology of sport should be twofold: (1) to trace culture, particularly the sport aspect, back to its beginning, and (2) to put
sport as an item of culture into its proper theoretical perspective.

Anthropologist Eldon Best gave special attention to games
and sports in his ethnographic research. His 1924 two-volume
work *The Maori,* contains extensive descriptions of the play
activities of this New Zealand group. He also treated these
events in his 1925 article, "The Games and Pastimes of the
Maori."

In 1931, the noted British social anthropologist Raymond
Firth wrote an article entitled "A Dart Match in Tikopia: A Study

in the Sociology of Primitive Sport." In this, he described the competitive dart-throwing match of old Polynesia, a festive occasion "very closely connected with the social organization and religious belief" of the Tikopians (Firth 1931, 65). Firth (1931, 95–96) also underscored the important role of sport in primitive society generally and suggested that the subject deserved "more attention than it had already received."

Anthropologist Alexander Lesser published his *The Pawnee Ghost Dance Hand Game* in 1933. This brilliant analysis of the game's role in the total culture process of this Plains Indian group is one of the outstanding monographs of twentieth-century anthropology.

In 1944, Morris Opler published a description of the "Jicarilla Apache Ceremonial Relay Race," in which he recognized the vital relationship between sport in that system and environmental adaptation. The following year, Marvin Opler (1945) published an analysis of Japanese style wrestling that he had observed at the Tule Lake relocation center in California. Generally, though, anthropologists during this period paid little attention to sport. For example, Alfred Kroeber (1948, 29), in his classic *Anthropology,* mentioned play as an important part of human society, but devoted no space to a discussion of sport.

During these years, social science literature was occasionally graced by contributions from nonanthropologists addressing sport-related issues of interest to anthropologists. For example, in 1939, Corrado Gini wrote an interesting piece on baseball and shinny as these two sports were played among the Berbers in Libya, and it was published in the *Journal of Rural Sociology.* Another important contributor to the anthropological understanding of sport and games during this period was folklorist Paul Brewster. Among his many articles on the subjects, perhaps the most significant was "The Importance of the Collecting and Study of Games" (1956).

Several scholars from the ranks of physical education also added to the limited literature in this area, describing the sport activities of particular primitive or preliterate peoples (e.g., Dunlap 1951; Stumpf & Cozens 1947) or stressing the importance of looking at sport from a cultural perspective (e.g., Frederickson 1960).

Despite these occasional forays into the subject by those in the discipline as well as by those in other professions, the anthropological study of sport remained an infrequent topic in the main stream of anthropology, and conceptual problems were at best unexpressed concerns until recently. This is witnessed to in the Human Relations Area Files, a compendium of anthropological data from approximately six hundred societies around the world. Of the 631 topical areas in the *Outline of Cultural Materials* (Murdock 1961), one system by which the data are filed, one of the areas, number 526, is labeled "athletic sports." Approximately 240, or 40 percent, of the societies in the sample have at least one reference under that category. The other 60 percent have no material at all under that heading. While some might see this lack of ethnographic material on athletic sports in the Human Relations Area Files as an indication that many societies simply do not have such events in their repertoire of behavior, I am inclined to interpret it as a historical comment on anthropologists' failure to treat sport as a significant aspect of culture.

In an attempt to appraise the extent to which sport has been included in anthropological ethnographies during the first century or so of the discipline's existence, I compiled and analyzed a standard list of well-known monographs. Seventy-five books were selected as representative of the "standard" ethnographies, and each of these was examined to weigh the amount of attention devoted to activities that could in any way be called sport. Of these seventy-five major works, published betweel 1861 and 1969, only twenty-six, or 35 percent, contained any reference at all to such phenomena. Of these twenty-six, only seven contained what would be called thorough descriptions of a particular sport, and only one provided any systematic analysis of sport activity (E. S. C. Handy, *Polynesian Religion*, 1927). More typical of the entire sample were the ethnographies that ignored sport and play completely (e.g., George Foster, *Tzintzuntzan*, 1967).

The year 1959 was a critical one in the history of anthropology's treatment of sport and games. That year, John Roberts, Malcolm Arth, and Robert Bush published their seminal article entitled "Games in Culture" *(American Anthropologist)*. This was one of the first systematic attempts in the history of the discipline to put definable parameters around the concept of games, and it served to stimulate productive theoretical debate regarding the general role of games and the special role of sport in human society among anthropologists.

Subsequently, during the 1960s, anthropologists began to pay more attention to sport. Robin Fox's "Pueblo Baseball: A New Use for Old Witchcraft" (1961) was widely read. In his 1964 presidential address to the American Anthropological Association, Leslie White gave some credibility to the anthropological study of sport by suggesting that the discipline provided a viable model for the analysis of professional sports, in particular, baseball, which he saw as a vital expression of the American cultural system itself (White 1965, 633–34). During the mid-sixties, there was a greater tendency than in earlier decades for ethnographic fieldworkers to take notice of sport and play activities among th people they were studying and include some of this material in their monographs. Also, at professional meetings of anthropologists, both regional and national, there were occasional sessions devoted to the reading of papers on sport and sport-related topics.

The sociology of sport began to come into its own during the late sixties and had a direct impact on its sister discipline, anthropology. Major sociological publications of the period included *Sport, Culture, and Society* (Loy & Kenyon 1969), *The Cross-Cultural Analysis of Sport and Games* (Lüschen 1970), and *Games, Sports, and Power* (Stone 1972). The latter included a popular piece by the anthropologist George Gmelch, "Magic in Professional Baseball," that demonstrated how the understanding of life in simple society could enlighten the understanding of contemporary sport behavior.

In a 1973 review of three books on sport, including the Loy and Kenyon and Stone works (above), anthropologist Joyce Reigelhaupt (1973, 378) noted that members of her profession had devoted little attention to sport and games during the previous twenty-five years. She then suggested that the time had arrived for the development of an anthropology of sport and that Clifford Geertz's (1972) essay on the Balinese cockfight would be "a logical starting point" (Reigelhaupt 1973, 380). While I am sympathetic with her sentiments, I question the logic of her departure. While the Geertz article is important to theoretical anthropology in general, it is of little direct value to the study of sport in particular.

Perhaps of greater significance for this period in the development of anthropology's interest in sport studies is the work of Edward Norbeck, who, in addition to other treatments of the topic of play, published an article that appeared in a special 1971 *Natural History* supplement on play. In this piece he underscored the importance of anthropology's taking the subject seriously. Then, in 1973, he organized a symposium at the annual meetings of the American Anthropological Association, held in New Orleans that year, in which papers on play were presented. These were published the following year in a volume edited by Norbeck (1974), *The Anthropological Study of Human Play.*

It was during those 1973 American Anthropological Association meetings, and partly in conjunction with the Norbeck symposium, that a handful of anthropologists who had been independently developing their own interests and doing research in sport and play began to discuss the feasibility of a special professional organization devoted to the treatment and dissemination of data related to these topics. At the same time, in other parts of the country and in Canada, those having similar interests were pondering the same possibility.

The following year, these diverse interests and perspectives jelled when a group of anthropologists and sport historians met in London, Ontario, in connection with the annual meetings of the North American Society of Sport History. It was at this meeting in May of 1974 that the Association for the Anthropological Study of Play (TAASP) was born. With a membership composed of individuals from a variety of disciplines (e.g., recreation, history, sociology, psychology, physical education, anthropology, leisure studies), TAASP has become an important focal point for the anthropological study of play in general and sport in particular.

In recent years, the number of anthropologists dealing with sport in their research, writing, and classroom instruction has increased. No longer is sport simply a topic of idle conversation and pastime activity among anthropologists; it has become a legitimate subject of serious study.

Still, the question remains as to why it has taken so long for anthropologists to make the study of sport respectable. Perhaps the most obvious factor underlying the discipline's hesitancy is that sport is not always as obvious in small-scale society as it is in modern, more complex systems. Some scholars have even argued that sport is nonexistent in primitive societies (e.g., Damm 1970; Guttmann 1978). Thus, it is understandable that anthropologists focusing on nonstate systems, as they traditionally have done, might see no need to look for or consider sport.

At the same time, I suspect that there are other reasons affecting the oversight of support in anthropology circles. Individual anthropologists have always tended to be preoccupied with particular dimensions of culture (e.g., economics, social structure, kinship, political organization,), often to the detriment of others, even though they make noises about the importance of holism and cultural integration. Also, though I have only limited data to support this contention, the class backgrounds and physical conditions of the founding fathers of anthropology suggest that they were not sport enthusiasts, and if they were, the sports were not those of the masses. Charles Darwin was the son of a prosperous physician, and though he was interested in shooting and dogs and associated with "the sporting set" at Cambridge, he was plagued with a debilitating illness for most of his life and did not manifest any notable interest in sports such as football (soccer), club ball, or cricket. E. B. Tylor's father ran a prosperous, family-owned brass foundry, and the son grew up in fairly luxurious surroundings and in a strict Quaker home atmosphere. By age twenty-three, his health was breaking down, adding to the suspicion that he was little interested in the physical competitions of ordinary people, although he did give some attention to games and sports in his writing. James Frazer was the son of a pious Presbyterian who managed a prosperous drug firm, and a woman from the family of a wealthy merchant. Because of strict religious upbringing, his younger years were marked by more intellectual than physical exercise. Franz Boas was the son of a well-to-do Jewish businessman, and though he spent much of his childhood leisure time outdoors, he was more interested in botany than in sport. He was described as "a delicate child . . . a cause of much of the fuss made over him by his mother and sisters (Kardiner & Preble 1961, 118).[1] Bronislaw Malinowski was the son of a Polish nobleman of the landed gentry, yet led a lonely childhood. Because he was so frequently sick, his mother watched and doted over him well into his adult years. Alfred Kroeber's father was a successful wholesale clock dealer in New Jersey whose wealth allowed him to send his son to the best tutors and schools in New York. A serious scholar even as a boy, he had little time for organized play, and was of "somewhat fragile" health throughout much of his life (Steward 1973, 4).

This apparent lack of personal interest or participation in the popular sport activities of their respective eras and localities does not in itself explain the lack of significant attention to sport behavior by a century of anthropologists. There is no data to suggest that an anthropologist-athlete automatically turns to the analysis of sport. This has not been the case in other areas. For example, among nineteenth-century anthropologists there were several trained as lawyers who devoted little time or energy to the explicit treatment of law in their research (e.g., J. J. Bachofen, Lewis Henry Morgan, J. F. McClennan). Nevertheless, an appreciation of sport from a participant's perspective can lead one to a scholarly interest in the subject. For example, in a fieldwork setting, the anthropologist may find that involvement in organized sport/recreational activities is a painless and convenient way to become a part of community life. In the process of this involvement, he may begin to ask questions that he would not have thought to raise otherwise, questions which eventually could lead to the analysis of sport as an important category of cultural behavior in itself (see Blanchard 1974).

Sociologists have been quicker and more effective than anthropologists in making the study of sport a respectable part of their discipline. The openness of the sociological community to sport as a legitimate academic subject is reflected in the many special courses that are offered in the undergraduate curricula, the number of "sociology of sport" specialities listed in the *Guide to Graduate Departments of Sociology,* the many sociology of sport textbooks and readers that are now available, and the enthusiasm with which the discipline embraces its own sport heroes. For example, most sociology students know that Herbert Blumer, the Berkeley sociologist and symbolic interactionist, was an all-American football player at the University of Missouri and played professional ball with the old Chicago Cardinals before taking an academic position.

The primary reason for its greater respectability in sociology than in anthropology is the fact that sport is more likely to be a major element in the social systems that sociologists study than in those treated by anthropologists. However, I would also suggest that there are additional social class and sport participation variables. While I cannot substantiate this statistically, I suspect that sociologists have generally been more attuned to and familiar with the values and norms of middle-class American society than have anthropologists. I would also guess that over the years more sociologists than anthropologists came to their respective disciplines with histories of athletic involvement. Unfortunately, only a detailed study of the childhood backgrounds of representative samples of sociologists and anthropologists could prove such a suggestion, but it is an interesting possibility.

The recent tendency for sport studies to become more common and respectable in anthropology poses an additional question: What factors have led to the emergence of the new interest in sport among anthropologists? To begin with, the popularity of sport throughout the world makes it impossible to ignore. It is especially evident in contact societies where culture change often involves the transmission of modern sports (e.g., basketball, soccer, baseball) into a traditional social setting. In such situations, the anthropologist cannot overlook the importance of sport. The growing interest in sport studies among anthropologists is also related to the general proliferation of topical specialties in anthropology. There are many anthropologists but few unexplored areas of human behavior. Sport represents one of the few remaining frontiers in the discipline. Finally, I would also suggest that in recent decades the social class backgrounds of American anthropologists have gradually shifted downward. No longer is it an avocation for the aristocratic (see Richardson 1975 for a description of a typical background of an American anthropologist). Persons with ordinary social credentials have begun to make significant contributions to the discipline, anthropology has become increasingly an applied science, and many anthropologists now openly admit to an enthusiasm for playing racquetball and watching TV sport specials like "Monday Night Football."

The Anthropology of Sport: Research and Teaching Objectives

The anthropological study of sport for both research and teaching purposes is a distinctive theoretical perspective that can best be understood and appreciated by a consideration of its major objectives. These include:

1. The definition and description of sport behavior from a cross-cultural perspective. This embraces the analysis of sport-related concepts that can be applied across cultural lines and the testing of propositions about the general role of sport in human society.

2. The study of sport in primitive, preliterate, tribal, non-Western, Third World, and developing countries. This is a distin-

guishing characteristic of anthropology and is essential to the salvaging of ethnographic data on sport behavior around the world.

3. The analysis of sport as a factor in acculturation, enculturation, and cultural maintenance. According to recent research findings, sport has the potential for serving all three of these functions in significant ways.

4. The use of sport as a perspective on other facets of cultural behavior. Sport as ritual reflects the fundamental tenets of the social setting within which it is played. Therefore, what is purported to be the ethnography of sport is often general ethnography and provides an unusual yet valuable perspective on other facets of culture.

5. The analysis of sport behavior in human prehistory. Although archaeology has provided little evidence for games and sports in prehistory, the problem is an important one, and there is new interest in exploring the issue (Fox 1977).

6. The analysis of sport language, in both the non-Western and the contemporary Western world. Sport jargons are important to understanding the mechanics of sport behavior.

7. Studying the role of sport in the multicultural educational environment. At this level, the application of anthropological understandings of sport behavior can have important results as a facilitator of communication and learning.

8. Developing and administering sport/recreation programs for special populations (e.g., handicapped, mentally retarded). This objective requires the input and expertise of physical anthropologists sensitive to both the physical and cultural dimensions of the sport experience.

9. The application of anthropological methods to the solution of practical problems, the development of special programs, and the administration of these programs in physical education, recreation, and intramurals. This approach is especially critical in multicultural, multi-ethnic, and multiracial situations.

10. The creation of attitudes conducive to cross-cultural understanding. As the sport-recreation scholars Cozens and Stumpf have noted: "If cultural anthropology teaches us anything, it teaches us to look beneath the surface of what we see and develop our tolerance of the other fellow's pleasures."

Perhaps the most comprehensive of the objectives of sport anthropology is the use of data about sport from other times and places in the understanding of contemporary sport behavior.

This approach affords valuable insight into such issues as the role of women in sports, sport and international understanding, sport and the aging process, sport and recreation for the elderly, and sport and violence in human society.

In general, the anthropological study of sport is a distinctive and important social scientific approach to the analysis and understanding of one of the most visible of human activities. It has great practical, theoretical, and instructional potential and should be a part of every anthropology curriculum.

Note

1. Boas's war experience and the apparent duel that left his face scarred were later developments in his life and cannot be used as indicators of an earlier interest in sport participation.

References

Avedon, Elliot, and Brian Sutton-Smith. 1971. *The Study of Games.* New York: John Wiley.

Best, Eldon. 1924. *The Maori.* 2 vols. Wellington.

————. 1925. *Games and Pastimes of the Maori.* Dominion Museum Bulletin, no. 8.

Blanchard, Kendall. 1974. "Basketball and the Culture-Change Process: The Rimrock Navajo Case." *Council on Anthropology and Education Quarterly* 5(4): 8–13.

————. 1981. *The Mississippi Choctaws at Play: The Serious Side of Leisure.* Urbana: University of Illinois Press.

Blanchard, Kendall, and Alyce Cheska. 1984. *The Anthropology of Sport: The Application of Social Science in Physical Education, Recreation, Athletic, and Leisure Programs.*

Brewster, Paul G. 1956. "The Importance of the Collecting and Study of Games." *Eastern Anthropologist* 10(1):5–12.

Coakley, Jay J. 1978. *Sport in Society: Issues and Controversies.* St. Louis, Mo.: C. V. Mosby.

Cohen, Eugene N., and Edwin Eames. 1982. *Cultural Anthropology.* Boston: Little, Brown.

Cole, Johnnetta B., ed. 1982. *Anthropology for the Eighties: Introductory Readings.* New York: Free Press.

Culin, Stewart. *Games of the North American Indians.* Twenty-fourth Annual Report of the Bureau of American Ethnology. Washington, D.C.: Government Printing Office.

Damm, Hans. 1970. "The So-called Sport Activities of Primitive People: A Contribution Towards the Genesis of Sport." In *The Cross-Cultural Analysis of Sport and Games,* ed. Gunther Lüschen. Champaign, Ill.: Stipes.

Dunlap, Helen L. 1951. "Games, Sports, Dancing and Other Vigorous Recreational Activities and Their Function in Samoan Culture." *Research Quarterly* 22(3):298–311.

Edwards, Harry. 1973. *The Sociology of Sport.* Homewood, Ill.: Dorsey Press.

Firth, Raymond. 1931. "A Dart Match in Tikopia." *Oceania* 1:64–97.

Foster, George. 1967. *Tzintzuntzan: Mexican Peasants in a Changing World.* Boston: Little, Brown.

Fox, J. R. 1961. "Pueblo Baseball: A New Use for Old Witchcraft." *Journal of American Folklore* 74:9–16.

Fox, Steven J. 1977. "A Paleoanthropological Approach to Recreation and Sporting Behaviors." In *Studies in the Anthropology of Play,* ed. Phillips Stevens, Jr., 65–70. West Point, N.Y.: Leisure Press.

Frederickson, F. S. 1960. "Sports in the Cultures of Man." In *Science and Medicine in Exercise and Sports,* ed. W. R. Johnson, 633–46. New York: Harper and Row.

Geertz, Clifford. 1972. "Deep Play: Notes on the Balinese Cockfight." In *The Interpretation of Cultures,* 412–53. New York: Basic Books.

Gini, Corrado. 1939. "Rural Ritual Games in Libya." *Rural Sociology* 4:283–99.

Gmelch, George. 1972. "Magic in Professional Baseball." In *Games, Sports and Power,* ed. Gregory P. Stone, 128–37. New Brunswick, N.J.: Dutton.

Guttmann, Allen. 1978. *From Ritual to Record: The Nature of Modern Sports.* New York: Columbia University Press.

Haddon, A. C. 1898. *Study of Man.* London.

Handy, E. S. C. 1927. *Polynesian Religion.* Honolulu: Bernice P. Bishop Museum, Bulletin no. 34.

Kardiner, Abram, and Edward Preble. 1961. *They Studied Man.* New York: World Publishing Co.

Kroeber, Alfred L. 1948. *Anthropology.* New York: Harcourt, Brace and Co.

Leonard, Wilbert Marcellus, II. 1980. *A Sociological Perspective of Sport.* Minneapolis, Minn: Burgess.

Lesser, Alexander. 1933. *The Pawnee Ghost Dance Hand Game: A Study of Cultural Change.* Columbia University Contribution to Anthropology, 16. New York: Columbia University Press.

Loy, John W., Jr., and Gerald Kenyon, eds. 1969. *Sport, Culture, and Society: A Reader of the Sociology of Sport.* New York: Macmillan.

Loy, John W., Jr., Barry D. McPherson, and Gerald Kenyon, eds. 1978. *Sport and Social Systems.* Reading, Mass: Addison-Wesley.

Lüschen, Gunther, ed. 1970. *The Cross-Cultural Analysis of Sports and Games.* Champaign, Ill.: Stipes.

Mooney, James. 1890. "The Cherokee Ball Play." *American Anthropologist* 3(2):105–32.

Murdock, George P., et al. 1961. *Outline of Cultural Materials.* New Haven, Conn.: Human Relations Area Files.

Norbeck, Edward. 1971. "Man at Play." *Natural History,* Special Supplement (December):48–53.

———, ed. 1974. *The Anthropological Study of Human Play.* Rice University Studies 60(3).

Opler, M. E. 1944. "The Jicarilla Apache Ceremonial Relay Race." *American Anthropologist* 46(1):75–97.

Opler, M. K. 1945. "A Sumo Tournament at Tule Lake Center." *American Anthropologist* 47(1):134–39.

Reigelhaupt, Joyce A. 1973. Review: (three volumes on sport). *American Anthropologist* 75:378–81.

Richardson, Miles. 1975. "Anthropologist—the Myth Teller." *American Ethnologist* 2(3):517–33.

Roberts, John M., Malcolm J. Arth, and Robert R. Bush. 1959. "Games in Culture." *American Anthropologist* 61:597.

Spradley, James P., and David W. McCurdy, eds. 1980. *Conformity and Conflict: Readings in Cultural Anthropology.* Boston: Little, Brown.

Steward, Julian H. 1973. *Alfred Kroeber.* New York: Columbia University Press.

Stone, Gregory P., ed. 1972. *Games, Sports, and Power.* New Brunswick, N.J.: Dutton.

Stumpf, F., and F. W. Cozens. 1947. "Some Aspects of the Role of Games, Sports, and Recreation Activities in the Culture of Modern Primitive Peoples: The New Zealand Maoris." *Research Quarterly* 18:198–218.

Tylor, Edward B. 1879. "The History of Games." *Fortnightly Review,* London: Chapman and Hall, n.s. 25 (1 Jan.–1 June):735–47. Also in *The Study of Games,* 63–76. *See* Avedon and Sutton-Smith 1971.

———. 1896. "On American Lot-Games as Evidence of Asiatic Intercourse Before the Time of Columbus." International Archives for Ethnographia, Supplement to vol. 9:55–67. Also in *The Study of Games,* 77–93. *See* Avedon and Sutton-Smith 1971.

Weule, Karl von. 1925. "Ethnologie des Sportes." In *Geschichte des Sportes aller Völker und Zeiten,* ed. G. A. E. Bogeng. Leipzig.

White, Leslie. 1965. "Anthropology 1964: Retrospect and Prospect." *American Anthropologist* 67:629–37.

PART V
The Humanistic Conflict in Sport: A Summing Up

The need for sport, vicarious and participatory, seems a felt need for millions; it fills a void; it will likely not go away and may even increase significantly in these last decades of the twentieth century and into the next.

> —John A. Lucas and
> Ronald A. Smith,
> *Saga of American Sport* (1978)

The world of American sport is rich in materials for the humanistic imagination; rich, too, in the actual experience of human realities basic to the humanistic tradition.

> —Michael Novak,
> "American Sports, American Virtues" (1985)

In attending to the varied voices that echo the positive and negative implications of contemporary sports experience, the reader of these pieces should perceive that there are no real clear-cut winners in this debate; that actually the humanistic viewpoints of both the positive and negative approaches to American sports are interrelated in philosophical intent; and that the stances of both sides appear to complement each other in a dialectic intended to direct the individual toward an understanding of self, as well as a clearer conception of his or her role in modern society through involvement in sports, either as participant or spectator.

Thus, if there is a single theme unifying the statements that comprise this symposium's attention to the sociocultural approach, the individualized experience, the literary-folkloric interpretation, and the academic analysis—no matter how diverse their viewpoints—it is one which emphasizes sport's obligatory mission to provide our citizens bountiful opportunities for self-fulfillment. Appropriately enough, the proponents represented here either overtly or indirectly espouse a sensitivity to the "sport-for-all" philosophy, regardless of any reproachful attitude their respective stands might take toward the denigrating trends in contemporary sports. From the sociocultural standpoint, Michael Novak's persuasive case for the need to insulate sport from the corruption of these trends connotes a generally optimistic outlook that sport's essentially religious function will continue to convert and inspire adherents. Even Christopher Lasch's pessimistic contention that sports have strayed from their original purpose of offering "a dramatic commentary on reality rather than an escape from it" reminds us that perhaps it is not too late to recover the true meaning of our natural relationship to sport—at least, according to Lasch's perception of what this role should be.

And while the apocalyptic vision of Robert Lipsyte condemns SportsWorld as a tangled wilderness of racism, sexism, commercial greed, and distorted values that exploit the individual and mirror the excesses of Western society, political scientist Richard Lipsky can weigh both the good and bad sides of sports and conclude confidently that their true worth lies in their natural ability to transcend any societal aberration to provide us with a much-needed refuge from the harsh realities of life. A similar attitude is detected in the intensely individualistic thought of James A. Michener in *Sports in America* when, after pointing out the multiple abuses pervading American sports, he affirms that they are actually a kind of last frontier and, as such, are fully deserving of our continuing surveillance and protection in order to keep them free from those influences which tend to divert sport's essential mission of "enlarging the human adventure." Like the critical postures of most of the contributors to this collection, Michener's candid opinions are humanistically motivated, no doubt to help foster a way of life that he has always valued highly.

Even when our fiction writers depict a sport-oriented character whose literary experience dramatizes the failings of modern life, they are carrying on a humanistic tradition that harks back to James Fenimore Cooper. It is one that discerns sporting experience, whether interpreted in a positive or negative sense, as having special meaning for the American way and our understanding of the worth and dignity of the individual. For as Michael Oriard has pointed out in his book on American sport fiction: "Although the reality of sport culture can be brutal or dehumanizing, in their essence the games celebrate life, the vitality of the spirit, and human potential; the best novels understand both sides well." So it is not by accident that John Updike, for example, has created a character conditioned by organized athletics as the central figure of his Rabbit Angstrom saga. The predicament of a successful ex-athlete frustrated by the unfathomable social demands of urbanized society in his quest to identify with the primal simplicities of nature is an archetypally American experience. It is a metaphorical situation, too, that can tell us much about the humanistic conflict and how it relates to the continuing search for personal identity and self-fulfillment in an increasingly dehumanized world. Surely, Michael Novak's comment that American sport is "rich . . . in the actual experience of human realities basic to the humanistic tradition" has been significantly attested to by the output of our creative writers, especially since the 1960s.

As we have observed, many of our academic scholars have also revealed through a prolific production of historical, philosophical, psychological, and sociological (as well as literary) treatises an underlying awareness of the nature-society antithesis at the heart of the humanistic conflict in American sports experience. The examples included in this collection are, unfortunately, only a small sampling of the sport scholarship produced in recent years, but they are sufficient to inform us that the academic community, which seems to have discovered the tip of a gigantic iceberg, may be on the threshold of coming closer than any other sector to uncovering new truths about the humanistic approach to American sports experience. Already a number of scholarly studies have pointed out how sport in American life, in both its mythic and historical senses, has come to signify not only the regeneration and renewal of the body but the human spirit as well. It is a duality reflected in the nature-society antithesis itself, one which is expressed even in the conventional American understanding of what we think sporting endeavor is supposedly all about. Thus the American psyche can relate to the athletic feats of a fictional Frank Merriwell or a real-life Dale Murphy as not so much physical in nature as they are spiritual in their ultimate import.

As sport has developed in this country, then, it has revealed to us a great deal about ourselves and what it is that makes Americans distinctive as a people, particularly as the characteristically American qualities of individualism, competitiveness, industry, ingenuity, and mobility have defined themselves through our identification with sporting experience. As I have observed in *The Sporting Myth and the American Experience,* our involvement in sport, either as participant or spectator, can reveal to us as much about our inner selves as about our outer preoccupations, probably in a more intimate fashion than in the way we relate to our day-to-day occupations. In his enlightening study, *Sport and American Mentality, 1880–1910* (1983), Donald J. Mrozek has impressively demonstrated how our culture's growing national consciousness during that period made us increasingly receptive to the self-actualization possibilities of organized sports. But if, as he says, the "emergence of sport suggested a reconciliation of man and nature . . ." or a way to recover the spirit of our pioneer heritage, its expansion and development in this century also mirrored how far apart these two entities have become as this country endured two cataclysmic world wars and a rising tide of attendant dehumanizing forces to arrive at our present point in today's still uncertain world.

Ultimately, then, the real winners of the "great American sports debate" will be those of us who are fortunate enough to profit by the insights and observations that these and future works in the literature of American sport culture will generate. As we approach the advent of the twenty-first century, there are signs that sport will not only continue to grow in popularity as a mode of self-fulfillment for both participant and spectator, but that it will also supply us with one of our most accessible avenues to relating healthily and naturally to the world around us. If this is the Age of the Spectator, as Benjamin G. Rader categorizes it in his history, *American Sports* (1983), it is also a time when the reaction to the authoritative stances of bureaucracy and technology has resulted in greater participation in sports whether one jogs, plays handball, or joins a church-league softball team. The final selection in this book, "Sport for All" from John A. Lucas and Ronald A. Smith's *Saga of American Sport* (1978), contains abundant evidence of the narrowing of the gap between watching sport and participating in it. Transcending television's and big business's mercenary attempts to involve more and more people in sporting activity are the expanding efforts of both the health-fitness movement, which has dramatically altered living patterns and created stronger ties to the natural world, and the metaphysical dimension of sporting experience, whose continuing exploration of the self is a telling sign that the real significance of sport's humanistic role in society is yet to be realized.

23
Sport for All

JOHN A. LUCAS AND RONALD A. SMITH

No nation in the world can even remotely compare with the United States in its obsession with watching sporting events. Enormous national wealth, an ever-increasing amount of individual time free from work, and a long tradition of highly organized amateur and professional athletics account for this passive state. And yet there is substantial data to indicate that participatory sporting and recreational activities are presently competing for both purse and time. The majority of American people have already entered an era where millions of choices are being made between spending money and time on passive, spectator sport and the even larger commitment toward lifetime sport for all. In significant numbers, Americans are turning to fun activities, exotic sporting, recreational, and lifetime physical activities. The tug between watching sports and participating in them will go on for a long time. Statistical evidences from Europe and the United States indicate that the participatory sport-for-all movement is growing more rapidly than the sedentary pastime of watching sport. It is entirely possible that within a generation the one will catch up with the other.

Sport for All as Big Business

A careful survey by the A. C. Nielsen Company, a prominent market research firm, established the extraordinary popularity of the American sport-for-all movement. According to this survey, swimming, bicycling, fishing, and camping were favorite pastimes. Tennis has since moved into the top ten with well over 30 million "players"—each of whom spends an average of $250 per year.[1] Golf is rapidly moving up the list into fourteenth place. Back in 1969, *U.S. News and World Report,* reporting on the role of recreation, play, and leisure, noted that affluent and leisured Americans have boomed it into an 83-billion-dollar enterprise— "the fastest-growing business in America."[2] In 1970, over 8 million bicycles sold for $300 million, 7 million people owned pleasure boats, $3 billion was spent on hunting and fishing equipment. Leisure authority Max Kaplan points out that the total expenditure for recreation by Americans is over one-fifth of our total consuming expenditures—a total of "well over $110 billion."[3] The leisure business reaches out and touches almost every single citizen. More Americans have more time on their hands and money to spend than ever before. Millions of dollars will be spent watching sports; billions will be spent in playing at sport, in the coming national involvement in lifetime sport for all.

The Fitness Dimension of Sport for All

Although the President's Council of Physical Fitness and Sport started during Dwight Eisenhower's administration and grew during the brief tenure of the physically vigorous John Kennedy, the massive concern with fitness during the sixties was a European phenomena. Switzerland has a well-organized fun and fitness course available to every citizen. Financed by the government and national insurance companies, Switzerland has 150 "parcourses"—each providing jogging and flexibility and strength exercises. The vest-pocket nation, highly organized and in love with the out-of-doors, has found parcourse programs enormously appealing. A massive West German sport-for-all program called "Trimm trab–Trimm-trab" has evolved into a national campaign and affected the lives of millions. Massive governmental programs of winter lifetime sports involvement have already become a tradition in Norway, Finland, Sweden, and the Netherlands. Even England, usually slow to move, has launched a nationwide program that The Sports Council calls "Sport For All." Other nations, including the two Chinas, and the entire communist-socialist bloc of nations, have organized and well publicized programs of lifetime sport for all. The United States, so much more amorphous in its national political and ideological control, has greater difficulty in convincing millions of Americans that the President's Council on Physical Fitness and Sports is correct in its slogan, "Physical fitness is beautiful, beautiful, beautiful." Author-Athlete Kenny Moore is close to the mark with his observation that places like Finland and Sweden

> are a very active culture beyond the top level of athletics, that there is a commitment to sports as something good for the people, as a means toward education. Here [USA] I get the feeling that sport is very vicarious, that it is a means of entertainment.[4]

Persistent good humor and an abundance of factual data from the medical profession, sport scientists, the physical education professionals, the media, and the business community, will probably alter America's uncertain attitudes toward physical fitness. In the vaguest sort of way, millions of Americans are becoming better informed, understanding what a classics scholar said over fifty years ago. "All our people," he said, "should emulate the physical fitness of Ulysses. We are no more protected from physical decadency by our Olympic games than were the Greeks by theirs."[5]

Mass participation in sport may become one of the most significant movements in the United States. Hiking, orienteering, climbing, cross-country skiing, the whole range of Eastern martial arts, all the racquet sports, swimming, weightlifting, rowing and paddling, volleyball, and scores of other relatively vigorous activities are being savored by an ever-increasing number. The Boston Marathon, with 2,000 fit runners, and the 6,000 men and women who race the San Francisco Bay-to-Breakers road race typify the largest group of fitness apostles—the runners and the joggers. Although Archibald MacLeish was referring to football, he might well have included any vigorous sport in his reminder that a "precise sense of participation" is one of the many rewards for the daily retreats into physical reeducation.[6]

Sport and the Existential-Humanistic Preoccupation

The awful truth that American competitive sport has frequently gone mad is countered by the intrinsic value of sport participation—a turning away from the winning preoccupation to a point of view which sees sport as a three-letter word, "F--U--N." According to the new sport humanists, and in a seemingly contradictory, existential way, the reduction of winning's importance actually heightens the value of the individual sporting experience. This old-new attitude gained momentum in the 1960s and 1970s, adding hundreds of thousands of participants to a sporting cult that did not in the least consider the winning edge of great importance. Only a few, however, were willing to go as far as George Leonard's catchy, glittering generality, "Winning isn't everything. It's nothing." Competition, like a little salt, adds zest to the game and to life, he noted, tempering his lead statement somewhat. When winning becomes the only thing, "it can lead only to eventual emptiness and anomie."[7] This existential-humanist disgust for the winning obsession created a new and less threatening environment, and large numbers joined the ranks of sport enthusiasts. For a short time, Jack Scott preached an anti-sports-establishment, anti-win-at-all-costs litany. He gained instant fame during the late 60s and 70s. Personal confusion and frequent philosophical contradictions led to his rapid demise. Nonetheless, as Scott predicted, this new renaissance in athletic thought will strongly affect sport and school physical education for the remainder of the century.[8] Competition out-of-bounds is an obvious sickness; the play element must be fused with the serious competitive spirit to give the lifetime, sport-for-all thrust a healthy and therefore more permanent cycle. Human development, both physical and spiritual, must be the goal of all sport competitors and participants. Joy and high emotion must commingle, and, as Central Michigan University's Charles Ping noted in quoting Nietzsche, man must experience "the ideal of truly exuberant, alive and world affirming man." "The nurturing of the expressive sense is one of the key justifications of an athletic program."[9]

Metaphysical Dimensions of Sport

More and more, there is fuller realization of sport's physical, recreational, intellectual, and even spiritual dimensions. Obviously, sport continues to touch the lives of millions, and newer battalions of Americans now see opportunities for lifelong involvement in sporting, recreational activities. Any new passion brings with it new disciples and a multiplication of creeds. The new politics, the new psychologies and philosophies of the decades of the 1960s and 1970s, also gave birth to an animated metaphysical dimension to sport. Whatever the truths and excesses of this contemplative and philosophically irrational preoccupation with sport, it definitely has opened up the possibilities of mass public involvement. The tendency to individual exaggeration is countered by the truism that thinking tends to make it so. In his book *Positive Addiction* psychiatrist William Glasser is convinced that running is the hardest but surest way to healthful positive addiction. The multiplication of particular kinds of addictions "strengthen[s] us and make[s] our lives more satisfying," is his medical and metaphysical prognosis.[10] There appears a growing realization that sport is much more than cheap entertainment—that it is capable of giving us a vision of beauty and an extraordinary experience, both physical and metaphysical. The 1976 Boston Marathon victor, Jack Fultz, thought it odd that late in the race "your mind moves away from the body. It wanders. You start to transcend the physical pain." The literature is replete with such remarks from golfers, weight lifters, swimmers, and other men and women involved in individual sports. The modern precursor to this mystical, irrational component might be Eugen Herrigel in his 1953 *Zen in the Art of Archery.* He continually speaks of the self-detached, egoless, spiritually minded athlete as the truly effective sportsman and human. The "unspiritual archer" can never compete successfully against the one immersed in "unbroken equanimity."[11]

Golf champion Tony Jacklin attributed some of his success to a mystical perception of sport—a state where everything is pure and clear, "a cocoon of concentration. And . . . I'm invincible," he said.[12] The current vogue of Eastern philosophies, yoga and transcendental meditation, and raised levels of consciousness techniques has had real but ill-defined impacts on professional athletes, serious and recreational sporting men and women.

Michael Murphy in his *Golf in the Kingdom* talks in terms of a
return of the human to the divine—through sport. George
Leonard does the same thing in his 1975 *The Ultimate Athlete.*
There are many more writers equally reverential about the metaphysical side of sport. Such talk is exciting, somewhat new, and
contains much truth. But it is unbridled, lacking balance or a
Grecian sense of sophrosyne. Several writers have helped in this
latter regard. Scott Kretchmar and William Harper conclude
that there is no rational answer to the question, "Why does man
play?" Excessive preoccupation with explanations is to be
avoided. Larry Locke rejects sport as educative. Sport is just
what it is, he says. Articulate educators, skeptical and seriously
concerned about the recent wave of literature giving moral, aesthetic, and even religious adornments to sport, are emerging at
the same time that such metaphysical sport literature is still on
the increase. "It used to be the things worth dying for were
abstract ideas," noted *New York Times* cultural reporter Richard
Shepard. The excessive passion for sport ideology is ruining
sport and "hampering the spread of ideology the world over."[13]
Olympic marathon champion Frank Shorter possibly summed up
this impatience with the overpassionate sportsman with his re-
mark that he has nothing but respect for the average guy who
runs. "What I can't stand," he says, are those "who make a cult
out of it. It ruins the whole thing to take it so seriously."[14] What
each of us must learn to do is to immerse ourselves in sport,
enjoy the game as something vitally important for that moment,
and yet as soon as it is over, realize its relatively inconsequential
nature.

The Future Sport-for-All Scenario—A Case for Optimism

It has been said that sporting events are almost the only thing
in life that has a conclusion. Pessimists (or as Herman Kahn calls
them, "catastrophists") declare that today's sports are actually
the funeral games of modern Western civilization. And yet there
is an almost infinite variety of choices between the Super Bowl
and a casual hour of frisbee play—between gladiatorial competition and the ephemeral enjoyment of sport. The ascendancy of
intellect is presently being met by a healthy, countervailing
sporting impulse. Our machine culture often fails us; men and

women who pursue lifetime sports may be looking for, and often find, what Max Lerner calls "new accessions of experience."

The expanding sport-for-all movement in the United States is important for its physical fitness implications. During the 1960s and 1970s, medical and physiological evidence mounted so steadily that sound health habits combined with regular, vigorous exercise are of vital importance in daily work and in making our leisure time meaningful. During this era, huge numbers accepted the self-evident declaration of the prominent physician Per-Olaf Astrand that "the human body is built for action, not for rest."[15] Regular exercise or "active recreation" has been dramatically forwarded as a prerequisite for good body function and to the quality of life. The American Medical Association, in a rare moment of sermonizing, recommended a lifelong commitment to the broadest concept of fitness in order that one may "live best and serve most."[16] The long argument between diet and exercise as more important in the prevention of heart disease seems resolved in favor of exercise. More and more, physicians, physiologists, physical educators, and nutritionists have thrust regular, pleasant exercise into the fore of cardiovascular medicine. *Time* magazine, on 23 February 1968, both admonished us and urged us with its essay "Don't just sit there; walk, jog, run." Psychological and social benefits are frequently cited. "What all of the experts are wholeheartedly against is nonexercise." The scientific and popular literature on human fitness is replete with titles like "Therapeutic physical exercise," "The road to fitness," "Can exercise improve your brain power," "The new aerobics—key to fitness at any age," and "Exercise: the new miracle drug." No doubt that all of this and more led to the extravagant national advertisement which proclaimed, "Not one of the top U.S. corporations has a fat president."

Playing games is increasingly important to millions of people. Games permit a respite from customary pattern, said Marshall McLuhan. They can provide many varieties of satisfaction— from the mundane to the sublime. When Swedish film director Ingmar Bergman was in his late fifties and contemplating his advancing years, he commented, "It's like climbing a mountain. The higher you get, the more tired and breathless you become, but your view becomes much more extensive." The new sport and recreational surge in the United States has embraced millions, motivated by thoughts as private as Bergman's view.

Should sport be spontaneous, uninhibited, unstructured, non-competitive, nonaggressive, nonviolent play for its own sake? Or does it mean daring, risking, bearing uncertainty, and enduring tension for a prize?[17] The options available are both extremes and all the subtleties in between. The postindustrial scenario should open significant recreational and sporting opportunities to all social and economic classes (except the diminishing number of poor). The quaternary society—a truly postindustrial economy—might very well contain a significant population participating in nonwork activities, marking "the third great watershed of human history."[18] There is much room for optimism in a realistic anticipation of a continued strong American economy where significant leisure will be available to more and more individuals. Just as significant, possibly, is the growing awareness that participation in lifetime sports can measurably enhance the quality of life.

Sport Alters American Living Patterns

It is an acceptable cliché that sport is a mirror of society. For some time now, the reverse has also been true. The extraordinary pervasiveness of sport in American society—especially the new lifetime sport involvement—has actually altered the lives of countless individuals. Recently, historians have generally accepted sport as a genuine area of exploration. The same is true of many psychologists, sociologists, physiologists, physicians, and philosophers. Learned societies of scholars from each of these disciplines look keenly at the effects of individual and collective sporting experiences. Like quicksilver, however, definitive statements about sport and play are hard to come by.

> Like any form of human behavior that has antecedents both in the predispositions of the species and in the specific cultures within which individuals grow and develop, the meaning to be derived from participation in physical play is almost impossible to dissect given our correct level of analysis.[19]

The new sport humanists, Stuart Miller, George Leonard, Bil Gilbert, Neil Amdur, and many others, may be unfamiliar with the older philosophies of R. Tait McKenzie, Clark Hetherington, Jay B. Nash, and Arthur H. Steinhaus. A close analysis of the modernists reveals a sport-for-all attitude precisely the same as those of the traditional educators. There is no essential philosophical difference between the attitude of Esalen Institute's Stuart Miller and that of the late physical education scientist Arthur Steinhaus. Miller's "new directions" sees sport as "a powerful psychological searchlight, teaching the player about himself . . . consciously used in the development of the whole personality. . . ." Steinhaus's classic essay "Fitness Beyond Muscle" concluded that "for the highest human accomplishments man must be strong in totality." The laudable message of the new sport humanists is very old. The new advocates of self-actualization through sport have no more hard evidence of sport's efficacy in this direction than did the old-timers who talked so convincingly about character building through athletic competition. The strong evidences from both directions, except in the physiological dimension, still tend to remain semiscientific. Exactly what sport does to the individual human mind and spirit is still uncertain. No doubt remains, however, that it is capable of profoundly affecting men and women, young and old.

In the year 1976, 15 million Americans drove, chipped, and putted over 300 million rounds of golf. Multiply this a hundredfold in a hundred different sporting directions and one begins to see the dimensions of this still new, sport-for-all, lifetime sports direction. "The vibrant dynamic feeling that comes from being more than just well" is an intellectual realization and a body feeling that is gaining acceptance at a remarkable rate in contemporary America. The response you get from moderate, regular, and joyous exercise "is so great," says Laurence Morehouse in his almost too casual text, *Total Fitness in 30 Minutes a Week.* "Functional wellness" "minimum maintenance," are terms he uses to emphasize that sport is necessary to us and can be fun. "Inactivity will kill you," he warns. The American free citizen, who both worships material abundance and feels entitled to his share of it, may slowly outgrow a narrow definition of wealth and emerge more expansive, realizing what Sebastian de Grazia knew. Work may make a man stoop-shouldered or rich or both; it may even ennoble him. Worthy use of leisure may perfect him, and in this lies its future. Through leisure man "may realize his ties to the natural world and so free his mind to rise to divine reaches."[20]

Notes

1. Neil Amdur, "Swimming Still Rated Top Participant Sport," *New York Times,* 24 March 1974, 1, Sports section.

2. "82 Billion Dollars for Leisure," *U.S. News and World Report* 67 (15 September 1969): 58.

3. Max Kaplan, *Leisure: Theory and Practice* (New York: John Wiley and Sons, 1975), 123.

4. Ken Moore, as quoted in Skip Myslenski, "U.S. Decathlon Star Knows Sacrifice," *Philadelphia Inquirer,* 13 June 1976, 7E.

5. Allan H. Gilbert, "Olympic Decadence," *Classical Journal* 21 (May 1926): 698.

6. See MacLeish's sport philosophy in Neil Amdur, *The Fifth Down* (New York: Coward-McCann and Geoghegan, 1971), 11–14.

7. George B. Leonard, "Winning Isn't Everything. It's Nothing." *Intellectual Digest* 4 (October 1973): 47.

8. John Lucas, as quoted in Neil Amdur, "The New Awakening in Athletics," *Washington Star,* 2 April 1972, c6.

9. Charles J. Ping, "Education and Athletics Are Worthy College Experiences," *N.C.A.A. News* 11 (15 March 1974): 7.

10. William Glasser, *Positive Addiction* (New York: Harper & Row, 1976), 2 and passim.

11. Eugen Herrigel, *Zen in the Art of Archery* (New York: Random House, Vintage Books, 1971), 78, 80, and passim.

12. Tony Jacklin, as quoted in Dudley Doust, "Mystical Perception in Sport," *Intellectual Digest* 4 (April 1974): 32.

13. Richard F. Shepard, "Time to End Sports, Opiate of the Masses," *New York Times,* 17 November 1974, 2 Sports section.

14. Frank Shorter, as quoted in Lawrence Shainberg, "The Obsessiveness of the Long-distance Runner," *New York Times Magazine,* 25 February 1973, 28.

15. See Per-Olaf Astrand, *Health and Fitness* (Stockholm: Universaltryck, 1973).

16. "Fitness of American Youth," *Journal of the American Medical Association* 163 (23 February 1957): 648.

17. For one person's view, see John P. Sisk, "Hot Sporting Blood," *Intellectual Digest* 4 (November 1973); 46–47.

18. Herman Kahn et al., *The Next 200 Years. A Scenario for America and the World* (New York: William Morrow and Co., 1976), 23.

19. Daryl Siedentop, *Physical Education—Introductory Analysis* (Dubuque, Iowa: William C. Brown Co., 1976), 27.

20. Sebastian de Grazia, *Of Time, Work, and Leisure* (Garden City, N.Y.: Anchor Books, Doubleday and Co., 1964), 414.

Notes on Contributors

WILLIAM H. BEEZLEY, who teaches sport and Mexican history at North Carolina State University, is the author of a forthcoming book on the folklore of college football.

KENDALL BLANCHARD is chairman of the Department of Anthropology/Sociology at Middle Tennessee State University. He is the author of a number of publications, among which are *The Mississippi Choctaws at Play: The Serious Side of Leisure* and *The Anthropology of Sport* with Alyce Cheska.

JOHN BRIDGES is a member of the Sociology Department at the University of Notre Dame where he teaches courses on mass culture. He has writen articles and participated in conferences addressing popular culture subjects.

LLOYD W. BROWN, a specialist in the literature of the Caribbean, is with the comparative literature program at the University of Southern California.

JOAN M. CHANDLER, a native of England and graduate of Cambridge University, is American Studies head at the University of Texas in Dallas. She has published widely in the area of sport and culture, particularly as television has affected this relationship.

GEORGE CORE, a member of the English faculty at the University of the South, is also editor of the *Sewanee Review*.

RICHARD C. CREPEAU, a member of the history faculty at the University of Central Florida in Orlando, is the author of *Baseball: America's Diamond Mind, 1919–1941*. He has published extensively in the area of American sport culture.

JEFFREY H. GOLDSTEIN is professor of psychology at Temple University. He has edited and authored a large number of publications, among which is *Sports Violence*.

ROBERT J. HIGGS, professor of English at East Tennessee State University, is the author of *Laurel and Thorn: The Athlete in American Literature* and *Sport: A Reference Guide*.

JACK HUTSLAR is executive director of the North American Youth Sport Institute, based in North Carolina. Originally in education, he has been involved with youth sport, recreation, and athletics for over thirty years.

NEIL D. ISAACS, whose versatility has combined the career of an English professor at the University of Maryland with that of sportswriter for a Washington newspaper, is the author of numerous publications, including *Jock Culture, U.S.A.*

CHRISTOPHER LASCH, professor of history at the University of Rochester, is the author of the influential study, *The Culture of Narcissism: American Life in an Age of Diminishing Expectations.*

RICHARD LIPSKY teaches political science at Queens College, City University of New York. A former athlete and sportswriter, he is the author of *How We Play the Game: Why Sports Dominate American Life.*

ROBERT LIPSYTE, who has been a sports journalist for *The New York Times,* is the author of a number of books, among them, *SportsWorld: An American Dreamland* and *Assignment: Sports.* He is currently on the staff of CBS News.

JOHN A. LUCAS and RONALD A. SMITH, the coauthors of *Saga of American Sport,* both teach at Pennsylvania State University.

CHRISTIAN K. MESSENGER is the author of *Sport and the Spirit of Play in American Fiction: Hawthorne to Faulkner.* He teaches English at the University of Illinois (Chicago Circle).

MICHAEL NOVAK, author of *The Joy of Sports,* has written prolifically on a wide variety of timely subjects. He is currently with the American Enterprise Institute for Public Policy Research in Washington.

ALLEN L. SACK is both a professor of sociology at the University of New Haven and project director of the Center for Athletes' Rights and Education. During the mid-1960s, he played football at the University of Notre Dame.

GREGORY S. SOJKA, who chairs the Department of American Studies at Wichita State University, has published articles on American literature, popular culture, and sport studies.

GARY STOROFF, who teaches English at the University of Connecticut (Stamford), has published articles on numerous authors and is now working on a study of Graham Greene.

WILEY LEE UMPHLETT is the author of three books on American

culture, including *The Sporting Myth and the American Experience*. He currently serves as an administrator at the University of West Florida in Pensacola.

DAVID L. VANDERWERKEN of the English faculty at Texas Christian University is co-editor of *Sport: A Literary and Conceptual Approach*. The author of numerous articles on sport, he also participates in conferences on sport.

WILLIAM H. WIGGINS, JR., is with Indiana University's Department of Afro-American Studies. He has published and participated in conferences concerning black American culture.

Select Bibliography

The following bibliography of American nonfiction and fiction is comprised of those books published since 1960 which, from the point of view of this collection, have had the most significant humanistic impact on American sport culture.

Nonfiction

Angell, Roger. *The Summer Game.* New York: Popular Library, 1972.

Axthelm, Peter. *The City Game: Basketball in New York from the World Champion Knicks to the World of Playgrounds.* New York: Harper & Row, 1970.

Beisser, Arnold. *Madness in Sports: Psychosocial Observations on Sports.* New York: Appleton-Century-Crofts, 1967.

Betts, John. *America's Sporting Heritage.* Reading, Mass.: Addison-Wesley, 1974.

Blanchard, Kendall A. *Mississippi Choctaws at Play: The Serious Side of Leisure.* Champaign: University of Illinois Press, 1982.

Bradley, Bill. *Life on the Run.* New York: Bantam Books, 1977.

Brodie, John, with James D. Houston. *Open Field.* Boston: Houghton Mifflin, 1974.

Bouton, Jim. *Ball Four.* New York: World, 1970.

Boyle, Robert. *Sport: Mirror of American Life.* Boston: Little, Brown, 1963.

Butt, Dorcas Susan. *Psychology of Sport.* New York: Van Nostrand Reinhold, 1976.

Cady, Edwin H. *The Big Game: College Sports and American Life.* University of Tennessee Press, 1978.

Coakley, Jay. *Sport in Society: Issues and Controversies.* St. Louis, Mo.: C. V. Mosby, 1978.

Coffin, Tristram Potter. *The Old Ball Game in Folklore and Fiction.* New York: Herder and Herder, 1971.

Cosell, Howard. *Cosell.* New York: Pocket Books, 1973.

318

Crepeau, Richard C. *Baseball: America's Diamond Mind, 1919–1941.* Orlando: University Presses of Florida, 1980.

Dizikes, John. *Sportsmen and Gamesmen.* New York: Houghton Mifflin, 1982.

Durso, Joseph. *The All-American Dollar: The Big Business of Sports.* Boston: Houghton Mifflin, 1971.

Edwards, Harry. *The Revolt of the Black Athlete.* New York: The Free Press, 1969.

——. *The Sociology of Sport.* Homewood, Ill.: Dorsey Press, 1973.

Evans, J. Robert. *Blowing the Whistle on Intercollegiate Athletics.* Chicago: Nelson-Hall, 1974.

Flood, Curt. *The Way It Is.* New York: Pocket Books, 1972.

Gerbert, Ellen et al. eds. *The American Woman in Sport.* Reading, Mass.: Addison-Wesley, 1974.

Goldstein, Jeffrey H., ed. *Sports, Games, and Play: Social and Psychological Viewpoints.* Hillsdale, N.J.: Erlbaum Associates, 1979.

Goldstein, Jeffrey H. *Sports Violence.* New York: Springer-Verlag, 1983.

Guttman, Allen. *From Ritual to Record: The Nature of Modern Sports.* New York: Columbia University Press, 1978.

Halberstam, David. *The Breaks of the Game.* New York: Knopf, 1981.

Higgs, Robert J. *Laurel and Thorn: The Athlete in American Literature.* Lexington: University of Kentucky Press, 1981.

Higgs, Robert J. and Neil D. Isaacs. *The Sporting Spirit: Athletes in Literature and Life.* New York: Harcourt Brace Jovanovich, 1977.

Hoch, Paul. *Rip Off the Big Game: The Exploitation of Sports by the Power Elite.* New York: Doubleday, 1972.

Isaacs, Neil. *Jock Culture, USA.* New York: Norton, 1978.

Izenburg, Jerry. *How Many Miles to Camelot? the All-American Sports Myth.* New York: Holt, Rinehart & Winston, 1971.

Johnson, William O. *Super Spectator and the Electric Lilliputians.* Boston: Little, Brown, 1971.

Kahn, Roger. *The Boys of Summer.* New York: New American Library, 1973.

Klein, Dave. *The Pro Football Mystique.* New York: New American Library, 1978.

Koppett, Leonard. *Sports Illusion, Sports Reality: A Reporter's View of Sports, Journalism, and Society.* Boston: Houghton Mifflin, 1981.

Kramer, Jerry, ed., with Dick Schaap. *Instant Replay.* New York: New American Library, 1969.

Lasch, Christopher. *The Culture of Narcissism: American Life in an Age of Diminishing Expectations.* New York: W. W. Norton, 1979.

Leonard, George. *The Ultimate Athlete: Revisioning Sports, Physical Education and the Body.* New York: Viking, 1974.

Lipsky, Richard. *How We Play the Game: Why Sports Dominate American Life.* Boston: Beacon, 1981.

Lipsyte, Robert. *SportsWorld: An American Dreamland.* New York: Quadrangle, 1976.

Loy, Jr., John W. and Gerald S. Kenyon. *Sport, Culture, and Society.* Macmillan, 1969.

Meggyesy, Dave. *Out of Their League.* Berkeley: Ramparts Press, 1970.

Merchant, Larry. *The National Football Lottery.* New York: Dell, 1973.

Messenger, Christian K. *Sport and the Spirit of Play in American Fiction: Hawthorne to Faulkner.* New York: Columbia University Press, 1981.

Michener, James A. *Sports in America.* New York: Random House, 1976.

Mrozek, Donald J. *Sport and American Mentality, 1880–1910.* Knoxville: University of Tennessee Press, 1983.

Murphy, Michael. *Golf in the Kingdom.* New York: Dell, 1972.

Murphy, Michael and R. A. White. *The Psychic Side of Sports.* Reading, Mass.: Addison-Wesley, 1978.

Novak, Michael. *The Joy of Sports.* New York: Basic Books, 1976.

Offen, Neil. *God Save the Players.* Chicago: Playboy Press, 1974.

Oliver, Chip, with Ron Rapoport. *High for the Game.* New York: Morrow, 1971.

Olsen, Jack. *The Black Athlete: A Shameful Story.* New York: Time-Life Books, 1969.

Oriard, Michael. *Dreaming of Heroes: American Sports Fiction 1868–1980.* Chicago: Nelson-Hall, 1981.

Parrish, Bernie. *They Call It a Game.* New York: New American Library, 1972.

Peterson, Robert. *Only the Ball Was White.* Englewood Cliffs, N.J.: Prentice-Hall, 1970.

Plimpton, George. *Paper Lion.* New York: Pocket Books, 1967.

Rader, Benjamin G. *American Sports: From the Age of Folk Games to the Age of Spectators.* Englewood Cliffs, N.J.: Prentice-Hall, 1983.

Rentzel, Lance. *When All the Laughter Died in Sorrow.* New York: Saturday Review Press, 1972.

Roberts, Michael. *Fans! How We Go Crazy over Sports.* Washington, D.C.: New Republic, 1976.

Rooney, John F. *A Geography of American Sport.* Reading, Mass.: Addison-Wesley, 1974.

———. *The Recruiting Game: Toward a New System of Intercollegiate Sports.* Lincoln: University of Nebraska Press, 1980.

Russell, Bill. *Go Up for Glory.* New York: Coward-McCann, 1966.

Sage, George. *Sport and American Society.* Reading, Mass.: Addison-Wesley, 1970.

Sample, Johnny. *Confessions of a Dirty Ballplayer.* New York: Dial, 1970.

Schecter, Leonard. *The Jocks.* Indianapolis: Bobbs-Merrill, 1969.

Scott, Jack. *The Athletic Revolution.* New York: The Free Press, 1971.

Shaw, Gary. *Meat on the Hoof: The Hidden World of Texas Football.* New York: St. Martin's Press, 1973.

Slusher, Howard S. *Man, Sport and Existence.* Philadelphia: Lea & Febiger, 1967.

Smith, Leverett T., Jr. *The American Dream and the National Game.* Bowling Green, Ohio: Popular, 1975.

Tatum, Jack. *They Call Me Assassin.* New York: Everest House, 1979.

Tutko, Thomas, and William Burns. *Winning Is Everything and Other American Myths.* New York: Macmillan, 1976.

Tygiel, Jules. *Baseball's Great Experiment: Jackie Robinson and His Legacy.* New York: Oxford University Press, 1983.

Umphlett, Wiley Lee. *The Sporting Myth and the American Experience.* Lewisburg: Bucknell University Press, 1975.

Underwood, John. *Death of an American Game: The Crisis in Football.* Boston: Little, Brown, 1979.

Vanderzwaag, Harold J. *Toward a Philosophy of Sport.* Reading, Mass.: Addison-Wesley, 1972.

Voight, David Q. *America through Baseball.* Chicago: Nelson-Hall, 1976.

Weiss, Paul. *Sport: A Philosophic Inquiry.* Carbondale: Southern Illinois University Press, 1969.

Wolf, David. *Foul! The Connie Hawkins Story.* New York: Holt, Reinehart & Winston, 1972.

Yeager, Robert. *Seasons of Shame: The New Violence in Sports.* New York: McGraw-Hill, 1979.

Fiction

Note that two influential sport-centered novels appeared in the 1950s, Bernard Malamud's *The Natural* (1952) and Mark Harris's *Bang the Drum Slowly* (1956), and are therefore excluded from this list. (For some notable recent works, see Introduction, note 5.)

Beckham, Barry. *Runner Mack.* New York: Morrow, 1972.

Brashler, William. *The Bingo Long Traveling All-Stars and Motor Kings.* New York: Harper & Row, 1973.

Charyn, Jerome. *The Seventh Babe.* New York: Arbor House, 1979.

Coover, Robert. *The Universal Baseball Association, Inc., J. Henry Waugh, Prop.* New York: Random House, 1968.

Deal, Babs H. *The Grail.* New York: McKay, 1963.

DeLillo, Don. *End Zone.* Boston: Houghton Mifflin, 1972.

Exley, Frederick. *A Fan's Notes.* New York: Harper & Row, 1968.

Foster, Alan S. *Goodbye, Bobby Thomson! Goodbye, John Wayne!* New York: Simon & Schuster, 1973.

Gardner, Leonard. *Fat City.* New York: Farrar, Straus & Giroux, 1969.

Gent, Peter. *North Dallas Forty.* New York: Morrow, 1973.

Harris, Mark. *It Looked Like For Ever.* New York: McGraw-Hill, 1979.

Hemphill, Paul. *Long Gone.* New York: Viking, 1979.

Herrin, Lamar. *The Rio Loja Ringmaster.* New York: Viking, 1977.

Jenkins, Dan. *Semi-Tough.* New York: Atheneum, 1972.

Kinsella, W. P. *Shoeless Joe.* Boston: Houghton Mifflin, 1982.

Larner, Jeremy. *Drive, He Said.* New York: Delacorte, 1964.

Maule, Hamilton ("Tex"). *Footsteps.* New York: Random House, 1961.

Neugeboren, Jay. *Big Man.* Boston: Houghton Mifflin, 1966.

O'Connor, Philip F. *Stealing Home.* New York: Knopf, 1979.

Olsen, Jack. *Alphabet Jackson.* Chicago: Playboy, 1974.

Roth, Philip. *Goodbye Columbus.* Cleveland: World, 1963.

———. *The Great American Novel.* New York: Holt, Rinehart & Winston, 1973.

Shainberg, Lawrence. *One on One.* New York: Holt, Rinehart & Winston, 1970.

Updike, John. *Rabbit, Run.* New York: Knopf, 1960.

———. *Rabbit, Redux.* New York: Knopf, 1971.

Whitehead, James. *Joiner.* New York: Knopf, 1971.

Young, Al. *Ask Me Now.* New York: McGraw-Hill, 1980.

Zuckerman, George. *Farewell, Frank Merriwell.* New York: E. P. Dutton, 1973.